To Sara,

May The Lord blessings be
with you.
Enjoy

Bruno Di Carlo

Salem monte Carlo
10-20-22

Vivi La Tua Vita
(Live your life)

YOUR FEET WALK, YOUR MIND TRAVELS

Bruno DiCarlo

ISBN: 978-1-66784-593-7 (print)
ISBN: 978-1-66784-594-4 (eBook)

Special thanks to my friend Robert Lovinger.

HELLO, MR. D?

FROM somewhere in a deep corner of my mind, I hear a questioning voice say, "Hello . . . Mr. D.?"

"Yes!" I answer.

But why do I answer? Why, when something in me says that I shouldn't? Maybe it's all the years of others admonishing me: "*Be polite ! No need to be rude! Be polite!*"

The voice continues with a tone of malice. "Hi, I'm Mr. C."

Again I think, "Why do I answer what I can't see?" Who or what is this strange entity that I hear but don't see? I briefly consider whether or not I should search for the source of this invisible voice before I answer again, but I find myself thinking again that I should be polite and answer it. Is it in my mind, or am I actually hearing this voice? If it's in my mind, I have already found it. If it's not? I look in my rearview mirror as I drive to work at 5:15 in the morning, but there's nothing in my frosty rear window besides darkness.

Around the time I was about six years old, something happened to me that imprinted in my mind the imperative to be polite and respectful to others. Growing up in a small town in Italy, we were taught that as we walked to school, or at any other time we passed an older person or anyone else, we were to acknowledge them with, *"Buon Giorno,"* even if they were complete strangers.

As a child, there were times when I wore shoes through which I could see my big toe waving at me as I looked down. My pants, like those of my dad and my brothers Vincenzo and Franco, had more patches than a rainbow quilt. My older brothers' overcoats became my overcoats when they were too small for them, but as I wore them my hands disappeared inside the sleeves, and they were so long that I could barely see my shoes. That was okay because I had an overcoat that didn't have any rips or patches, and I also liked the fact that it smelled like my brothers.

Thursday, October 1st of 1962, on my first day of first grade, there was no need to wear my brother's overcoat, as the mild weather of the *Abruzzi* region made it possible for us to wear shorts to school. But I did have my brother's shoes on. Good shoes they were, and I loved them as they made me feel bigger. They were solid ankle boots with some scuffs on the toes from Vincenzo kicking rocks, an old can or anything that rolled, so that he could make believe it was the soccer ball that he loved so much but which we couldn't afford to buy.

The heels on both shoes were worn out on the outside, maybe my brother was bowlegged. The shoes were a bit big on my feet, but my grandma stuffed some paper in the front so that my feet didn't float around. But most of all, I loved those shoes because my big toes didn't stick out through the front of them as I walked to school. If I couldn't see my toes, then yes, they were good shoes. The pants that I wore were mine, but the shirt was also my brothers', as at one point or another they also had worn the same shirt that now I had on.

The good part was that we wore a *grenbiule* uniform over our underclothing, so no one was the wiser about what I was wearing under my uniform, as everyone wore the same uniform, rich or poor: same color blue for men or women, with a white bow tied under our chin. The uniforms hung down like a potato sack to the kneecaps, and girls were not allowed to wear a belt with it because it would show the body form. We wore those uniforms from kindergarten to fifth grade. Try that one today.

From my street, there were seven kids who walked together to school. Myself and another kid named Mario were of the same age. We were in the same classroom and were the youngest of the group. He was one of my best friends, and to this day we remain the best of friends. That morning walking to school, we were excited to be starting the new school year, but also a little afraid of the fact that we were going to a new classroom and a new teacher. Mario was a little more shy than I was, so I stayed close to him to give him comfort, but I was just as scared as he was.

We had about a mile and a half to walk to school, and as children do, I forgot the lesson that my grandmother taught me, to be polite and respectful to others. So as we walked along we did what children do best: just ignored everyone. I don't remember passing anyone who I forgot to give that "good morning," to, but I must have passed by someone who took it upon themselves to let my *nonna* know that I didn't. Now, remember the fact that texting didn't exist and we didn't even have a phone on the farm, but by the time I got home my grandma knew that I had passed by her *commare*, Anna, and I didn't acknowledge her.

As far as the first day of school went, I don't remember anything memorable about it, but I remember every detail of what happened when I got home as if were yesterday.

My grandma was the one who was at home for my siblings and me. My parents ran the farm and they were gone from sun-up to sundown.. As I approached my front door, it magically opened and my grandmother was there to greet me.

"*Bentornato!* How was your day?" she asked me.

My reply was something like "okay," as I tried to walk by her to go change into my play clothing. I was ready for my snack and wanted to go out and play.

"*Un minuto!* Wait a minute," she said to me. A little annoyed, I turned around to face her. As I turned around, *nonna* Maria had pulled a chair from under our kitchen table and sat herself down in front of me. The first thing she did was to put her index and middle finger under my chin and push it up so that I was looking at her eyes and not her feet.

When I was much younger and she wanted to make a point about something, she would sit herself down on the floor so that we could be eye to eye with her. In later years, due to her arthritis and bad knee, she took to sitting down on a chair, but always using those two fingers to make sure that you looked her in the eyes.

"How come you didn't say good morning to *commare* Anna?" she asked.

Signora Anna's home was located about a half kilometer down from the school, and pas-sing under her balcony was the only way you could go to get to school, no way around it. She loved to sit on her second floor balcony so that she could have a view of that half kilometer of the street coming toward the school. She would see you coming up from the time you were still a dot in the distance, and she would fix you with her eyes. To be more precise, to me, she seemed to fix you with one eye. Yes, one of her eyes looked up and the other looked down, and it followed you as you passed by. Sometimes you tried not to look up, but that eye had power, and you looked up and said, "*Buongiorno, Signora* Anna." She would greet you back, but she would never acknowledge you first.

Did I see *commare* Anna? Play dumb, see what happens. "I didn't see her this morning ..." But even before I finished my words, my eyes were looking at my *nonna's* feet, and I knew that she wasn't going to buy it.

"Hey, look at me !" she said, as she pushed my chin back up. "You passed under her balcony and she told me that you never looked up to greet her."

"No, *nonna,* she wasn't there." Continue the lie.

"HEY! DON'T PLAY *STUPIDO* WITH ME! *Commare* Anna would never miss being on her balcony for first day of school. Look, she told me that you were with Mario and I know that when the two of you are together, both of you turn into two old women, so it's okay, but don't lie to me. It's important to me that you pay attention to what's going on around you and be polite and acknowledge others."

"But why, grandma? I barely know her," I said, with the most whining voice that I could muster. She paused for a moment and then said, "Okay, okay, do you notice sometimes when stray dogs come around into our yard and they approach our dogs?"

"*Si, nonna,* I have seen them."

"What do you see the dogs do?"

I didn't know that this was going to turn into a test on my first day of school. "I don't know, grandma. What do they do?"

"What they do is circle each other and sniff at each other's butt. Do you know why?"

"I don't know, grandma. Maybe they just like to sniff each other's butt."

I'm expecting some world-shattering revelation from my grandmother, and the only thing she wants to teach me is why dogs sniff at each other's butts.

"*Testa dura di cucuzza!* You are smart but you have a hard head. Let me tell you why dogs sniff at each other's butt. It's their way of saying hello. It's their way of greeting each other. If two dogs can say hello to each other, you better learn from them and say hello to another human as you pass by them and be polite!"

"*Si, nonna, as* long as I don't have to sniff their butt."

"*Vai via,* go change, and go and play."

So the next day as I walked to school I saw *Signora* Rosa and with a big smile I said, "*Buongiorno, Signora* Rosa*!*" And then I jumped out of the way from the splashes that *Signora* Rosa made by emptying the night chamber pot down the sewer. Further down the street, "*Buongiorno, Maestro Ercolino!*" I said to one of the only two carpenters that our town had. *Maestro* Guglielmo was the other. They could build you a crib, a door, a window, or a casket. I guess they were *maestros* of their trade.

THE VOICE

"DO I know you? Have we met before?" I ask.

Even as I speak, the thought is in my mind as to why I keep answering what I can't see, so definitely it's got to be my imagination. And then I hear a sound, the sound of a voice like I never had heard before as it says again to me, "Hi, I'm Mr. C. I gave you a glimpse of me once, and lucky for you the coin flipped in your favor. But now . . . I'm back!"

As soon as I heard those words I started to have a sense of recognition of the voice, but not enough to know who it was. I couldn't place the voice as anyone I knew, but in the back of my mind there was recognition but no face to go with it. Then a bulb went on in the next instant, as I recognized the voice that I could hear from the entity that I couldn't see. Now I knew the face to go with it. The voice was from a well-known actor, governor, bodybuilder, and author by the name of Arnold . No last name is needed, everyone knows him as the one who said, "I'll be ba-a-ack!" in a famous movie. But I was hearing it as, "I'm back!"

Again the now familiar voice said, "I'm the rest of your mortal life. For every moment I give you to think, 'I got this,' I will take two to let you know that you don't. I'm the shadow that will control every breath you take. I will be omnipresent in your life and the life of those that you love the most!"

Then the voice changed again to one that I didn't recognize and it became one that sounded seductive but also menacing as it said, "I'm the thief in the night!"

But this thief isn't happy to just take from you -- he'll take but he doesn't leave. He will penetrate the deepest recesses of your mind, body and soul. And even when you think you have succeeded in eradicating him, he will quietly hide for a while, just enough for you to believe that you are safe, and then . . . "TAP, TAP . . . BAMM!"

Maybe it's good and bad. Angels and demons, night and day. And then as I pull into my parking space in front of my workplace, it goes quiet.

I'd had my first encounter, or maybe my first brush, with Mr. C., about two years before my first surgery that I will soon undergo.

The big C, the unspoken word. The unspoken word that for so long has terrified billions of people. Growing up, if any of the adults, including my parents, were to speak of cancer, they would not use the word. They would say "*Quella brutta malattia.*" That ugly sickness.

The thought was that if you didn't speak the word *cancer*, it would go away. I should have kept quiet.

About a year after I had my cancer surgeries, I had occasion to be talking to a friend of mine in Italy. I was inquiring about a mutual acquaintance who I knew had been sick, but I wasn't aware that he was dealing with Mr. C.

And thanks to the wonder of the Internet and satellites, as we are looking at each other on our phone screens, I asked my friend. "*Come sta?* How is he?"

"Not too good," he answered.

"Is he in the hospital?" I asked.

"No!"

"At home recuperating, then?"

"No!"

"He's not in the hospital and not at home . . . where is he?"

"At the cemetery!"

I'm stunned for a moment, but I recover quickly.

"*E morto*? He died?"

"*Si*," he answered.

"When? How?"

"He died a couple of weeks ago."

"How did he die?"

I can see the moment of doubt on my friend's face as we are staring at each other's faces.

"He died of that sickness," he said.

"What sickness did he have?" I asked him, hoping to have a little clarification.

"Hey *Bruu*," my friend said, using my nickname from when we were children," he died from *quella brutta malattia*." The ugly sickness. The unspoken word.

I wanted to say to him, "Like the one I have?"

But I didn't have to say it because the look on his face said it for me, as maybe he saw a solitary tear running down the side of my face.

"I'm Mr. C. I'll always be there for you. Your friend is dead. You're alive." I hear the seductive, menacing voice in my mind as I wipe the tear from the side of my face.

And then it went quiet again.

Two years earlier, my first brush with Mr. C. came when after an annual physical at my primary doctor 's office – with blood and urine taken and that fun part, a digital exam – the doctor's opinion was that my prostate felt bigger than normal (from the length of his fingers I thought that he was examining my colon). "But we will wait for the PSA results to see if you might need to see a urologist," he said.

My PSA was over eight. Time to see a urologist.

My wife was with me as we went to meet my urologist, who I will call Dr. Urologist. After another fun examination and a review of my blood test, he said to my wife and me as we sat in his office, "The decision is yours. You are still young . . . barely 60 and way too young to have your prostate so enlarged. We can try medication to shrink the prostate, but my recommendation at this point is to do a biopsy. It's for peace of mind, to make sure that nothing is going on that we would have to worry about later and end up needing surgery or treatment."

My wife and I are sitting side by side as Doctor Urologist talks to us. We look at each other and she says to me, "Have the biopsy. As the doctor says, it's for peace of mind."

On the day of my biopsy, as the nurse comes out to the waiting area and calls my name, my wife squeezes my hand to pass on some of her strength as we exchange a chaste kiss for good luck.

I follow the nurse to a small room that looks like a miniature operating room with monitors, computers, a surgical bed, sealed containers for disposal of needles and similar items that might be contaminated, pressure cuffs, and all sorts of other tools. On a table at my side, I see a funny looking rod sitting there.

I'm instructed to remove all of my clothing from the waist down. There is a sheet on the bed to cover myself with after I strip down. It's funny to stand in the middle of a room fully dressed from your hips up, but with nothing on below. I am confident that this procedure will go well, and I'm not worried at all as I sit on the bed and pull the sheet over and tuck it under the lower part of my body.

A few minutes later I hear a knock on the door, and Dr. Urologist and a nurse walk in. After exchanging a few pleasantries, he instructs me to lie down on my side and to bring my legs into the fetal position. I feel the breeze blowing up my rear as the nurse pulls and then lifts the sheet that I had meticulously tucked around and under my bottom, and now my posterior is completely exposed.

Dr. Urologist reassures me that there is nothing to worry about. He will be using a spray to numb the area of the prostate where the biopsy is to be taken and there should be no pain. After a couple of minutes I feel the doctor's hand on my hip as I see him reach beyond him while he is bending down at the waist to look up my posterior. I feel a foreign object entering a dark place. The nurse must have sensed my discomfort with the operation. I feel her reassuring hand on my back as she says, "Relax. . . . Don't tighten up."

I feel what I think is the rod I had seen on the table, but I'm not sure, as I hear, "Take a deep breath."

And as I take my deep breath . . . I'm shot. I mean, I hear a sound as loud as a gunshot in my gut. I jump, my body levitating off the table like a coiled spring that has been pushed down and then released. Then I feel a sort of a pinch and a rip inside of me.

"Did that scare you? I should have warned you," Dr U. says, as the nurse does her best to keep me down on the table. "It's the biopsy being taken. The instrument is spring-loaded and when released, it sends a set of very small claws to go and collect pieces of live tissue to be sent for biopsy. The area should be numb. You'll be okay, relax."

I feel like I am in the movie *Alien*, when the entity comes out of some poor bastard's gut and the only thing you see is a snake mouth full of teeth. With each shot Dr. U takes I feel the bi-te from the alien inside me.

Bang! I feel the next biopsy being taken. "Relax, only 12 more to go," Dr. Urologist says.

I think that any man who has had a biopsy of the prostate feels the loss of modesty. (I think of this as a man thing.) Women start at a very young age being poked and examined. Having a baby probably eliminates just about any sense of modesty that a woman might have left. Not for men. Barring sickness, most adult males don't have a digital examination until their later forties, or maybe even fifties or sixties, and then to have this foreign object getting to the place that should be left as a dark place . . . Although, as Jerry Seinfeld used to say, "Not that there is anything wrong with it."

Then there is the waiting for the biopsy results to come back. In between you deal with one and a half weeks, and maybe it is closer to two weeks, of pissing blood and the burning of passing that blood and urine, and wondering, "Do I have cancer?" I swear that they do use that little monster from the movie *Alien* to rip those little bits of flesh out of your insides. And that pretty nurse is always there watching and making sure that whatever sense of modesty you might have left gets completely neutralized.

Two weeks to the day, at the same ten o'clock time slot, we are ushered into Dr. U's office. The nurse asks a couple of questions about medication before leaving the room. My wife and I sit side by side waiting for the doctor to come in. There is a quiet in the room so we can hear each other's breath escaping from our lungs. We both seem to be looking around the room to find something to focus on or talk about. My wife says something about the doctor's diplomas on the wall. "Where did he go to school? Can you read it from here? I don't have my eyeglasses." I pat my shirt pocket, knowing that I have left my eyeglasses in the car as I say, "No, I don't have my glasses, and those diplomas are too far up on the wall to see."

A thought comes to my mind as I answer my wife. Wouldn't it have been smarter to check those medical school diplomas at the first appointment, before I came here to see him to have a biopsy?

And we sit there waiting and trying to ignore the fact that shortly we will hear, "Good news, Mr. D.," or "Sorry, Mr. D."

On one side of the room that we are sitting in there is a full-sized bust of a grown man's lower torso and genital area that is split in half to offer a view of the prostate. My eyes keep on going to this little gland no bigger than a walnut that is the cause of all of my troubles.

My wife and I sit there still trying to make small talk and believing that all is okay. After all if, you don't name it, it goes away.

And finally the doctor comes in and he seems to be in a good mood. We shake hands all around and hellos are exchanged, and then he sits at his desk in front of us. On the desk is a file that has been sitting there all the time we have been waiting. We watch the doctor closely as he turns a couple of pages, to see if we can pick up from his facial expression some idea of what the verdict would be, and then he looks at us and says, "Good news, there are no cancer cells showing from your biopsy."

Just like that a ton comes off our shoulders. I can feel tears on the side of my face and from the corner of my eye I see my wife wiping tears off her face.

I'm thankful I have been told I don't have cancer. After all, why should I have cancer? We eat our fruit and vegetables and salads faithfully. We watch our intake of carbs and artificial sugars, and don't eat too much red meat. We have poultry and fish two, three, four times a week. We lead an active life, have a few drinks a week. I have been told that the enzymes in red wine burns the fat in our arteries. Cheers!

Gave up smoking long ago. My wife's only experience with smoking came as a teenager with couple of friends deciding to try it. Got caught by her dad on the first try. "Don't do that again," she was told. She says that she never smoked again because of the look of disappointment she saw on her dad's face as he caught them smoking that cigarette. Nothing there to warrant the big C.

Just a bit over two years from my prostate biopsy, Mr. C. decided to show up and tap me on the shoulder. It came with a call on my wife's phone. Reason the call came on my wife's phone is that I keep my old flip phone in my car uncharged and shut off. If I have a need to use it, I just plug it into my cigarette lighter and use it, and yes, my car is old enough to still have a cigarette lighter. I don't have a smart phone. My phone, my flip phone, when first acquired, was state of the art. We bought it for my son as he was going away to his first year of college. That was in the year 2000. It is now 2017. My son is now 34 years old and I'm still using his flip phone. That is great material for a commercial.

When people ask "Do you have a smart phone?" I'm tempted to want to use the common answer, "No . . . I have a stupid phone." My phone is not stupid, it just has a stupid owner.

Once at a party with mostly family members around me, everyone is making fun of the fact that I use a flip phone and they all have smart phones. To make it more personal, someone made a reference to an episode that happened a while ago. My son at some point had called to tell me that he had misplaced the keys to his car and asked if I could go by to pick him up. Needless to say, my phone was in the car, and the call went unanswered and the voicemail unheard. About six months later, I'm in the car, stuck in traffic, on my way to Boston. I decide to fill the time by making a phone call to one of my friends. As I power on my phone I see that there is a voicemail from my son.

Without looking at the time and day, I instantly call my son back and ask.

"Hey, where are you?"

"Just got home from work," he answers.

"Oh, you found your keys?"

"What keys?"

"YOUR KEYS!! You left me a message that you lost or misplaced your keys and you needed me to pick you up." There is silence for a moment and I can almost hear his mind searching. Then he says, "Dad , that was six months ago that I left you that message." Well, I guess he found his keys.

Back at the party, one of my children says, "Dad has a stupid phone that he doesn't charge or answer." I take offense at having them call my phone stupid as I say , "I don't have a stupid phone. Maybe a little retarded, but not stupid." Everyone stops talking, eating, and breathing, and they are all looking at me. You might have thought that I told them I just killed the Queen of England. (We love you, Elizabeth). "Dad, don't use the 'R' word. That word has been banned, and is very offensive to special needs people."

"But I was referring to my phone! It's an inanimate object!"

"D-A-A-A-D-D . . ." with that long "a-a-a-a-a." And then I see that my son-in-law Tim 2 – both of my sons-in-law are named Tim, so to tell them apart we call them Tim 1 and Tim 2 – is wearing a t-shirt with big block letters that says,

SPREAD THE WORD
TO END THE WORD
WWW.R-WORD.ORG

A cartoon comes to mind that I had seen in the comic pages of one of our local newspapers, *The Boston Herald* . There is a UFO hovering over a city and the two Martians in the craft notice that everyone walking around is either talking on a phone or carrying a phone. A quote appears in the little cloud over the spaceship that says, "We are too late . . . this planet has already been colonized." That, for a long time, was my feeling about smart phones.

GROWING up in Italy, for both young men and women alike, one of the first things you learned was how to ward off things like *"il Malocchio,"* the evil eye, being bad-mouthed, death, bad weather, your car getting stuck, evil spirits, or anything bad that you didn't want to happen to you or your loved ones. I do know that there is a big difference between your car getting stuck and dying, but in a moment I will explain. And yes! The method that you learned to ward off all bad things was also used to ward off cancer.

Fai li corni. The horned salute. There is more to the two-horned salute than most people are aware of, or from what they have learned by seeing it in some *Mafioso* movie.

First step in two parts is to know how to use it properly and when to use it. Second, as important as step one, is to know to start with your right hand. The left hand is used only when doing a double-horned salute using both hands, and doubles should be used only in extreme emergencies, something like the black pestilence or a nuclear explosion. Now pay attention.

Close the middle two fingers in the palm of your right hand. Good. Now fold your thumb to enclose your middle and ring fingers in the palm of your right hand. Extend index and pinky to form a fork. If you have a pinky ring on, it is even more effective. This is done with the palm up, and this particular form of salute is a generic one used for warding off everything and anything. Now hold your left arm across the middle of your ribs so that your open palm touches your upper arm, up against your biceps.

With the palm of your right hand up and your two fingers extended, bend your arm at the elbow so that your fingers, hand and forearm are pointing forward. You are now ready. Start a back and forth motion with your right arm, while holding your left arm in place across your stomach, with the palm held lightly across your upper arm so that your hand makes a stopper for your right arm's biceps in the back and forth motion . . . yes, just like that. Your arm is now your personalized pitch fork. Back and forth you go, just as if you were stabbing a wild beast that want to rip your head off.

And then there is the horned salute that's used as you see a funeral procession passing by, or it could be an empty hearse maybe just going down the street to fill the gas tank, or as you drive by funeral homes in general. This horned salute usually is done discreetly as the funeral procession passes by, or a hearse passes you on the highway, or if you are driving by a funeral home. Automatically fold your fingers, but hold your hand palm down with your index and pinky finger extended. At this point, if you can, you turn your body to discreetly hide your right hand close to your body to cover the back and forth motion pointing to the ground and not in front of you, while your left hand reaches for your testicles and gives a good scratch while you say, *"fa li corni."* Pump and scratch, but always discreetly, in case there are women or children around.

But!

Women are also very fond of the two fingered horned salute to help ward off any evil, but not many of them scratch their vagina as they do the horned hand shuffle. Maybe scratching one's vagina is not as effective as one's testicles . Once again, women get the short end of the stick.

There was a lady that lived in our neighborhood while I was growing up who didn't have a problem adding a scratch while doing the horned shuffle. We called her *Za* Rosetta. The word *Za* means *Zia*: aunt. She was not one of my aunts, but the expression was used as one of respect toward her as she was a friend of our parents, and a neighbor, and an older member of our community.

We were at a family party to celebrate my cousin Liliana's *Prima Communione*, First Holy Communion. After church, we all went to my aunt Delia's house for *il ricevimento*, a reception in honor of Liliana. The main room of the house, *il salotto*, the den, was cleared of furniture and a row of chairs was set up all around the outer walls of the room so that people could sit side by side. Soon my aunt, my mom, and others that were there to celebrate and help would start to come around the room with trays of cookies, small sandwiches . . . and drinks. And I don't mean tonic. I'm talking about *Sambuca, Marsala , Stock 84 ,Ramazzotti* and *vino*.

This was a booze fest and pastry orgy. We usually had or saw cookies only for Christmas and Easter, and even then they were only put out when we had guests. And the guests always had first dibs. When one of these parties was given, most children tried to take one of those seats around the room or tried to squeeze in between parents or relations. If you made it into the circle, you got served just like any adult in the room. That afternoon I was sitting next to our neighbor, *Za* Rosetta, and she was sitting holding her young daughter, Loretta, on her lap. The child was about a year of age.

Someone came by, not a neighbor but a man from our town, and seeing mother and child sitting there he said, "*Ma che bella bambina.*" What a beautiful child.

"*Grazie,*"she replied as the man moved on. And as I was sitting there with a cookie in one hand and a glass of Marsala in the other, I saw her take her daughter's hand and help her re-create the horned hand. And to my surprise, the young child had no problem holding her chubby fingers straight out. I saw *Za* Rosetta with her other hand take the child's hand to encourage her to scratch as she said, "*fa li corn mamma se ca quest ti fa lu malocchio.* Do the two-horned salute, my child, because that man will give you the evil eye."

The more I looked, the more I realized that the little girl was very well schooled in the point and scratch, and you know what they say about babies: "They are like little sponges, they learn fast."

For good measure she added her own horned hand to the back of the man as he continued down the other side of the room. Point and scratch, point and scratch. Repeat until satisfaction is achieved. And as I was looking at this set of mother-and-child horned salutes, she turned toward me and said "*tu pure Brunuu' fa' li corni.* You too, Bruno, do the two-horned salute." And not to disrespect my neighbor I held tight to my glass of Marsala in one hand, tucked the cookie under my folded middle and ring finger and did the shuffle. I didn't even know the man and I was giving him the salute. Be polite.

"*A la Salute!!!*"

Hello, Mr. D. I'm Mr. C.,
It Says, With A Tap On My Shoulder

"I'M Mr. C.," it says. "I'm the big dog. You're no longer the Alpha dog. You're no longer king of the hill, nor king of your kingdom or domain. No more *Pater Patriae*, father of your fatherland or your country, no more *dominus et deus*, lord and God.

"I'm Mr. C!!! I will own your mind, heart, and soul. I will be in your dreams and I'll walk with you for every step you take. I'll be the shadow that will follow you the rest of your mortal life. I'll make you cry like a newborn baby when you meet me and they will not be tears of joy.

When you think that you have no more tears to shed, I'll only be getting started with you.

I will take over your life and inflict pain like you've never known before.

I will bind your guts. Having a bowel movement will make you understand. It will give a new meaning to old saying, "shitting bricks."

Cancer: "*Cane che na' conosce padrone.*" That dog does not recognize a master. According to my wife, those are her mother's words.

After my first surgery and continued use of OxyContin, my intestines are completely bound up and the pain in my mouth and throat and tongue and teeth and every surface in my head have multiplied by thousands as I try to push that ball out of my bowels while sitting on a toilet. Sometimes I want to reach up into my bowels and rip out that ball that has formed in me.

Five days have passed since my surgery, and still I'm not able to have a bowel movement. Again today I'll try. After spending half an hour sitting on the throne, as I flush I see only a few pellets in the bowl.

Strangely, they remind me of the area around my vegetable garden in my back yard, where those fucking rabbits . . . I refer to them as rabbits, not bunnies as the rest of my family does. Those fucking, fucking rabbits eat every head of lettuce. Every sprout of young green beans gets chopped off at the neck with no mercy and leaves me contemplating the decapitated green beans and lettuce and snap peas. As a thank you, those fucking rabbits leave beyond a nice pile of pellets just like the ones I see in the toilet bowl.

Prior to my first surgery, toward the end of February, on a nice mild afternoon with a beautiful sun shining down and a promise of good things to come for us gardeners – we are always hoping for an early spring to get a jump on our planting season – I was walking around my back yard with my granddaughter Autumn and grandson Sammy. They were a few feet ahead of me when I saw Autumn stop and say "Look, *nonno*, little balls!" And then she reached to pick some up.

"NO! DON'T TOUCH IT! THAT IS SH . . .!"

Oops, almost said the shit word in front of my grandchildren. I correct myself and tell them that it's "poop." Everybody poops, even rabbits. Growing up for me the word that was used for shit was *ca ca'* or *cacca'*. A posting I had seen on Facebook reminded me of another episode from my childhood, when if my parents didn't want me to touch or go near something they always would say to me, "Don't touch that, it's *ca' ca'*." The posting that I had seen on Facebook was in Italian and it was a cartoon of a young boy being told by his parents every time he did something or touched something not to do it because it was *ca' ca'*, just like when I was a child. Then in the next frame of the comic strip, in the little cloud over the baby's head were the words, "These people live in a house full of *ca' ca'! Why can't they move to someplace where there isn't as much *ca'ca'*?"

"I'm Mr. C.! I'm going to bring havoc into your household finances. Everything you saved for and hoped to get, like that special trip, or your retirement funds. I'll take all of it."

I spent seven years restoring a 1967 Chevelle convertible, one of the few toys that I all-owed myself to have. I worked on that car with my son and my friend Marty.

Marty is one of those special friends that you have in your life who would never ask "Why?" He'll just say, "Sure!" Or," no problem, I'll be there." If you say to him, "I'll meet you at midnight, just bring a shovel," he doesn't ask why. But he'll say, "Should I bring an extra shovel for you?"

Someday I wanted to pass that car to my son. I wanted it to be his car, and maybe someday he could pass it on to his son or daughter. I hope that God grants him the same blessing that He gave my wife and me to became parents.

Gone. Sold and used the money to pay bills. That commercial you see on tv that portrays an older couple walking hand in hand toward the sunset, or the other couple holding hands across the two bathtubs looking at one of those beautiful island sunsets? Don't hold your breath that you're going to have any funds left over to even consider having one of those vacations or having the strength for it. Mr. C will devour all of it.

I'm angry. Not because I have cancer. I have accepted Mr. C. in my life. I have accepted that my life is forever changed. I have got past the "Why me?" phase, and what helped me with that was an episode that happened one morning as I went to one of those endless doctor appointments . While I was sitting in one of those endless waiting rooms, I happened to be sitting next to a gentleman who had his nose removed and most of the left side of his face.

Yes . . . the nose and most of the face was gone. After a few minutes of sitting there we started a conversation and the topic went to why I was there and then to what was the type of cancer I had. He had started the conversation by asking me, "Are you waiting for someone?" As if by appearance I looked like I didn't belong there.

In a couple of minutes I tried explaining to him what I was going through, and maybe from the tone of my voice and the sounds that came from me, as I couldn't put my words together and my words sounded like sucking water through a straw full of holes, I got the impression that I would get some sympathetic words. He turned to face me and I could see that he had a gauze patch over the nose and side of his face. "Cancer is hard. It's a noose around your neck. Do you have days where you just wonder why this is happening and why it's happening to you?" he asked, while pointing to his face.

Oh, my God, this man knows exactly how I feel. "Yes, that's exactly how I feel," I said to him.

"Why me? Why did this happen to me?" With a kind but knowing smile he said to me, "Look around you." He used his hand as he did to make a sweeping motion of the waiting area. "Why not you? What makes you special?" And as he continued on he said, "I have had a round of chemotherapeutic treatments, one of radiation, and now the cancer has metastasized to a different area and I'm having radiation again. My life the last few years has been a rollercoaster ride. If I try to get off while this ride is moving, odds are I will get badly hurt or even get killed, so I'm staying on for the ride and see where it takes me. And when it stops if I don't make it . . . Well, no one has come back and complained about it. How bad can it be?"

I'm angry, not because I have cancer but because someone, like the many someones who enter our lives either by choice or not, who we trust to do their job because it is their job, didn't do his. We look at these professionals and think of them as gods. Sometimes they look at us as a patient – just a patient.

I'm blessed for the people that came along as I met Mr. C. But my first step wasn't a good one, and I'm angry because an individual didn't do his job, and he didn't have the common sense to say, "Let's have someone look at this."

A BUMP—DON'T WORRY ABOUT IT

A little over two years before my diagnosis I felt a bump on my palate. I brought it to the attention of my dentist that I will call Mr. D. "Mr. D., can you check this bump on my palate as part of my oral cancer screening that you do for me every six months and you charge me $195 dollars, US dollars that I pay out of pocket because I can't afford to buy dental insurance?"

"Open your mouth. Let's see!"

After probing around for few seconds he says, "It's probably just a salivary gland that is clogged. It happens, it's common. Nothing to worry about," he says as I feel him tapping the roof of my mouth with one of those picks that he uses to clean teeth.

Later I learned that the names of our salivary glands are the parotid, the submandibular and the sublingual glands. The parotid glands are located in front of the ear and beneath the ear. A canal called the Stensen's duct drains saliva into the mouth from the gland into the area of the upper cheeks. The submandibular/sublingual are located deep inside the mouth toward the back of the jaws and they produce over 70% of our saliva. They enter the mouth under the tongue to dump saliva through a canal called the Wharton's duct. The sublingual glands are located under the tongue and they provide saliva under and around. There are close to 1,000 small glands called minor salivary glands that coat the surface in and around the mouth and throat, not any bigger than a couple of millimeters.

"The receptionist will see you out front, nothing to worry about. See you in six months."

"Thanks doc, see you in six months. What? Oh yes, the $195. Sure, I'll see the receptionist up front . . . Yeah, I know I'll save 10% by paying cash."

10% OFF

SIX months later I'm back for my faithful six months cleaning and my oral cancer screening that I pay out of pocket.

"Looks good, no cavities. See you in six months." he says, and in a moment I have my feet on the side of the chair touching the floor, but I think about the pesky bump that occasionally – if food hits it just right – gives me a stabbing pain. Nothing to keel over from, but just enough to know that it's there.

"Oh, okay. But doc, can you take a look at that bump on my palate?"

"Well, let's see it." I lie back down as he puts his mask and gloves back on. He has his little mirror on a stick that he's using to prod the area. Then I feel him poking around with his finger at the spot in my mouth he says. "Yeah! Just one of the glands, don't worry."

"Okay, doc, see you in six months. What? Oh yes, the 10% cash discount. I'll see the receptionist up front."

I Have Work To Do

THE magic words for most adult males are "Don't worry." I say most adult males because women are smarter than that. If you want to raise a red flag for women and see a raging bull, the magic words are also "Don't worry." So what you get is two complete opposites.

For males, "Don't worry" means a green light, don't think about it, don't talk about it and it will take care of itself. And of course I'm one of those males for whom if you said, "Don't worry," I'll take that at face value.

I'm back home and I get the full blast of my wife's questions. "Honey, did you ask the doctor about that thing growing in your mouth?"

"Yes!" I answer.

"Yes, what?"

"Yes, I did!"

"And?"

"He said not to worry."

"But what is it?"

"It's a gland."

"What's the matter with it?"

"It's clogged."

"So what is he going to do about it? Can I see it?"

"OKAY," I say, as I tilt my head back with my mouth open for my wife to look in my mouth. "I don't see anything. Wait, let me put on my eyeglasses," she says. My neck is starting to hurt so I sit on one of the kitchen chairs with my head leaning back. "I still don't see it," my wife says.

"Give me your finger," I say, and without waiting for a response I take her index finger and place the tip of it on the lesion in my mouth. I feel her finger move around a bit and then the tip of her finger seems to find it, because her finger stops moving dead on the spot. "I can feel it! Did the dentist feel it? What did he say?"

"He said don't worry."

"But what does he mean, don't worry?" By now my wife's voice has a pleading tone to it, but to me it sounds like nagging. I can hear the annoyance in my voice as I answer her in a way that a loving husband shouldn't answer his wife.

"WHAT DO YOU MEAN, 'WHAT DOES HE MEAN?' I TOLD YOU HE SAID DON'T WORRY AND DON'T WORRY MEANS DON'T WORRY, AND I'M NOT GOING TO WORRY ABOUT IT!"

"It's got to be something. I felt it! There is something there!" she says to my back as I'm walking down our entrance stairs toward the front door. I have some yard work to do.

I needed to throw another stone before I walked out as I stopped with one foot on our foyer and one on our front steps. I yelled up at my wife standing in the kitchen, "Hey, the dentist gives 10% off when we pay cash . . . Maybe we should start to pay cash for everything and ask for a 10% discount."

SIX MONTHS LATER—KEEP AN EYE ON IT

AS Dr. D. is done with my cleaning and I have that nice clean tingling feeling in my mouth and the chair is pushing my posterior up to a sitting position, Dr D. says, "All good, no cavities, see you in six months."

This time I remember before I start to get off the chair to ask Dr. D. about the bump on my palate, and with both of my legs still on the table I say, "Hey, doc, can you check that bump on my palate? The other day I was having a piece of nice crusty bread and I think a piece of the crust poked it and I saw stars."

"Let's take a look."

Still with both feet up I feel the back of the chair going back down. Dr. D. is standing al-most in front of me with his index finger poking around in my mouth and applying pressure at different spots as he says, "Does that hurt when I push on the area?" As he asks the question, he touches the very spot where the bread poked me, and I feel my body jump. He still has his fingers in my mouth as I try to give a half nod with my head that says, "Yes, it does hurt."

Didn't the fact that my body jumped off the table give away that it did hurt? At the same time I nodded, "Yes, it hurts," I was shrugging my shoulders to say, "Maybe it didn't hurt too bad." Denial?

"That sensitive area is between the hard and soft palate. When some of these glands get clogged they can get very sensitive. We'll keep an eye on it. See you in six months."

"Okay, doc, see you in six months. . . . What's that? Yes, I'll see the receptionist up front for my 10% off." When I walk into my home, my wife is there. I can't see her yet, but the car is in the driveway and I know she's home.

Both of us have Monday off and we always try to have all doctor appointments on Mondays so as not to disrupt our work schedule or lose any income. When she knows that I have a doctor appointment, she turns into the Soup Nazi from the Seinfeld show. Today I'm barely up the first step and she's in the kitchen and she can't possibly have seen me yet, but I hear, "What did the dentist say?"

"All good! He'll keep an eye on it," I yell, as I walk downstairs to my basement to change into my work clothes. I'm busy, the deck needs painting.

SIX MONTHS LATER—NOTHING TO WORRY ABOUT

"HELLO, Dr. D., this thing on my palate hurts most of the time. I had a banana for breakfast and I saw stars and definitely it's getting bigger," I say to him before he even has a chance to answer my greetings.

"Sit back so that we can take a look."

I don't know why he uses the term "we." It's not likely I'm going to help him look in my mouth. I feel him poking around the roof of my mouth with the handle of the little mirror he uses when he does the cleaning. My palate is very sensitive and after the first poke he scales back the pressure he's using with the mirror handle. Maybe the moaning coming from me gave away that it hurts.

"I want you to see an oral surgeon. They'll probably scrape the surface of the area and for a couple of days you are going to feel like you had a hot cup of coffee and burned the top of your mouth. Nothing to worry about."

"Nothing to worry about." The famous words. And yes, the $195 for the oral cancer screening, and let's not forget that with cash I'll get the 10% off.

The Soup Nazi is at the door waiting as I get home. "Honey, what did the doctor say? Did you tell him that it hurts all of the time when you eat?"

"Yeah, I told him and he's sending me to see an oral surgeon. They'll scrape it off and it will be like having a hot cup of coffee and there is nothing to worry about." That was a mouthful.

Waited three weeks because I didn't want to take a day off from work. The first appointment available on a Monday was three weeks away. The doctor I was referred to was not available, so I made an appointment with one of his associates who I will call Dr. F.

Nice man and seemed very knowledgeable about what my problem could be, but very evasive about treatments or removal. After the examination he told me that before we did anything we needed to have a CT scan of the area and maybe we would need to have a biopsy done. "Nothing to worry about, just to be on the safe side." Another "we."

So, I would have an appointment at a local hospital the following Monday. On Saturday I got a call from the hospital to do the pre-registration. I was told that when I went in for my appointment I needed to have a check with me for $195 to cover the deductible on my insurance or I could give them my credit card now. After a week I got a call from Dr. F. that the CT scan was inconclusive and I will need to have an MRI. Two more weeks for a Monday appointment.

Again on the Saturday night before my appointment I received a call from the hospital for pre-registration and again I was informed that I would need to have a check for $900. The woman on the phone also told me that they take credit cards if needed.

I do carry health care insurance, as I should. Because of the new Affordable Care Act mandate there isn't a choice. If you choose to go without insurance the fines could be as high as the cost of the insurance itself. I'm paying over $1,500 a month for my wife and me. My in-network deductible is around $3,400 dollars a year individually. My out of network deductible reaches close to $13.000. And that's thousands. My deductible used to be $50 for emergency room, $500 for medical, and $100 for prescriptions. My cost yearly was about $10,000 (and that was for a family of five: my wife, me, and our three kids). I now have two individual policies as the kids are grown with jobs and carry their own insurance coverage. To keep the monthly payments down I was forced to take a higher deductible with less coverage and payments almost double what I had before.

With the high deductible to pay the out-of-network cost because everyone I see is a specialist, plus taxes paid on earned money to make the monthly payments, plus the monthly payments, as of now the cost for my health care for two people is just over $30,000 a year.

Congress passed a 3,000-page bill with just a, "Just sign it, we will read it later and fix it if need be. Don't worry." The famous words again: "Don't worry." Our healthcare was in trouble, but like a small baby it just needed a diaper change; it didn't need to be blown up .

Two weeks later I got a call from Dr F.'s office that an appointment had been set up for me to go in for a biopsy, and from the look of the scans there wasn't much to worry about. On the day of the biopsy they would probably remove the growth because it showed that it was just a surface growth on the palate. Nothing to worry about.

Bob- Physician Assistant

NOW enters one of many people who along my journey have became what my wife refers to as my "guardian angels." His name is Bob. He is the physician's assistant at my general practitioner's office. As the insurance company required approval and referral by the doctor, Bob noticed that I had gone for scans and that I was booked to go for a biopsy. He decided to call me to get more information about the procedure that I was booked for.

He called. Later on I found a voice mail from him. Needless to say, I never got his message from the phone I don't turn on, so I didn't return his call. He took it upon himself to call my wife to inquire about the scans and biopsy coming up. She's also a patient in their office.

My wife explained to him about the biopsy and removal of the growth to be done in the office of the oral surgeon. My wife told me that she couldn't even finish her sentence when she heard, "NO!" in a very loud tone from Bob. "NO! I'm sure he's someone very capable, but I'm going to recommend an ENT (ear, nose and throat specialist) to do the biopsy and take another look at the scans. I will call their office today and within the next couple days I will get Bruno to see them ."

My wife says that I only caught a percentage of what was being said because I didn't keep still long enough to hear all of the conversation. When she told me about the conversation she had with Bob the only thing I got out of it was that I was seeing a specialist to do the biopsy. The fact that he was an ENT was completely lost in translation.

Now, understand that from my side of things, when my wife told me that Bob had called and that he wanted me to see another doctor, the only thing I could think of was that I would need to write another check to another doctor.

With my wife leading as my number one guardian angel – and when I say leading, I mean shoving and pushing to get me to see the ENT – she canceled the appointment with the oral surgeon and took the appointment that Bob had scheduled for me the following Monday. How convenient. I didn't even have to take the day off.

The nurse ushered us into what I realized was the doctor's private office instead of an examination room. She instructed us to take a seat across the desk and the doctor should be in shortly. As my wife and I sat side by side, before the nurse left the room I asked her what to do with the CDs of the scans that I was holding in my hands. When we got the call that we had an appointment I was instructed to pick up copies of the scans on CD from the hospital and to have them with me when I came in. She took the CDs from me and put them on the desk as she left the room.

Less than five minutes and the doctor came in. He's probably in his late sixties or early seventies. Why that thought came to mind or what difference his age makes, I don't know and have no idea.

Dr. R.

HE introduces himself. "I'm Doctor R.." We shake hands all around. He has a soft tone in his voice and instantly I feel my body relax in the chair I'm sitting in. "I'll need a few minutes to review your scans," he says, as he picks up the envelopes that the nurse had put down on his desk. There are two CDs in the envelope, an MRI and a CT scan.

He has the scans on his computer monitor in front of him and he's alternating back and forth, reviewing one and then the other again. From where I'm sitting I can see the side view of his face as he sits sideways from us while reviewing the scans. A couple of times he gets closer to the computer screen to see the scans better. Once I saw him wrinkle his brow, but nothing too telling as to what he was seeing in those scans. As we sit quietly waiting for the doctor to finish his review of my scans, the only thing that I find to do is to keep looking at my watch and almost down to the second, 21 minutes later the doctor turns the computer monitor toward us.

"This is the area where the growth is located," he says, while making a circle with a capped pen over the area of the screen that shows a combination of a skull and lots of black and gray. The spot right beside the hole that I know is my left nostril is where the doctor's pen is now tapping at and the scan shows a dark area.

"We don't have a clear view of what's beyond this area. I need to do a biopsy to get a clearer understanding of what's going on and decide on treatments."

Sure, cha-ching, I hear in my mind, as my wife says, "Do we need to go to the hospital for that?"

"No, we'll do the biopsy here."

I see him reach for his phone and I hear him give instructions to the nurse to set up a room for it. My wife has been holding my hand as we sit there and as I hear the words "biopsy to be done here and now," I give her hand an involuntary squeeze. I think the doctor must have noticed it, because promptly he says, "I'm going to numb the area so you'll feel nothing. Nothing to worry about."

The biopsy felt like someone took a pair of pliers and just ripped a chunk off my palate, and when I say a chunk I'm not exaggerating. It reminded me of my prostate biopsy without the sound of the shot. But I think this sound I heard is worse because I heard the ripping of the flesh being taken from my palate. As I'm moaning, the doctor looks at the tip of the claws that he used to rip flesh out of my palate with a glow of satisfaction on his face, and he says, "Yeah, this is a good sample."

As we are ready to leave, the nurse informs us that in four days, Friday morning, or at the latest Friday afternoon, we will have the results and she will give us a call.

And this is a good place to introduce another of my guardian angels. Next to my wife, they would be guardian angels number 1 and 1A.

Dr. Peter Fredhenson, A Doctor With A Soul

DR. Fredhenson is an ear, nose and throat specialist. I have known Peter for about 25 years. He performed two sinus surgeries on me (Deviated Septum, non cancer related), about three years apart. We became friends. Not every-Saturday-night-dinner friends, but enough of a friendship that we had each other's phone numbers and when the cell phone became the norm, I always had his private number and we had each other's home numbers. Any time I had need of a referral, or any of my family or friends were in need of a consultation or recommendation, Peter was there.

At this point you may ask why, if you have such a good doctor as one of your friends and on top of that he's an ENT, why didn't you call on him when needed? Furthermore, my wife and I own a hair salon. I have been a hair stylist for the last 44 years and Peter sits in my chair for a haircut on an average of every four to five weeks. After I had my sinus surgeries, Peter would come to get his hair cut and carry with him his medical bag. And even before I would cut his hair he would say, "Let's go to the back room and take a look." He would check how I was healing and remove crust buildup around the healing area and mucus to allow me to breathe better.

So why at some point didn't I say to him, "Hey, Peter, I have this thing growing on the roof of my mouth, what do you think?" If I had done that he would have said, "Let's go in the back and I'll take a look."

Well, to answer as simply as I can, in my mind I was already seeing an expert related to teeth and mouth. I was always under the impression that the dentist I was seeing was the expert on my teeth, tongue, and the rest of my mouth. After all, why else are they scrubbing my tongue with their little piece of gauze and running their finger around my gum line and poking around? And every six months I'm paying for my oral cancer screening. Oral to me meant my mouth and anything near it. That was his job – the job that this doctor, or dentist, never did to the level that he should've done to live up to his oath.

PRIMUM NON NOCERE

EVERY doctor, physician, dentist, therapist and anyone else who puts a "Dr." in front of their name took that oath.: "*Primum non nocere*" or "*Primum nil nocere.*" First, do no harm.

Every medical student or health care professional knows those words because they are a fundamental principle known world-wide.

"First, do no harm."

Some people would argue that according to those words it's better to do nothing than to do something and cause more harm. Sometimes any intervention can cause more harm than benefits. In my case the harm of doing nothing almost took my life with stage four cancer.

I'm angry because the choice was taken from me. I'm angry because someone made a life decision for me. If that someone had said to me, "I don't like the way this looks, maybe you should have a medical doctor take a look. Nothing to worry about, just for peace of mind." And if I had then said to him, "Why bother! If you think it's nothing, it's nothing." And if he had then said, "No, it's best that we get you to see a medical doctor." And if my answer was, "No, doc. I'm okay." ... If all those "ifs" were the case, you could say to me, "He told you to see a medical doctor and you didn't, so now shut the fuck up and move forward with whatever life you have left."

But no! I never had a chance to make that decision. All because my dentist either didn't have the knowledge to understand, or he didn't care. But I think he should have known because besides being a dentist, he is also a teacher in one of the most respected dental schools in the world. And if he didn't know what he was dealing with, he should have had enough in him to say to me, "It's nothing, but let's have someone else look at this."

For over two years I heard, "Don't worry." Every six months I paid my fees to have a professional do my oral cancer screening and for every time I heard "Don't worry," I assumed that I had a professional doing his job. But we all know what the equal is of the word assume.

ASSUME = ASS-U-ME.

I really thought the magic was in that little piece of gauze that my former dentist used to pick up my tongue so that it wouldn't slip off his fingers and he could use it to wiggle my tongue around and side to side. That was my protection against cancer. I should have followed my parents and grandparents and all before them and used the two-horned salute and scratch. Bend your arm, pull your elbow back, point those two fingers as you roll the others in, and back and forth, pump and scratch. I probably would have had better odds with that, than the odds I had putting faith in my dentist.

I didn't ask the question to my friend Peter until P.A. Bob made the appointment with Dr. R. I finally called him and asked if he knew of this doctor that was going to do my biopsy. Honestly, I thought that if Peter could reach through the phone, he would have strangled me. Not because I wasn't using his expertise, but because I hadn't told him about the problem I was having.

"How long has this been going on?" he asked.

"About one, to one and a half years, maybe a little longer." I was ashamed to say two years.

"ALMOST TWO YEARS? ARE YOU FUCKING KIDDING ME?"

"No . . . I thought the dentist . . ."

"BRUNO!!! ARE YOU FUCKING AROUND WITH ME? WHAT THE FUCK! WHY DIDN'T YOU CALL ME ? I SAW YOU LAST WEEK FOR A HAIRCUT. WHY DIDN'T YOU TELL ME?"

For all of the years I have known Peter, I never heard him once use a swear word. I think at this moment he was trying to make up for the last 25 years.

"I don't know, Peter. The mouth? The dentist? They are the experts . . ." I heard this little voice come out of me. I think Peter felt that I was on the verge of crying. In the months to come I would be doing a lot of crying, but let's not jump ahead too far.

"Okay, okay." Peter said to me. "Who did they make the appointment with?"

"Dr R."

"Oh, good choice. We use him all the time. When are you going in to see him?"

"I saw him last Monday."

Turns out that Dr. R. is part of the same practice that Peter his part of. All of them are associated with the Mass Eye and Ear hospital (M.E.E.). In the next few months I would get to know all of them on a first name basis. Doctors, nurses, and even all of the parking attendants for the valet parking at the hospital.

". . . and Dr. R. set up an appointment for me to see a surgeon."

"Who's the surgeon that he recommended?" Peter asked.

"Dr. L."

"Oh, he's good! No, he's great! He is the best you can have."

The Biopsy

THE Friday following the Monday of my biopsy, my wife called the office of Dr. R. to in-quire about my results. She was told that there were no results yet. That same Friday night I got a call from Peter to tell us that there were no results. I had added Peter to the list of doctors to be able to access my medical records.

He also said to me, "I spoke to Dr. L. and even though we don't have the results yet, you will need to have surgery regardless of the results of your biopsies. I think that the growth . . . the tumor ... goes from your palate into your nasal cavity and needs to be removed. You need to be at Doctor L.'s office Monday morning at 9 am."

Well, I guess I will meet the surgeon. How convenient, Monday again.

"What do you think this thing is?" I asked Peter.

There was a small pause on the line and then Peter said, "It's too soon to tell. We don't have results yet from your biopsy and I don't want to spec-ulate. From past experience, these tumors are surface tumors and most of the time benign, but we need to do this one step at a time. From the look of the scan it's bigger than a surface tumor and things may be a little more involved than what we can see from the scans. Can it be cancerous? Yes, it can. We will find out."

I'm thankful for the many things Peter did for me and my family through my ordeal. But there is one thing that on a personal level helped me deal with what was to come. He was always up front with me and I never heard him say to me, "Nothing to worry about."

Dr. L.

WHEN we meet my surgeon, Dr. L., I am hoping they will have the results of my biopsy, but as we check in at the front desk, my wife asks the receptionist if they have our results, and she tells us that they are not in yet but the doctor will have more information.

So, we meet a young woman who is the physician's assistant to Dr. L. She seems about the same age as one of my daughters, mid to late twenties. As the introductions are made I neither catch nor retain her name. She is very pleasant as she asks all of the questions regarding medication and medical history, and a few minutes later Dr. L. walks into the examining room followed by a young man who is pushing a computer stand in front of him.

"Hello, Mr. Di Carlo," he says as he extends his hand toward me. "I'm Dr. L." We shake hands all around. He's young, not baby young, but I think about late forties, maybe early fifties. He didn't waste any time in preambles and he sat at the desk on the side of the room. He made a couple of entries on the keyboard in front of him and turned the computer screen toward my wife and me.

"I would have liked to have results from your biopsy, but we don't have them as yet. Most of these tumors are benign but I wouldn't know that for sure until we have results. The tumor needs to be removed. I will surgically do it as there's no other way to treat it. If you look at the screen," Dr. L. says, pointing at the screen and making a circle around an area on the screen like Dr. R. had done in his office with the tip of his capped pen. "The tumor looks to be contained in this area, but we also know that it extends toward the nasal cavity and by the scans we can't tell how far up it is. I will know that when I do the surgery. These tumors over time tend to grow in size and if left in place it will move into your sinus and it would make it almost impossible for you to breathe through your nose."

Dr. L. takes a pause for us to digest the information. I notice that every word Dr. L. speaks is being typed in the computer by the young man working at the computer stand. "... And if you don't have any questions we could schedule surgery in two weeks."

Strangely the only question that I can come up with is, "How long would I have to take off from work?"

"Everyone is different. Give yourself a few days, or maybe a week. Use your judgment but keep in mind that you are going to have a surgical removal of a tumor and no matter how minor it may be, your body needs time to recover. If you feel that you're up to it, by all means go to work."

I must seem a little worried, because Dr. L. gets up from where he's sitting and comes over to my side. My first reaction is that our meeting is over and I start to stand up to shake hands, but Dr. L. puts a reassuring fatherly hand on my shoulder for comfort, or maybe to keep me sitting in my chair. I find myself looking up at him as he stands on my side of the chair and says, "Don't worry, we will take good care of you. I'll see you in two weeks. My assistant up front will set up the appointment." As he says that, he puts his hands in the side pockets of the smock he's wearing. He is looking down at me and maybe this is the time to stand up and shake hands and say, "Okay, doc, see you in two weeks," but instead I ask a question. "Dr. L., do you think the surgery could be scheduled on a Monday?"

His hand comes out of his pocket and lands on my shoulder again and with a light squeeze he says. "No. Monday is the day we reserve for office visits. But look at it this way: You can have your follow up visit after your surgery on a Monday."

Throughout the appointment, with everything that was talked about, the discussion never touched the subject of cancer. Maybe the doctor feels the same way as my people of old; that if you don't talk about it, maybe it goes away. For me now the hard part is going to be the waiting and the fear of finding out, and I don't think that not to speak of it will make it go away.

MEET MR. C.

ON Wednesday, February 22nd, 2017, I'm at work at my usual time of 6 am. After my morning routine of making coffee and doing a couple of loads of laundry and putting them in the dryer, and some dusting and mopping of the floors, I do my walk-around of the shop and all seems to be ready for the work day and for when the rest of my coworkers get in later in the morning. I make my way to the front desk, and as I look at my day's schedule of appointments, I don't see anything unusual. About a half dozen haircuts, a couple of colors, some children's haircuts – a good, full day of bookings. I should be done by 7 pm. Yes, that is my average day at work, 12 to 14 hours.

Wednesday is one of the three days that my wife works at the shop with me. The rest of the week she is either babysitting our grandchildren or food shopping, or cleaning the house, or going to the bank, the cleaners, or doing any errands that anyone needs help with. I'm glad that I'm at work 12 hours a day because at least I know when my day is done. That Wednesday morning my wife came through the shop doors at about 9:30. A little unusually early for her because normally she comes in at about 10 to 10:30. As she walked in I was at the front desk scanning a credit card for the 9 am appointment I had just finished.

Usually as she or our coworkers come in, they all go toward the back of the shop where we have an area to hang our jackets and coats. Today instead she stayed by the desk until I completed my credit card transaction. As I finished I looked at her and said, "Hi, good morning."

"Hi," she answered, and as she spoke she put her hand on my wrist. As she did that I could see that she had tears in her eyes.

We had seen my surgeon a week the past Monday and almost two weeks since my biopsy, but with the weekend in between I wasn't expecting an answer yet. But every day and every time the house phone rang or I heard my wife's phone ring I would hold my breath. In the back of my mind I knew that eventually that call would come and as I looked at my wife's face with tears streaming down, I knew that she had taken that phone call and that life was changing for me and my family.

"Can we go in the back?" she said as she turned and walked toward the back of the shop. I followed her to our back room and pushed the door ajar as I entered it.

"The doctors office called. They have the results of your biopsy . . ." and for a moment I thought that her tears were tears of joy.

"The biopsy showed positive for cancer cells and Dr. L. wants you in his office as soon as possible."

There, just like that, I learn I have cancer. Meet Mr. C.

My wife leaned into me and we hugged each other. She is sobbing in my arms, but for me – a person who cries when I hear "America the Beautiful" play at a ballpark or at any other event – I don't have any tears as I find myself comforting my wife. Did everything stop? Did I break down? Cry? I look at the door to our back room, still ajar, and I see a couple of our coworkers walk by. The waiting has been as hard on them as it is for us. I smile at them to reassure them that everything is okay. At the same time, I see my 9:30 appointment walk in. At the risk of seeming rude, I close the door all the way so that we can have a little more privacy. My wife's hands are around my upper arms, not hugging me but almost holding me up.

Maybe she thinks I'm going to faint after I hear the news that I have cancer and she would need to hold me up. Nothing happens. I smile at her and say, "I'm okay."

"I'm sorry," she says as I separate myself from her hug.

"I have to go back to work. I just saw my next appointment come in. I'm good, don't worry," I tell her.

As I separate her gripping hands from my arms, I know that maybe we should stay behind the closed door and have a good cry, but I have no time for that. I have a full day of bookings, and I need to go and make some money. No time for crying or cancer. No time to die.

At about one o'clock that afternoon, I went into the bathroom to wash my hands before lunch and I had my first breakdown over the news of having cancer. The sobs came from the pit of my stomach as I stood over the toilet urinating. I started to shake and as I was still urinating I found myself urinating all over the edge of the toilet bowl, floors, and some on myself.

After I wiped everything down, including my shoes, I was glad I had black pants on and the wetness didn't show through. I washed my face and when I came out I was glad none of my coworkers were near the hallway. I quietly snuck into our unused pedicure room and closed the door behind me.

Hate Enters My Heart

THAT night driving home, I had the first thought of hate toward my dentist. I was scheduled to see him in March for my six-month cleaning.

How long has it been since I have been complaining about that growth? When did I tell him about that growth on my palate?

I remembered that the last two times I saw him, I mentioned that it hurt. So that makes what? A year? Was it two or three times before the pain came that I had asked him about that bump on my palate? That makes it, what? Two, two and half years since I first noticed that bump. Over two years I have been carrying cancer and nothing was done about it. Two years is a long time. Did the cancer spread, and did it get worse over the two years?

I feel the tears coming down my face, followed by sobs. I'm on Route 24 driving home and I realize that I'm going over 80 miles an hour. I see my exit up ahead and as I get to the end of the ramp there is a gas station on the right. I pulled into one side of the parking area and cried and cried.

Why did my dentist choose to wait over two years?

Why couldn't he have said to me, "Let's get you to a medical doctor and see what this is about?"

Over two years have gone by. I'm thinking, "Can I die from this? My God, I hate that man. I hate him from the bottom of my stomach, from the very place where my sobs are coming from. I hate him."

Monday February 27th

THIS meeting with Dr. L. is to discuss the results of the biopsy and to go over details of the surgery, not that I have anything to say about it. Now that we know we are dealing with cancer, the point of attack would be different. My daughter Elisa is with us. She'll be the note-taker.

The three of us walk down the hallway to my examining room hand in hand. We sit holding hands. Dr. L.'s office is on the top floor of the M.E.E. hospital, and as I look straight ahead in the distance outside the window I can see the CITGO sign near Fenway Park, home of the Boston Red Sox. I wonder if I will get to see another Sox game.

I know that that's stupid and that having cancer isn't necessarily a death sentence, but at this moment I feel that the hammer is coming down. The tears come as I put my face down in my hand because my wife doesn't let go of my other hand. She gets up and she hugs my head to her chest. I'm shaking. This is a dream, I think to myself. She hands me some Kleenex as she says, "We will get through this. Let's listen to what Dr. L. has to say." And almost on command, Dr. L. comes into the room.

As usual, he has a nice smile on his face. He probably feels that it's a good starting point for delivering the news, "Hi! Mr. D. . . . meet Mr. C."

I'm asked to sit in the examining chair while my wife and my daughter remain sitting on the chairs they had taken on the opposite side of the room as we came in.

We exchange "hellos" and "good mornings" and shake hands as Dr. L. settles at his desk with the computer in front of him. He does the same thing as at our last meeting, as he touches a few keys and the screen comes alive. He scans down a few pages to what I imagine is my biopsy report. He takes a few minutes to go over it, and as the last time, he doesn't give much away with his facial expression.

"We have the biopsy reports," Dr. L. says as he turns toward me. "They confirm that there are cancer cells present . . ." My wife has come to stand about a foot from my side. She doesn't want to be in the way but she wants to be able to hear what the doctor is saying, and his next words are, "You have a very rare form of cancer called ACC . . ."

A.C.C. ADENOID CYSTIC CARCINOMA

THIS is a switch. Dr. L. goes from talking about cancer to talking about music. It must be a new group I never heard about, ACC. No, maybe he meant AC/DC.

"What, doc? AC/DC? No, I never was into them. Highway to Hell . . . Okay, I guess it's good music if you like them . . . but I'm more an Eagles Hotel California kind of man . . .Fleetwood Mac . . ."

I get a little smile from Dr. L. as he says, "Funny, Mr. D. I said ACC. Adenoid Cystic Carcinoma. It's a very rare form of cancer."

". . . rare form of cancer." From there on, I have no idea what Dr. L. says.

My eyes fill and a sob come up from the pit of my stomach. My hands are in my lap, and they seem to have a life of their own because I can't seem to bring them up to wipe the tears running down my face. Present in the room are Dr. L., his P.A., the young man on the computer taking notes, my daughter and my wife now standing next to me. And I'm all alone.

Everything goes into slow motion and then everyone is still. As I look around from Dr.L. to the P.A. to the computer boy to my daughter and my wife, I can see a rainbow of colors bouncing from one person to another and everyone in the room seems to be engulfed in those colors. All of them in color, and all removed from my black and white self. I never felt so alone as at that moment.

Thankfully, my wife hands me some Kleenex, as Dr. L. makes to get busy reviewing some more information on the computer. Maybe he wants to give me time to compose myself, and I guess he is not going to put his arms around me for comfort. Or maybe physicians need to remove themselves from the impact of delivering this kind of news, probably on a daily basis.

"Hello, dear Mr. or Mrs. So and So, there is someone I'd like you to meet. HERE IT COMES! Meet . . . MR. C.! DA-DAAA!"

Dr. L.s' pointing to a picture on his computer screen and he's pointing to an area in the center of a gray mass. "This is the edge of your hard palate, and here," he says, pointing to a different area, "is your soft palate. I'm hoping that the cancer is contained in the hard palate, but I won't know that until we do surgery and more biopsies. It appears that the tumor is growing toward your nasal cavities. The cancer in these tumors is usually contained. The tumor is about this size, ..." he says, making a circle by connecting the index finger and thumb on his left hand, while pointing at the circle with his right index finger. "With cancer, as we remove a contained tumor, there is a need to go beyond the edge of the tumor itself because we need clear margins."

I'm in a daze and just nod. "Clear margins," I say, as if I know what clear margins are. But my wife pays more attention than I do and just as she is going to ask about clear margins, Dr. L. puts up a hand like he is a traffic cop and continues, "When we remove a tumor, we need to go beyond the tumor itself because of microscopic cells, so we need to create a safe area that sometimes goes about a half inch beyond the tumor. In your case I don't know where the safe area is. We do biopsies as we go along. We still send tissue to the labs after surgery to have them reviewed. It looks like, at this point, with the size of your tumor, I will need to remove at least one of your teeth. And if I need to remove more because they are in the area of the tumor, I will do that. I don't think that the cancer is in the bone, but as I said, if it is, if need be I will remove the bone above your teeth."

The bone? Remove the bone in my face?

Right at this moment the only thing I see is myself with my face half collapsed because Dr. L. removed the bone from my face. I will be the new Two-Face, from the Batman movies: one side somewhat decent looking, not handsome but not bad looking, the other side a collapsed, flat looking face with an eye hanging from a string. Just like in a cartoon, my eye is going up and down, "boing, boing, boing." Maybe that will be the new way of doing things when shooting a movie. The view from one side of the face will be for drama with real people, and when doing the other side of the face, with an eye hanging from a slinky, it will be the cartoon side.

Wait! I think they did that already.

"Boing, boing, boing"

"There is more. I'm going to try to prevent an opening from happening into your nasal cavity, but I'll need to chase this cancer," I hear Dr. L. say.

But my mind is stuck and I'm still seeing my eyes hanging from a string as I ask, "That is good, right, doc? Surgery? No opening? No hole?"

"Yes, Mr. Di Carlo, that would be a good thing, but I want again to stress the point that biopsies on the day of surgery will decide what will be the best course of action as we surgically remove . . ."

We? Does he mean that I will have a part in this ? When he says, "we," does he mean, "Mr. D., pass the scalpel. Not that one, the other one."

". . . the tumor. And we have a great dentist on staff who will fit you for an obturator if need be." My wife and I have puzzled looks on our faces. Obturator? What the fuck is that? But Dr. L. is not in his first rodeo. He explains. "A prosthetic." Did he say prosthetic? What the fuck?

Rocco, one of my childhood friends, almost lost both of his legs in a bad truck accident but thankfully after many months and after many surgeries and skin grafts, and lots of prayers, doctors were able to save one of his legs. He recovered and now he has a prosthetic limb.

So? Again I think, what the fuck is he talking about? Did this cancer spread from my mouth to my legs? And then what? A fucking dentist is going to make a prosthetic leg for me?"

My mind is jumping around. I never did drugs in my life but I think that now I know how some people might feel with drugs. At this moment I know that Dr. L. is talking, but I don't hear him. I feel heat spreading from the core of my body. It feels like these little lightning bolts hitting from the inside out. I can actually feel the heat reaching the tips of my ears. My hands are sweating, and I try not to dry them on my pants as they are still sitting flat on my legs. I feel a trickle down the side of my face. Are those tears? No, not tears, because I feel them further up on the side of my face. I'm sweating. The heat in my body has reached every extremity. Is that pain I feel in my chest? Should I say something? Maybe it's just the bile in my stomach acting up. I find myself taking a deep breath and I'm trying to do it with just slightly parting my lips, so as not to give away what's happening, and it makes me lightheaded. For a moment I think I blanked out because I felt my wife's hand on my shoulder as she asks, "Are you okay?"

"Yeah, I'm okay." I answer as I hear Dr. L.'s voice again. He is still speaking, but I don't know what he is saying, and either on purpose or without realizing it I interrupt and ask, "What about the prosthetic the dentist is going to do for me?"

For a moment Dr. L. has a confused look on his face, as the flow of information that he is passing on to us is at a different place from where my question was bringing him back to. For a moment, he seems to have an annoyed look as maybe he is thinking, "Hey, pay attention," but it is only a fleeting moment. Then, with a great smile, he says, "Sure, let me explain it a little better." I'm sure it was only my imagination that he would be annoyed by my question, or my lack of attention.

"It's a prosthetic, or an obturator. We refer to it either way. Dr. J. is the specialist on our staff. After we remove the tumor, Dr. J. will take a mold of your mouth and by the time you come out of anesthesia, the prosthetic will be in place. We will teach you how to remove it, clean it, and for probably six months to a year Dr. J. would need to make adjustments to it, because the tissue around the area will shrink as it heals. The obturator will protect the area that is affected from the surgery and will prevent a hole opening to your nasal cavity.

"I know that there is a lot to absorb. For now, I think it's best we concentrate on your surgery, but I need to make you aware of the kind of cancer you have. ACC is a very sneaky kind of cancer that likes to hide, and one of the favorite and first places that ACC likes to jump to is the lungs. ACC hides in the nerve lining, and the lining of your nerves becomes a highway for the cancer. I don't want to alarm you, but we need to do surgery soon, and for good measure you would need to do a round of radiation therapy, as the mouth is full of microscopic receptors that give the cancer plenty of places to hide in. Dr. B. is going to be your oncologist/radiologist. In the next couple of days, I will get you to meet with him.

"After a period of recovery from your surgery, he would direct you to what is the best course of action for you. There is a possibility you might need to do also a round of chemotherapy. If it's the case that you need it, it will be done before the radiation treatment. Sometimes, in some cases, you could be receiving both chemotherapy and radiation treatments at the same time. I know I'm jumping ahead, but I need to prepare you for what is ahead. This is a dangerous cancer."

Everyone seems to be looking at me. I don't know how to react. Should I be strong and be the model patient who says, "Yes, doc, I get it," or just break down and cry?

Dr. L. has a soft glow on his face as he says, "Mr. D., what's important is that when you wake up your cancer will be gone. There are extremes that I need to make you aware of. I feel that your tumor is contained and by the look of it from your blood work, it doesn't seem that it has spread anywhere else . . . But blood work doesn't show this cancer, only a CT or MRI would show that. I know it sounds drastic when we talk about removing teeth and maybe bone, and the prosthetic. But what's important is that by the time you wake up you'll be cancer free. Block the noise, don't read about it, and soon it will be over." He finishes with a big smile on his face.

I say, "Okay," and shake my head as a yes, up and down like a marionette on strings as I wipe tears off my face. My wife, the Rock of Gibraltar, stands next to me squeezing my shoulders and I find myself leaning my body toward her.

" DOES THAT HURT?"
"NO SIR! MAY I HAVE ANOTHER SIR!"

NOW the shaking in my chest is getting to the boiling point. My wife, standing next to me, is doing her best to keep herself together and soothe me at the same time, but this is a lot to absorb. The young man taking notes on his computer takes pity on us and hands my wife a box of Kleenex.

My surgery is Tuesday the 7th of March. Today is the 20th of February, George Washing-ton's birthday. Happy birthday, George. Two weeks to wait. At this moment I wish that they could just wheel me in and cut the fucker out of me.

On our drive home, close to one and a half hours because of traffic, my wife and I are very absorbed in our own thoughts. Maybe we exchange a half dozen words the all way home. As they sometimes say, "Silence is golden."

As we approach our home she tells me that she needs to do some marketing and asks if I would like to go with her. "I'm kind of tired. I'll stay home, but I'll help unload when you get home." Safe answer. "Okay," she says.

ADENOID CYSTIC CARCINOMA

IN my mind I already had a plan for when I got home. I'm going to dive into the web. I want to read more about this disease regardless of being told not to.

There are many articles and testimonials and opinions to read. A few things catch my eye as I bounce from one article to another. Some of what I read makes the tears come to my eyes and the sobs start. I'm glad that no one is home. I feel like I'm losing all control of my lacrimal glands as they seem to have developed a mind of their own. I randomly choose an article from *The Pan African Medical Journal.*

"Adenoid Cystic Carcinomas for the Palate: Case Report and Review of Literature." Uday Shankar Yaga, et al. Abstract." Adenoid Cystic Carcinoma is a malignant neoplasm that can affect either the major or minor salivary glands of the oral cavity." Okay, I already know that. Three Frenchman – Robin, Lorain and Laboulbene (none of them have Dr. in front of their name), in articles published in 1853 and 1854 – described the cylindrical appearance of this tumor. In 1859, Billroth (I have no idea who he is) first described ACC under the name "Cylindroma." Around 30% of lesions affect minor salivary glands, particularly the palate. The disease seems to show peaks in people around 50 to 60 years old, and it seems to effect women more than men.

Whoa! Perfect, I'm 60 years old. Dr. L. didn't tell me that I'm in the perfect age group for it.

"Clinical findings include slow growth." Okay, that's good, I think. ". . . local recurrence, perineural invasion." What does that mean? Is that what Dr.L. meant when he said that it hides in the nerves?

". . . Distant metastasis . . . Cribriform, tubular and solid . . . The solid is the most aggressive form . . . A unique feature of ACC is the propensity for perineural invasion even with early stage tumors . . . ACC is recognized as an extremely difficult disease to treat." Fucking great. I get the difficult one. Conley and Dinman describe it as, "ACC is one the most biologically destructive and unpredictable tumors of the head and neck." Jackpot!

As I scroll down, there are illustrations and pictures of different stages of the disease before and after surgery.

I see so many big words: neoplasm, cribriform, pseudolumina, pseudo-spaces, histopathologic-logical, isomorphic, eosinophilic, intraosseous epi-thelial, myoepithelial. It's too much. My stomach feels like a windmill. I think I'm going to throw up as I close the computer screen. Dr. L. was right when he told me not to read about it.

SURGERY

MY surgery was scheduled for Tuesday March the 7th. I had to report at M.E.E. by 6 am. With my faithful sidekick that my wife is, we left the house at 4:30. Normal ride in is an hour. We are trying to account for the morning commute traffic. By 5:30 I'm in front of the hospital. We beat the commuter traffic. The hospital offers valet parking, but as we pull up front by the hospital entrance we see a big sign announcing that valet is between the hours of 6 am and 7 pm. There is a parking garage that I can see in my rearview mirror about a quarter of a mile behind me.

The hospital faces Charles Street, a one-way street, and there is no way I can back up for a quarter of a mile. I drop off my wife at the entrance to spare her the walk back, while I drive around the block to backtrack toward the parking garage. I walk back as quickly as I can. I can see my wife stand-ing on one side of the lobby as I pass the glassed entrance to M.E.E.

"Did you check in?" I ask as I enter the lobby and approach her.

"No! The checking in for surgery is up on the surgical floor and they don't allow anyone up there until 6 am," she answers. I look at my watch. Only a few minutes to go.

At exactly 6 am we go up to the surgical floor located on the 7th floor. There is a spacious waiting area and a reception desk to one side. As I approach the desk there is no one there yet, but there is a signup sheet that instructs me to put down my first name and time of arrival.

We find a place to sit and after couple of minutes of fidgeting around I take a magazine that's on the table in front of us. I look at the date on the front cover and see that it is over two years old. Bored, I turned the first page, annoyed at the fact of a two-year-old magazine. A thought comes to mind: I have my new phone in my pocket. Yes!

The week leading to my surgery, my family decided that I should have an iPhone. Their thought was that if I was going to be in the hospital for a while, it would be important that they would be able to be in touch with me if they needed. So I asked them, "Don't they still have room phones in the hospitals?" And the answers were "That's not the same," or "You'll love it, dad!" or "When you get home from the hospital and we are at work or out, you can text us."

"I don't want to text. I don't know how. Why can't you call me on the house phone?"

"We'll teach you how to text so you can reach us faster!"

"Why can't I use the house phone to reach you?" I say again.

"Dad, we can't always answer our phones. You need an iPhone. If you text us we'll be able to text back much faster."

After a few minutes I hear my name called, "Bruno." Just like that, on a first-name basis, like we are the best of friends. I had done phone pre-registration on the Saturday previous to my appointment and at this point I just needed to sign some forms. I was expecting a clipboard and pen, but instead the receptionist points to a scanner on my right. "Those are consent forms for the insurance company. Just sign on the monitor."

I'm looking around but I don't see the little make-believe pen attached to a string. Is it attached to a string just in case someone decides to steal a pen that doesn't write? I don't see the pen anywhere, so maybe someone did steal it. Using the universal sign of bringing my hands up with palm up, I ask, "Where is the pen?" I almost feel like I'm in church and I'm reciting the Our Father prayer. If you are Catholic you know what I mean.

"No need for a pen. Don't use those anymore. Just use the tip of your finger." What??? The tip of my finger? What? It worked!

The tip of my finger signed my name, and even as I dot the i in my last name and sign a few more forms with the tip of my finger, I think of switching fingers to see if it works the same with every finger. I don't and keep on signing forms and after a while I don't have any idea of what I signed. The pleasant young lady explains every page put in front of me on the little monitor, but I don't read any of it. Just sign and nod "okay" to anything she says just like I understood everything, but in truth I don't understand anything. Then I am instructed to have a seat and the nurse will call me when ready. I go back to sit next to my wife. We lean against each other, not quite cheek to check but head to head. She is gripping my upper arm with both hands, like she is about to sink in the deepest of holes and wants to be saved. I pat the top of her hand against my arm as I hear:

"Bruno!"

"Yes," I answer as I put my hand up shyly, almost like a half wave. I feel like I am back in grade school as the teacher calls my name and I didn't study.

"Hi. I'm Jen, I will be your nurse. Come with me and we'll get you ready." My wife is getting ready to follow me in, but Jen says to her, "We'll get him ready and then I'll come out to get you."

Just like that, no kisses, no hugs between wife and husband. Our hands extend as I'm walking away without letting it go. Maybe our hands were trying to hold on to the last bit of normalcy. Our fingertips are the last to touch as I walk away. With that last touch, we lose the last of our old normal.

In the months to come I will hear a lot of, "You'll get used to your new normal." I was very happy and satisfied with my "old normal." I will shed many tears thinking of what I lost; what I always thought belonged there. To be able to eat, or drink a cup of water, talk, breathe.

What's to be thankful about that?

As I'm following the nurse through the doors of the unknown I have a strange thought. In my mind I am hoping that when Jen comes out to get me, I will hear her say, "This way, Mr. D., your table for two is ready." An after-Valentine's Day dinner. I always choose to celebrate days like that ahead of time, or after so that I don't have to wait two hours for a table as I don't have that time to waste. Well, soon I will have plenty of time to waste.

"Take everything off," Jen the nurse says, looking like a game show host as she slides the curtain back with one hand to reveal a miniature hospital room and with the other points toward the inside. There are monitors and wires and pressure cuffs hanging. Looks like I will be here for a while. "Remove all clothing including underwear. Your watch and that chain around your neck and your wedding band. Those two green bags on that chair are there for you to store your personal belongings," she says while pointing to one side of the room where a lonely chair stands with two green plastic bags on top of it.

As I started to unbutton the top button of my shirt, my hand touched the chain around my neck with Christ on the cross dangling there. "Can I keep my chain on? I would like J.C. to be with me," I asked with a hip note in my voice, not to be mistaken with the hip as the upper thigh bone or the hip as the sharp edge of a roof. I meant hip as cooler than cool, and the answer I got was, "No, you can't keep your chain on. If you believe in him he'll be with you, so no, you can't keep your chain on." She had a smile as she closed the half moon curtain and said, "I'll be back to check on you soon."

I stripped down as naked as the first day. As I felt the breeze coming up my butt, I realized that the room was on the cool side. Even my privates felt that something was going on and they were trying to go back to the beginning. It may sound crazy, but as I stood naked in the middle of the room with my privates shrinking I thought of an episode from the Seinfeld show.

In one of the scenes, a young lady walks in on one of the show's characters, George Costanza, as he is changing his clothing after coming out of a cold water pool. The naked George stands there trying to cover himself, but it's too late as she's seen it all. His privates have shrive-led from the cold water. She looks at him and laughter comes as she points to his privates.

"It's shrinkage from the cold!" he indignantly yells at her.

I was stripped of everything: the chain (my religion), the wedding band (my marriage), and my clothing (my modesty and privacy). To complete the circle, I was even stripped of the "Mr. Di Carlo." When you are a young man and even into your twenties, thirties and forties, it's okay to be called by your first name by family and friends. But beyond that you should be addressed as Mr. or Mrs., and I think I have earned that title, but today I again became just a first name.

I put on my hospital-supplied flapper that would give even someone with the best of bodies nightmares. "The opening goes in the back," Jen the nurse had said. I tried to walk around the room to practice a bit to see if I could find a way to hold the two open flaps together on my hip side in case I was asked to walk down the hallway. Hip as the upper thigh bone.

I decided to sit at the edge of the bed while I waited for the nurse to come back. I found I was getting a wedgie from the flapper so I pulled the sides from under my ass. I pulled the sheets up to my belly and tried to tuck it under my ass. Still didn't quite do it, so I brought my legs on the bed and tucked a pillow under my upper back and leaned back. A little better. Now I could bring the sheets all the way up under my chin. Still not much better as the flapper was caught in my in ass crack again. I pulled both sides out, and there, that was much better. Even my privates were starting to relax again as I felt the cool sheets hugging my ass and testicles. I heard a little voice that said, "Get ready boys, we're going commando."

They were in for a rude awakening.

I heard the nurse's footsteps stop by the curtain as she asked, "How're you doing in there? Are you done changing?"

"Yes," I answered.

"Good, I'm going to get an IV started."

Jen the nurse was so gentle that I didn't even realize the needle was in my hand. As she finished putting tape around the area where the needle went into the top of my hand, she pointed at the hair on my wrist and said,

"Sorry, that will hurt when they pull the tape off." After a small pause she said. "I'll ask your wife to come in now so that she can sit with you."

She closes the drapes as she walks away and I'm alone in my little alcove. I lift the sheets to adjust myself again and as I look at myself the thought that comes to my mind is why do they need to have everything off? The cancer is in my mouth. Why does my wedding band need to come off? I wonder if, when the anesthesia takes effect, they take a peek under the sheets.

A smile comes to my face as I see a group of nurses and doctors standing around placing bets on the patient's size before they take a peek. Small, medium, large. "He's got big feet. My money is on large." Or "He's a little guy, kind of short. I got my money on a small." Or "Long fingers, definitely a medium or larger."

Just then, my wife is escorted into my room. As she walks in I hand her my watch, my wedding band, my Christ on the cross and my wallet. Now I'm just a first name, almost completely anonymous. Jen informs us that soon some of the doctors will come by.

The surgical nurse is the first one to show up, followed by the assistant to the anesthesiologist, and then the anesthesiologist. Dr. L., my surgeon, is the last to stop by. Everyone who comes in is wearing the same blue garb, men and women, no distinction in what they wear. Dr L. is his usual very pleasant and smiling self. He reassures me that soon it will be over and what's important is that when I wake up my cancer will be gone. He then pulls out a magic marker, and the way my wife described it later, he put an x on the left side of my face and signed his initials under it.

"See you soon," he says, as he gives my arm a squeeze and walks out.

My nurse is waiting by the side of the open curtain as Dr. L. walks out. As soon as he's gone she takes his place at my side. She is holding a syringe in her hand and I watch her remove a little cap from the tip of the needle. Then she brings the syringe up at eye level and looks at it. Does she push the plunger to remove air bubbles? I don't know because I don't see much movement in her fingers, but she seems satisfied with what she sees as she inserts the tip of the needle into one of the ports on the sides of the IV going into my hand.

"This will help you relax. This is the good stuff." Wink, wink.

As Jen is disposing of the syringe in one of those special containers marked with biological warnings on the side, the surgical nurse comes back and she tells me that they are ready for me. I don't know if I'm ready for them, but my wife leans in and gives me a hug and a kiss. "See you soon," I say to her as they wheel me out of the room.

(Months later when my wife and I speak of that moment as she watched me being wheeled away, she tells me that all she could do was to pray that all would go well. As she prayed, she had a surreal feeling that this was not really happening. But it was.)

I wonder as I'm being wheeled down a white hallway and see white fluorescent lights pass by above me, if my wife was thinking this was the last time she would kiss me without a plastic mouth. As I look again, everything we pass by seems to be white.

Reminds me of when as I child out on the farm, as I would lie down on a grassy meadow and look up at the blue cloudless Adriatic sky, so bright that after a while of looking up and wondering what lies beyond, everything turned brighter and golden white. Maybe it was the sun burning my pupils.

Now, looking up as I'm wheeled down the hallway, all that I see is white above me and around me and I feel almost hypnotized by it. I hope that that's not a hint, because I think the only thing that's missing is a bright light and me floating toward it. As the surgical nurse rolls me into the operating room, I see that the rest of the gang is here – the anesthesiologist, her assistant, Dr. L., and another nurse I hadn't met. The nurse pushes my bed against the surgical table and then asks me to scoot over to it. All in a motion as the surgical nurse transfers the IV bag from the hook on my bed to the hook on the stand next to the surgical bed, the other nurse that I hadn't met yet is putting a syringe in the port at the top of my hand. "Count back from ten," she says with an angelic smile on her face. Wonder if this is another sign.

"Nine . . ." And that is all I remember.

NOT until five hours later. I'm glad as I open my eyes that the first thing I see is my wife's face leaning in toward me. "Hi," she says. And I can see moisture around her eyes.

The surgery took a little over three hours. From there I was moved to the recovery room. As I blink my eyes and try to reply to my wife's greeting, my mouth feels like it's full of cotton balls. I want to reach up and touch my mouth, but one of my hands is all hooked up to IVs and the other has some other device hooked to my finger, and my wife is holding tight to the free fingers. I move my tongue around gingerly but I don't feel anything. All is numb. I try again and I think I feel a difference from one side of my mouth to the other. Is that a little ridge between the center of my palate going toward the left side of my mouth? I think I found the prosthetic.

"Hello, Mr. D. Welcome to your new normal." Well, at least *it* is addressing me as "Mr."

Was that Arnold again?

I blink my eyes. Maybe I'm still under the influence of the anesthesia. As I open my eyes and find some focus, I see another familiar smiling face leaning in and Dr. L. says, "Hello, Mr. DiCarlo, how are you feeling,?" I like Dr. L. He understand the importance of "Mr."

For a moment I thought that it was Mr. C. talking to me again, but Dr. L.'s smiling face is there as I answer him with a small nod and something that sounds like "okay."

"All went well. I removed one of your teeth and part of your palate. I didn't remove the bone above your teeth and there is no hole from your palate to your nose. Dr. J. made the prosthetic obturator that is in your mouth now. It needs to remain in place for a few days to protect the area that we treated surgically and to prevent a hole from opening into your nasal cavity. The best part is that now you should be cancer free, but we will know more when the biopsy comes back. Soon we'll bring you up to your room. Rest, and I will see you in the morning."

"Okay, doc," I said again as he walked away.

Wait! Did he say I should be cancer free or did he say I am cancer free?

I'm still under the drug's influence and maybe I misunderstood what he said. I feel that there is still some influence of the anesthesia in my body, because everything I hear is partial as I fade in and out, but I'm pretty sure that I heard him say that there is no hole into my nose and that I'm cancer free. A couple of days later I found out a funny fact from my wife as she told me that I had made her blush when the doctor told me that there was no hole to my nose. "Why, what did I do?" I asked her.

"Well, when Dr. L told you there was no opening from your palate to your nose cavity, you got all excited and your response was, "Now I can still kiss my wife.""

"I did? I don't recall any of that," I said.

But there is one thing that I remember. Something happened as I was being transferred from the recovery room to my room. I was moved from the recovery room to an elevator in the same area of the floor that I was on. I felt okay, but I know that I was still drowsy. I was on the bed. They rolled me into the elevator and as the doors closed I saw that there was a man by the back wall of the elevator. He appeared to be an older gentleman and he was wearing a collar as priests do. I took him to be either a retired priest or the hospital chaplain. I was looking at him upside down because he was behind my head. I don't know why, but I'm pretty sure that for whatever reason, I asked him to pray for me. He handed me a prayer card and, still standing behind me, he put his hand on my shoulder and prayed over me. I was still drifting in and out as I thanked him for praying over me and I asked him if I could make a donation someplace.

A couple of days later I remembered about the episode, and before I went home I wanted to find out who the priest was so I could get in touch with him and find out where I could make a donation. None of the nurses knew what I was talking about, and they didn't know of any priest.

When we reached the 11th floor where my room would be, the nurse stopped by the room entrance. There was a flurry of activity in what was going to be my room. From where I was I could see a clock on the wall and that it was just a couple of minutes past 2 pm. Also I could see the foot of another bed and someone's feet under the blanket, and that meant I was going to have a roommate. He was in the first bed by the door and there were two doctors and a nurse near the foot of the bed. Beyond them by the window, I could see someone putting sheets on what was going to be my bed.

"Good! A room with a view."

In what seemed a couple of minutes or maybe longer because I was still fading in and out, the nurse wheeled me into the room. As I passed by the first bed I saw a man in it, and I just lifted my hand to say hello. He did the same back at me. The nurse that had wheeled me in helped me get into bed and as soon as I was in bed she got busy hooking me back up to a heart monitor. Next came a saline IV tube that she inserted on the port on my wrist and then an oxygen monitor on my finger. There was a bulletin board on the wall in front of my bed with my name, my doctor's name, and the nurse on duty's name.

Just as I was pulling the sheets over my legs, another nurse came in and she told me she'd be my nurse until 5 pm. She thanked the nurse who had wheeled me to the room and told her that she'd take it from here. She was young and very pleasant, and after introducing herself she checked the I.D. bracelet around my wrist and asked my name and date of birth. Satisfied by my answers she said, "You're almost ready for your pain medication. I will get it ready for you. It's important that we keep ahead of the pain."

A few minutes later she was back with a little plastic cup. With her feet she maneuvered the pedals under the bed to bring the back of the bed up while she informed me that the medication she'd be giving me was liquid OxyContin. She handed me a little pill cup. She told me that because of my mouth surgery I will only be getting the liquid and not the pill form, so that it will be easier for me to swallow. I took a little sip and it seemed to go down okay. My mouth still felt numb and the medicine had no taste to it.

My wife remained with me until about 6:30 pm. At my insistence, because I remembered that the valet service would shut down at 7 pm and I didn't want her to be walking around in a dark parking lot, she finally agreed that she would go. And then I remembered that I didn't use the valet service. Oh well. Minutes after my wife said goodbye and I was about to doze off, I heard a voice asking, "You're awake? I'm your nurse until midnight and I've got your medication." She wiped off the previous nurse's name and wrote hers on the bulletin board.

I must have dozed off longer than a few minutes, as I didn't realize the other nurse was gone. The new nurse was holding the same little cup as my first nurse had as she came beside me by the bed. Need to stay ahead of the pain. It felt like I was ahead of the pain, as I didn't feel any pain and I was very drowsy. As soon as the nurse left the room, I felt I needed to make a trip to the bathroom. As I looked at all of the wires and clips hooked to me I decided that I would need some help and pushed the call button and hoped the nurse would come back. She did.

The nurse came almost instantly, but she told me I should be able to do this on my own and in a flourish she showed me how to unplug the oxygen and heart monitor and then as she helped me stand by the side of the bed she instructed me how to roll up the IV tube around one hand so it didn't kink up and how to push the IV post in front of me.

Together we walked toward the bathroom side by side, but I could feel her hand on my back. I don't know if she was holding the flaps of my johnny together so that I didn't flash my roommate or people in the hall-way, or she was afraid I'm going to faint or fall. She walked me in to the bathroom and gently closed the door, saying, "I'll be by the door if you need me."

It took me a couple of seconds to start my urine flow because I had to roll up my johnny under my chin and use my chin to hold up the johnny, leaving me completely uncovered. At this point I didn't care. I needed to take a good piss and it was what I was going to do. I had one hand holding the rolled up IV line and making sure it doesn't kink up, and that left me one hand to help me do my business.

"Oh, what a relief that is." Wasn't that an Alka-Seltzer commercial?

As I came out of the bathroom, the nurse was there waiting for me. She guided me back toward my bed again, walking beside me while hold-ing on to my johnny. As I sat at the edge of my bed she demonstrated how to hook up the monitors. After finishing, she stood back and said, "Now, if you need to get up or go to the bathroom, you can do it on your own. Anything else I can do for you?"

The only thing that came to mind was to ask, "What time is dinner?"

"Sorry, you are in a strict liquid diet," she said.

Seemed that overnight, every hour or so someone came into the room for either me or my roommate. At about 5:30 am, a new nurse came in to give me my OxyContin. She asked again my name and date of birth. I wanted to say, "It's the same as three hours ago." She handed me the little cup and watched me swallow the medicine. She asked if I would like some water. I said yes. A few minutes later she came back with a pitcher of water and a cup. "Just a few sips at a time. You are on a liquid diet until the doctor sees you." Well, isn't fucking water a liquid?

Around 7 am a nice lady walked in, and after wishing me good morning and telling me what a delightful day it was outside, she asked if I had filled out the menu sheet for my breakfast order

Hmm. Food. Maybe this is my chance. "No, I don't have a menu. I didn't fill one out."

"No problem, I have one here in my pocket. You can check off what you like and maybe you can even look up what you would like for lunch," she said as she passed me a little menu and a pencil.

I marked off some scrambled eggs with a side of bacon, a link of sausage, blueberry muffin, yogurt, and for good measure a cheese Danish. Just as I was deciding on juice, I saw her looking at my chart and I heard, "Ho, ho. It says here you are on a liquid diet. Sorry. I can't take your breakfast order. I'll be back around lunch. Maybe by then the doctor will change your orders." And as a clincher she took the menu back.

The Obturator—the Blob

AT about 7:30 am, a group of five people come in and all of them are wearing scrubs and stethoscopes around their necks. One of them introduces himself and tells me he is an assistant to Dr. L. and he is going to examine me. He asks if it's okay for the others to observe as they are medical students. I say "okay." He asks if it's okay for him to bring the back of the bed up, and again I say, "okay." He leans in and starts to feel around my neck glands. The rest of the circle leans in around my head to see where his hands are touching. He then stands back and says, "I need to remove the prosthetic."

"WHAT? NO!" I said, "Dr. L told me that it needs to remain place for a few days and then he will remove it."

The assistant looks down at me with a face that asks, "Why is this guy arguing with me?" But with a smile he says, "I just spoke to Dr. L. He said that the obturator needs to be removed to prevent a hole from opening up between your palate and your nose cavity. If the prosthetic is left in place too long the pressure from it might cause a rupture."

"A rupture?"

Was I still under the influence when I understood from Dr. L. that the obturator needed to remain in place to *prevent* a hole from opening up? And now this guy is telling me the complete reverse; that it needs to come out to prevent a hole from opening up?

The assistant to Dr. L. is standing leaning in with his hands near my mouth waiting for me to open it. We're having a little standoff. I guess if Dr. L. said that it needs to be removed. "Doctor's orders," he says. And I slowly open my mouth.

He has his two thumbs under my chin and with his two index fingers nails he hooks up the sides of the prosthetic and pulls. I feel a little pop as the obturator dislodges, and as he takes it out, I get my first look. It's bloody, it's misshapen, and on each side it has hooks. It's a blob covered in blood, mucus, and I don't know what. He deposits the obturator in a plastic tray that one of the interns is holding and asks me if I can open my mouth a little wider and lean my head back. As I lean back I see five faces about a foot away trying to take a look into my mouth.

"Looks good," he says to the group as he points toward my mouth. They all seem impressed.

"Thanks, Bruno," the assistant says. "Dr. L. wants you to remain on a liquid diet for at least another day. Maybe tomorrow we'll start you on some soft food. You'll need to be able to swallow before we send you home. Rest. We'll come by later and Dr. L. will come by later also." When later? I think. But what I try to say is, "Okay" to their backs, as the group shuffles out of the room. Instead, what comes out is a mix of spittle and some kind of sound I don't recognize.

This is the first sound that I've heard coming out of my mouth since they removed the obturator, and this is not the sound of my voice. I look around the half-closed curtain to see if my roommate is there in his bed and I'm glad I don't see his feet. I don't want him to think that I'm half crazy talking to myself as I do a voice test. "Hello! Hello!"

In my mind I am saying, "Hello!" But what I hear doesn't sound like it. Or maybe it sounds like it should, but I don't hear it as it should sound. I sit up in bed and look around the curtain again and I am satisfied that I'm still alone. Maybe my voice sounds funny because my tongue is glued to the bottom of my mouth, safely cradled in place against my bottom teeth, afraid to explore the new surroundings without the obturator in place. I want to reach up with my tongue to feel what it's like, but I think, "Will it hurt when I touch it?"

Before the interns came in, the nurse had given me my10mg of OxyContin, so there shouldn't be any pain. I decide to take the plunge.

I feel my tongue shake as I tentatively reach up toward my palate, but instead of reaching to the left side I reached to the right side of my mouth. Yeah, feels the same. A little sensitive, but it feels the same.

Okay, that part of my mouth still there, a little numb but I can feel teeth and palate. As I slide my tongue toward the center of my mouth I feel the reassuring resistance that my palate offers as my tongue moves over it. Then just as I reach about past center I feel my tongue being released.

Half of my tongue feels pressure, the other half is able to wiggle freely. I slide my tongue back toward the right side of my mouth. As I do that, I realize that I'm drooling. I look over to the table on the side of the bed and thankfully I see a box of Kleenex. I grab a bunch of it and wipe my mouth and chin. As I look at the Kleenex I see blood, mucus and spittle on it – not an appealing combo.

I feel warmth coming up through the pit of my stomach. Boy, they keep these hospital rooms hot. I feel like I'm going to throw up as I lean my head back against my pillow and take a couple of deep breaths, but after a moment of head lightness I feel okay. I hear someone shuffle in-to the room and I see a face peek through the side of the half-closed curtain.

My roommate is back. He has his face bandaged from under his eyes to the top of his lips. His nose and his cheek bones are not visible. He gives me a wave, and I do the same, and neither one of us says any words.

"Okay, okay, try again," I say to myself.

Again I reach up with my tongue and again it goes toward the right side of my mouth. As I slide toward the center it reaches that mid point where half of my tongue is on solid ground and the other half is at the edge of the precipice doing a balancing act. I like the reassuring pressure that half of my tongue is getting on the right side of my mouth from teeth and palate.

I don't know how long I remain with my tongue floating halfway up against the right side of my mouth, because I lean my head back and closed my eyes.

The warmth is throughout my body, but now I can feel some tears coming down the side of my eyes and drifting toward my ears. I doze off. The drugs are working. As I come to, I find that my tongue is still at the same reassuring spot between my gum line and my palate on the right side of my mouth. I let my tongue down safely into the cradle of my lower teeth and wipe the drool from my chin.

I take a deep breath and say to myself, "*Dai . . . forza.*" You can do it. Most of the time that I find myself in a situation that I need to reason things out, or if I need to get a source of strength, my thoughts revert to my native and childhood tongue as again I think, "*Dai forza!*"

I feel my tongue reaching up to the right side of my mouth and this time I resolve to make sure that it doesn't stop there and continues on moving toward the left side of my mouth. I've reached the center of my palate and I feel the precipice as my tongue is released as it crosses from right to right-center to the center left side of my palate. Then I'm over the precipice and . . . nothing.

There is nothing there. For a moment my tongue is floating. I move it to the side and I find an opening, and as I push through it I find my cheek. I move back toward the center as I wipe the drool coming out the side of my mouth. I tentatively push my tongue up to explore the top of this new opening and feel something.

I was expecting the smoothness that a palate usually offers, but the touch that my tongue feels is foreign. It's floppy, it's jagged, it's slimy. My tongue retreats down and it's shaking in

place between my lower teeth. My mouth feels like I need a water pump to remove all of the drool that's there and keeps finding its way down my chin. My chin is also shaking. My tongue stays down in its safe zone, and I'm thankful that the curtain between my bed and my roommate's bed is closed. The tears come and the shaking that I was feeling I realize is from my crying. My head is back down on my pillow with my eyes closed. What happened? What's happening? Is it a dream? Yes, it's a dream.

But I realize that it's not a dream. I open my eyes and wipe the tears away as I find again I'm talking to myself, "*Dai Bruno . . . ma che' fai? Di cosa ai paura?*" Come on. What are you afraid of?

I reach up to the left side of my mouth and let my tongue feel around. There is a lot of empty space in the cavern that my tongue is roaming around. A cavern with a cathedral ceiling and there are either stalactites or stalagmites hanging down. I never remember which of the two is the one that grows from the ceiling as the calcium drips down, and which is the one that grows from the cavern floors as the calcium drips down and builds up. Maybe I can Google it? Nah.

I don't feel pain as my tongue explores the soft bits that are hanging from where my palate used to be. As I move to explore the left side of my mouth I find a hole that I recognize as similar to when in the past I had some molars removed and that feeling of nothing but open real estate. I feel like one of the 49ers as they made it over the mountains and saw what was or will be California for the first time. "Go West, young man." But for now I'm just exploring the left side of my mouth.

It's now about 8 am. I need to make a trip to the bathroom. I look at the call button on the side of the bed. Maybe I should call for help from the nurse, but she was good yesterday teaching me what to do, so I should try to do it by myself. I try to remember the steps my nurse had followed the day before. I shut the monitor that the little cuff attached to my finger is hooked to so I don't get the "blip, blip, blip," that the machine would produce. Next I slide the pressure cuff down my arm past my wrist. The last step is to roll the IV line up so I don't trip over it and make sure not to kink it up. I'm free to go.

It isn't very easy to urinate while one of your hands is holding the IV line and the post to make sure you don't fall over. And with your chin, you are holding the rolled up johnny. That kind of gets in the way of your vision. Well, then, just let it go, and as far I know the bowl is in front of me, but my aim probably isn't too good because I can't see the bowl too well. I hope that I'm not pissing everywhere.

As I stand in front of the sink washing my hands I decide to take a look inside my mouth. I try to open my mouth and I can only go as far as to see my tongue because there is a sharp pain all over the side of my face as I try to open my mouth wide enough to see my palate, or the area that used to be my palate. I lift my chin and try to see if I can take a peek that way. No dice.

"Oh, fuck this!" I say to the image in the mirror and just walk back to my bed. I hook back up and sit at the edge of my bed looking out my window. From my window side on the 11th floor I realize that I can see all the way across the Charles River, and as the morning sun from the east is shining over the waters of the Charles, the river has taken on a silvery color as it snakes under the Longfellow Bridge that spans from Cambridge to the Back Bay. I can see that there is heavy morning traffic crawling along the top of it. It took a few seconds for my eyes to adjust to the shining of the river as my eyes focus on the John Hancock building, and not far from it on the right I see the Prudential Tower. My eyes goes back to the river and I follow it in reverse of its flow. In the distance I can see the iconic CITGO sign on top of one of the buildings near Fenway Park. Just like my first visit in Dr. L.'s office.

There are all kinds of people going in and out of my room for my roommate and myself. Every couple of hours it seems someone is taking my vitals. I don't understand why the same person that takes mine can't do my roommate's vitals so as to avoid just about every hour someone else either seeing me or my roommate.

Doctors and assistants seem to be also on different time schedules. The moment you doze off, you get someone who asks, "Are you asleep?" I was until you woke me up! Everyone who comes into the room, in departing leaves you with the same words, "You get your rest now!" Until someone else wakes you up. My nurse comes in and again informs me that today I will just have liquids. I answer with a question, "When is my pain medication due? I want to stay ahead of the pain." She looks at her watch and then at the chart hanging at the foot of my bed and says, "You have another hour to go. In a scale from one to ten what would you say your pain is?"

Is this a trick question? Should I say a high number?

To me it feels like an 11. The first couple hours after taking the pain meds it seems like the pain gets very dull, but at just about the two hour mark it feels like someone is slowly opening a door and for every inch that door opens the pain increases by a notch. I say between six and seven. Not too high, not too low.

"Well, if it's between six and seven, we'll wait another hour. If you don't need anything else, I'll be back then." Damn. I should have said 11.

Before the hour is gone by I'm ringing my buzzer because the pain is very intense. The level of throbbing is so high it feels like I have an army of little people in my mouth with knives and they are all reaching out to stab and stab and stab. I try to take few sips of water and it feels like I'm swallowing a Mack truck. Unknown to me, they had cut my dosage of OxyContin from 10 to 5mg.

As the nurse comes in due to my repeat buzzing she looks a little annoyed as she asks, "Where is the fire?"

I guess that's an attempt at a joke but she sees the look of distress on my face. I try to communicate to her the level of pain that I'm in, but what comes out is a mumble jumble that doesn't resemble speech. "Are you in pain?" she asks.

"YES!" A noise comes out that sounds like, "Eeesss." Where the fuck is my voice?

"Okay, one to t . . ." Before she could even finish her "one to ten," I interrupt her and try to say "eleven," but no matter how hard I tried the words just aren't coming out the way they should.

". . . LEVEN, . . . LEVEN."

"Okay! I'll be right back," she says as she leaves the room.

I lean back and try to take some breaths as I wait for the nurse to come back with my meds and again I find myself in between tears cursing the man that did this to me. That fucking dentist. I hate him.

It took some ten minutes, but the nurse comes back with a syringe and goes right to the port on my hand and injects the sweet nectar of relief. "You're going to feel some warmth," and as she says the words I can feel the heat traveling to all of my throbbing pain receptacles. I lean back as the narcotic takes effect and fall asleep.

My wife must have walked in at some point and quietly waited for me to wake up. It's always nice to see the face of those who love you as you open your eyes. "Hi," she says as a greeting.

She looks tired. Even in my narcotic fog I can see dark circles under her eyes.

"I didn't want to wake you up. How are you feeling?" she says, as she leans in to give me a kiss. I find myself turning to the side and offering my cheek. I don't know if I did that because of the foul taste that I feel in my mouth or if I don't want her to feel my mouth as it is.

I fade in and out as my wife does her best to carry a conversation that I don't seem to register. As the day goes along the doctor approves giving me two 500 mg of Tylenol in between my doses of OxyContin. As long as I take my meds I feel I can deal with the pain. Around 6:30 pm my wife departs, again at my insistence because I want her to be able to make the car valet pickup before they close at 7 pm.

I'm alone again. The nurse from the night shift gives me my medication and reminds me that I would need to have some solid food before they can dismiss me and allow me to go home. "Make sure to try to keep on sipping some water." They keep on telling me they want me to have some solid food before I go home, but I don't see anyone bringing me any solid food. And strangely, as I finished my thought, the nurse comes back in and says, "Good news. Dr. L.'s left word that we can start you on solid food for breakfast."

Where is Dr. L.? I think to myself.

Every three hours the nurse comes in to give me my medication, and with the Tylenol in between I'm able to stay ahead of the pain. I'm having a hard time breathing if I lean back in my bed, but after a few adjustments of the bed controls, I'm able to find a somewhat comfortable position. Just before falling asleep, the nice lady from the cafeteria came by for me to fill the breakfast card for my choices. I do a do-over of the previous morning when she told me I couldn't have any of the choices I made because of my liquid diet. I choose scrambled eggs, sausage, jello, muffin, and a cheese Danish. All nice and softly chewable.

At 5:30 am, I get the "Are you awake?" I wasn't, until you woke me up. Someone is here to draw blood, and at almost the same time my nurse comes in with my pain medication.

Food, Solid Food

AT 7:30, a young lady comes and leaves the breakfast tray on my side table. I was partly asleep but it wasn't a solid sleep. As she puts down the breakfast tray I can see her silhouette but can't quite make out all of the details of her persona. Maybe the fact that I haven't had any solid food for over two days, or knowing that the night before I had filled that breakfast order, or maybe just the combined aroma of coffee and food that I smelled in my semi-comatose state, brings me out of the meds coma that I was in.

For a moment, I had forgotten where I was and that I'd had surgery. I stretch my arms over my head and this big yawn was coming out of me. For a moment it is like that great feeling you get on a Sunday morning when you get to sleep late and you wake up without that alarm clock, fully refreshed and the entire world is yours. For the short moment that I don't know where I am I have a small smile on my face. It doesn't last long because my mouth doesn't make it to the halfway point to get through that yawn before the pain comes. I freeze with my mouth halfway open as it all comes back to me.

The surgery, the pain and where I am. I think I have ripped something out in my mouth as the pain is so sharp. As I slowly close my mouth, the pain seems to subside. I wait a couple of minutes and test opening my mouth about halfway and it seems okay as I don't get any more pain. I raise the back of my bed to bring myself to a sitting position and reach behind my back to flip my pillow on the long way from my neck down the middle of my back and finally find a comfortable spot.

I pull the top of the side table toward me and the aroma of the food assaults my senses again. I uncover one of the plates and find the scrambled eggs. They look good, so I decide to start with them. The nurse had said to take small bites to allow my stomach to get used to solid food again.

I take a small portion of scrambled eggs, almost like I am feeding one of my little grand-children, and tentatively bring it in to my mouth. I'm barely able to open my mouth to allow the fork and the little bit of food through the opening to my salivating mouth. I gingerly deposit the food on my tongue and almost immediately shift it to the right side of my mouth to avoid getting food in the cavern that is the left side. After all, I don't want to get any food on that new shining Mack truck that's parked there where my teeth and part of my palate used to be. I'm chewing the small bits of food slowly and carefully but as much as I try to avoid the left side of my mouth, every time I swallow I feel some of the food is finding its way to the left side of my mouth and hanging around the cave.

I try to take an even smaller amount of food in my mouth so I won't have to chew it and can just swallow it. It doesn't help, as I can still feel food stuck in the area of my surgery. I take a little sip of water and lightly swish the water around. As I do so, I can feel some of the bits of food coming loose. I take another sip of water to repeat the process and I don't feel the small bits of food anymore, but what I feel is something foreign. With my tongue and what palate I have left, I'm trying to establish what is in my mouth. Most of my mouth is numb and my senses are not fully working but I know as I slowly open my mouth that something is there that doesn't belong. I feel some of the water drool down my chin as I'm reaching in to get what is sitting on my tongue. I don't want to swallow and I think even my breathing has stopped as I robotically reach into my mouth. My body is a statue with just my elbow to my fingertips moving as the rest of me is waiting to see what my fingers pull out.

"*What! What the fuck is that?*" I think as I look at my fingers, or what my fingers are holding.

And I really, really don't know what my fingers are holding on to, or what I'm looking at.

It's about the size of a nickel, and it's bloody and jagged. There is mucus dripping from it, food particles and other indeterminate substance stuck to it. As I'm looking at this foreign object in the right palm of my hand, just like magic I feel something else on my tongue. This is amazing. It's like the gift that keeps on giving. I switch the blob to the palm of my left hand and reach in with my right hand and surprise, there is another blob sitting there. I put them side by side in the palm of my hand and they look almost identical. I can feel the heat rising from the pit of my stomach as I feel panic setting in. I reached for the call button for my nurse and hit it.

I actually hit it with the palm of my hand, and then I hit it again. I'm in a frenzy, and now I'm using my index finger to stab the call button over and over again, as if the nurse were in that call box and she would appear from it. Instead, the only thing I'm doing is upsetting my roommate, who looks around the half closed curtain and asks, "Are you okay?"

This is the first time in over two days that I've heard his voice. For a moment I thought I was in a cartoon because his voice sounded to me like when as a child I watched the Hanna-Barbera cartoon characters. I don't know if it was Porky Pig or Bugs Bunny or some other character that he sounded like. Later I learn that for my roommate, this was his third return of cancer and this time his nose was removed because cancer had invaded the cartilage and the nose had to be removed.

As I'm hitting the call button, I feel more of the unusual substance in my mouth, and when I reach in I find two more pieces of blob on my tongue, making about four pieces of different sizes and shapes as I hear my roommate again. "Are you okay?"

The only thing I can do is to show him the open palm of my hand with the bloody blobs and bits. I don't know what they are. That prompts him to hit his call button. Our room door must look like a Christmas tree with all those call lights flashing. I'm moaning and I think that I'm speaking but I don't even know what I'm saying. I feel drool flowing down my chin and make no attempt to wipe it, and thankfully the nurse comes in followed by another nurse.

"OKAY, OKAY. We got it the first time," both nurses say as they come in. I see my nurse looking at my extended hand as she approaches my bed and the other nurse goes toward my roommate's bed. They came in so fast that both nurses looked like fighter jets splitting up to pursue the enemy jets or like Snoopy pursuing the Red Baron on Christmas Eve.

. . . And An Opening

"WHAT you got there?" she asks, while she puts on a pair of surgical gloves and then takes my hand by the fingertips. I try to talk to her but no words come out. Instead what I hear is something close to a whistling or the sound of blowing bubbles through a straw full of holes, or a combo of whistling and blowing. And as I close my mouth, I feel a draft going through from my mouth into my nose.

The nurse is standing beside me and I find myself pushing toward her like I want to jump out of bed, but she has one hand on my shoulder and the other holding my hand with the blobs. At some point I close my hand with the nurse's fingers in it and I think maybe I was hurting her, because I can feel her trying to get me to release her fingers.

I do release the grip on her hand and I see that both of our hands are covered with blood and blobs and bits of food. I feel the drool moving down past my chin down my throat to the hollow under my Adam's apple. "Bruno, calm down," she says to me as she reaches for a wad of Kleenex and wipes my face, and as she moves past my mouth I can't help but beg.

"Call the doctor. CALL THE FUCKING DOCTOR!!!" But that's not what I hear and I don't think that she understands me as I reach for her or I should say grab her with my bloody hand on her arm. "Bruno!!! Calm down," she says again and gently pushes me down so that I'm leaning back. I let go of her arm and I can see a bloody hand print where I had grabbed her arm, and for good measure there are bits of blob stuck to her uniform. Defeated, I lean back.

"Okay, okay, let's take a look. Open your mouth, please," she says as she reaches into her pocket and comes out with a flashlight. I open my mouth like a robot. My eyes are staring someplace on the ceiling above my bed. "Oh, okay, I see," she says.

With my eyes shifting from the ceiling to her face I try to ask her, "What do you see?"

My voice sounds strange and I'm afraid to speak again when I hear what my voice now sounds like. I knew there was a change in my voice, but at least I had a voice. Since those bits dropped out I don't know what is coming out of my mouth. The few words I had tried to speak as I was trying to communicate to her what was happening when she first responded to my call didn't sound like me. There is some alien form that has taken over my speech. This is like one of those black and white episodes of *The Outer Limits* from 1963. Maybe I never spoke at all, and it was all completely in my head.

"Call the doctors. Something bad is happening!" I beg her in my head. I hate him! Hate that fucking dentist from the bottom of my soul. And the tears roll down my face and mix with drool, blood, and blobs.

I hear a trickle of water. Drip, drip hitting the floor and as my eyes travel to the side table I realize that in my struggle either I or my nurse knocked over the water pitcher. I want to speak but I don't want to hear the jumbled sounds. I'll keep the conversation in my mind. I just hope that I don't start to hear those great answers that I usually give to myself.

"Yeah, I see it," she says as she reaches into her pocket. She comes out with scissors that at the tip look like pliers. I see her hand coming up toward my mouth like a dentist (that fucking dentist, I hate him) ready to pull a tooth. I try to follow her hand and the pliers, but they both dis-appear under my nose in the cavern where the big Mack truck is parked in what used to be my mouth. As the pliers disappear I wonder what else she has in her pockets, and then I feel her attacking something that is hanging from the roof of my mouth. Don't scratch the new truck.

"Here it is," she says triumphantly as she shows me the tip of her pliers holding a bigger blob than the other four that had dropped onto my tongue and I had pulled out of my mouth.

"It's gauze! Just surgical gauze. The doctor used it to pack and protect the area after the surgery."

She's looking at it just as I'm doing, and as she turns it side to side she says again, "Just surgical gauze, nothing happening with your mouth. I'm surprised that they didn't remove it when they took your obturator out." Then she gave the blob another spin and finally deposited it in a paper tray.

"But what happened? Did a hole open up? Why did the hole open up? Why do I feel a draft up my mouth to my nose?" I don't know how much of what I say the nurse understands, but to placate me she says, "Bruno, I'm going to let the doctor know what's going on and I'm sure either he or his P.A. will come by. It will probably be later on this morning, Everything will be okay. Try to get some rest."

"Okay," I try to say, but what I hear is something that sounds like "Aay." I don't know where the k or the o of "okay" are.

"I'll let the doctor know, and I'll be back soon with your meds. You are due for your Tyl-enol ," she says as she walks out of the room.

"But the hole? What's going on?" I find myself asking in my mind to a back that's walking away.

A few minutes later someone comes in and takes my food tray away. I'm not that hungry anyway . They keep the OxyContin coming every three hours. I don't know if it's to keep my pain at bay, or to keep me calm.

"I Was Afraid This Would Happen"

DR. L. came by at about 1:30 in the afternoon. I want to be angry because it took this long for a doctor to see me, but Dr. L. has his usual disarming smile on his face. "Mr. Di Carlo, how are you doing? You look great!" he says by way of greeting. I still like the fact that he addresses me by my last name.

"The hole. Something happened!" I say as I feel air coming through my mouth to my nose. I don't think that he understands what I'm saying because my voice squeaks like a toy being chewed by a dog, or like the voice of a child after taking a breath of helium from a balloon. Heck, I don't even understand what my mind is trying to tell my mouth to say.

"Let's take a look," Dr. L. says as he takes a flashlight out of his pocket. I guess everyone in a hospital walks around with a flashlight in their pocket. "I was afraid this would happen. The tissue has separated, creating an opening." I'm looking up at him with a questioning look. I already know that a hole has opened up because when I speak I sound like that squeaky toy that my dog Brandy used to chew on.

"We are going to keep an eye on it. For now there is nothing we can do to change what's happened. I'll see you later this afternoon. I was told that you haven't eaten solid food as yet, so you are going to need to try again to have some solid food before we can send you home." Again, that great smile on his face as he leaves the room.

Really? We're going to keep an eye on it? We can't even keep both eyes on it? Just one eye?

That's the best we can do?

A few minutes later the nice food lady comes into my room and wants to know if I have decided on my dinner. I just shake my head no. I don't want to speak because I don't want her to hear my squeaky voice. "I have a menu right here," she says as she hands it to me with a pencil. "Look at it and see if there is something that you like." She tells me her name, but either because my mind is still asleep, or the stupor of drugs, or because my life is falling apart, I don't register her name.

I saw her another dozen times within my four admissions, but I never asked her name and her I.D. badge always seemed to be turned around and I couldn't see her name.

On Monday, February 12th 2018, almost a year later, I'm sitting with my wife in the coffee shop at the hospital on the 7th floor. It's 7 am and we're waiting for a 9 am appointment with Dr. L. I look up and there she is.

My mystery lady is sitting one table over from where we are sitting. I find myself looking at her and she notices that I'm looking. I don't want to intrude because she's with other people. We finish our breakfast and we are leaving to go to the 11th floor where my doctor's office is located.

We are walking away from where she's sitting with her friends or coworkers. We're two tables away as I let go of my wife's hand and I go around another table and turn back toward her table. My wife looks at me with a questioning expression, but she follows me.

As I approach her table I'm about to say, "Sorry to intrude . . ." but even before the words come out of my mouth she says, "Hi, how are you ? How are you feeling? I was wondering if you were going to say hello."

Oh, my God, she remembers me.

And in the most natural way she stands up and gives me a hug. This is my mom's hug, my grandmother's hug, my sister's hug, my best friend's hug. All of them combined. My wife is now at my side and I try to explain to her who the lady is. I still don't know her name and the most I can do is to tell my wife how this lady helped me with my food.

Less than a month later, but a year and one day after my first surgery that was Tuesday, March 7th 2017, I'm sitting in the same coffee shop on the 7th floor of M.E.E.. This time I'm by myself at 7 am waiting for an appointment with another doctor. His name is Dr. J. You'll meet him later. My appointment is at 9:15. I look across the way and I see her again and this time as I look up and catch her eye, I do a little wave with my hand. Even before she waves back, I'm up walking toward her to say hello. She's with another lady that I also recognize as one of the hospital workers. I had seen the other lady before, but I also don't know her name. We hug each other and exchange pleasantries. I feel that it's time I should know her name. I decide to reach up for her I.D. badge, but before touching it I ask her, "May I?" while pointing at her badge that is still turned the wrong way. Her eyes say yes, and as I take one corner of the badge and turn it around I see her name. "Beatrice."

"Bea. Sweet Bea," she says. "That's my name." Another of the many angels that have entered my life.

Going back to that afternoon after my first surgery when I didn't know her name and she is helping me make choices for my dinner, Sweet Bea sees the indecision in my face, and she says, "Would you like some help?" Without waiting for my response, she opens the menu and says, "Okay, we need something soft for you, so let's start with some scrambled eggs, oatmeal, and maybe some jello. Let's add a nice blueberry muffin, a cheese

Danish, and some yogurt. No coffee, too hot. What about some nice prune juice?" Isn't that breakfast? Maybe it's the only soft food they have.

I nod yes and see a triumphant smile on her face as she folds the menu. "I'll get right to it, and I'll get you some fresh water for your pitcher."

And just like that she's gone. I answer her as she is walking out of the room and again the voice I hear is strange to me. This alien, foreign entity is answering for me as I say, "Okay, thanks." I'm in *The Twilight Zone*.

Either I have my own personal concierge, or maybe she has just taken pity on me. In less than ten minutes she's back with my breakfast tray. In one hand she is holding the food tray, and with the other she expertly makes room on the table by moving around my phone, charger, Kleenex, water, pitcher, and cups. With a swipe the used Kleenex that I had piled on the table earlier disappears into her pocket, and voilà! She slides the foot of the table under my bed as she puts the food tray on the table and in a continuous motion, as she sets the tray down on the table, her hand is on the side of my bed where the controls for the bed are. Like it or not, my back is being pushed up and it stops as my chest touches the table.

The food tray is inches from under my nose. "Smells good, doesn't it?" she says as she removes the cover from the scrambled eggs dish while at the same time filling my cup with fresh water. And it does smell wonderful. This is my third day with no solid food. I need to make an effort to eat if I want to go home. I know that I will eat because about now my stomach is making a mating call for the food in front of me.

"I had the cook use a little more milk and cheese in your eggs. That should make it a little easier for you to swallow. Take your time. I'll be back later to collect the tray."

I'm looking at the food and the aroma is inviting, but at the same time I'm feeling it's repulsive. My stomach feels that there is a storm brewing in it. Is it because I'm hungry, or because I'm going to throw up? I haven't eaten in three days. What can I have in me to throw up?

Va bene . . . dai ce la fai. You can do it, you've got to eat.

I uncover the oatmeal dish and take a tentative taste with the tip of my tongue and the only taste I get from it is that is hot. I fill another spoonful, blow on it some, and when it feels to my lips that I can put it in my mouth,

I take the plunge. Where did it go? I feel around in my mouth with my tongue and realize that most of what I put in my mouth is now lodged in the cavern next to the Mack truck. I reach for the nice cup of ice cold water that my concierge filled for me.

I take a drink and try to swish the water around my mouth to dislodge the food. I don't know what could be worse as the cold water has gone straight to my brain. It feels like I just inhaled a full bowl of ice cream in one bite and the pain that came with it is biting at my mouth, my throat, my teeth.

I look around and the box of Kleenex seems out of my reach. The best option is to spill everything out of my mouth into the oatmeal bowl. I still feel the food lodged in the place where my palate used to be. My brain, my mouth, and any parts of my head connected to my former palate are throbbing.

I unplug myself and go to the wash basin located by the bathroom door and fill a cup with warm water. As I bring the cup up and water gets past my lips, I have almost instantaneous relief. Sweet warm water is sloshing through my mouth and I feel the pain slowing down some. And strangely enough as I'm standing there I don't feel air escaping through the hole in my mouth.

Hey, maybe the hole is not that big after all. Maybe the healing process has started already and the hole is closing up. I spit out what is in my mouth and I see some bits of food mixed in with water. I fill my mouth again with water and the heat of the water feels soothing.

I take a bigger swallow this time and I feel like I have a full cup of water in my mouth. I'm swishing around and around and I can feel the pieces of food dislodging as they swish around with the water in my mouth. My head is up and I'm looking in the mirror when out of my nose comes a jet stream of a gray matter, followed by red and white blobs of blood clots. Food, water, and whatever other substance keeps coming out of my nose and shooting across to the mirror. It's like a hose that has been kinked up and now as it's released, the stream shoots out.

What the fuck? WHAT THE FUCK???? I wipe my face, my chin, and part of the mirror, and defeated, I make my way back to bed. I wave at my roommate as I walk by. Over the last three days of sharing this room still we haven't done much more than wave to each other or exchange a grunt. As soon as I finish hooking up to the monitors I find myself looking at the food tray. I know that I need to have some solid food, but it is starting to be easier said than done.

THUNDER AND LIGHTNING

THE oatmeal doesn't look too attractive anymore. I put the cover back on the bowl and take the cover off the scrambled eggs. Looks a little more solid than the oatmeal. It should be easier to control it in my mouth. I take care to keep the food on the right side of my mouth while lightly chewing on it and I find that by barely touching the food with my teeth and just swallowing it, it seems not to get stuck in the empty space. As the food travels down my throat I experience something new.

There is thunder and lightning in the back of my throat. It feels like that distant storm forming at the horizon that you don't know yet the strength of. You can see some light flashing and you hear the rumbling, but distance and landscape block the view and the sounds and might of things to come. I feel the pain as the little bits of food travel down my throat, but it's almost a numb pain. "You can do it," I tell myself, knowing that my new friend OxyContin is doing a good job keeping me numb .

It takes me about 20 minutes to pick my way through the scrambled eggs and the muffin. I take a small bite of the cheese Danish but it feels too scratchy as I try to swallow it, so I take a napkin and wrap the Danish in it and put it under the dish cover. I pile a bunch of Kleenex inside the oatmeal bowl so that some of it will get absorbed and disappear. I only take a spoonful of the yogurt. The coldness of it bothers me, so I stick some Kleenex in that also.

Almost everything I swallow feels like razor blades, but I want to go home. I need to make it look like I had some of the food. I put covers back on every dish to better camouflage the food that I'm trying to hide.

Around 5 pm my nurse comes in and she has my friend Oxy with her. She looks at me and at the same time looks at my food tray and goes right for it. "Let's see how good you did," she says.

She lifts the cover to every dish that I had covered to look inside them. She picks up the knife on the side of the tray and moves tissues and napkins out of the way to look under them. Then she stabs the napkin that my Danish was wrapped in. With the knife she collects the rest of the scrambled eggs that I had spread around the dish in a neat pile in the center of the dish. "Not my first rodeo!" I think she's going to say, but instead she says, "Hmm, not too hungry?" She then takes the Kleenex out of the yogurt cup.

"I had some," I mumble.

"Have you brushed your teeth since surgery?" is her reply.

I had tried earlier that morning with the mini tooth brush that was in the kit furnished by the hospital along with mini shampoo, soap and little plastic basin. Just like checking in at a hotel. Almost.

". . . Eeess." Yes, I say in my mind.

If my nurse doesn't understand my answers, she never gives it away with a "What? Can you say that again? What did you say?" She is very attuned to her patient's feelings and needs.

"Okay. This evening we need to start something that you will need to do for a while, even for the rest of your life."

"What, brush my teeth? " I think I say, but I have no idea what I actually say. My nurse smiles at me and continues on as she reaches into her pocket and pulls out a little red tub with a peel-back cover on top of it. I'm still astonished by what these people can pull out of their pockets. They say that doctors and nurses do magic, but maybe it's these coats they wear. Maybe it's like Joseph and his Magic Dream Coat.

"This is Peridex," she says while pointing at the little tub. "It's a solution that you will have to use to rinse your mouth every time you brush your teeth, or after every time you eat. It helps the healing process and it will sterilize the area that's been affected by the surgery. This is a good time to start because you just had some food."

She then takes a cup and empties the little tub into it and passes it to me along with the little plastic tub that was in my hospital kit to use as a spittoon. I point toward the bathroom and want to ask if I should go over to the wash basin, but she says, "No, you should be able to rinse here, just spit in the little basin."

"Okay!" I mumble.

"Try not to rinse too hard," she says, "but give it a good swish to remove the food particles, and try not to swallow it. You should be able to take the contents of the cup in one gulp."

"Okay," I nod.

I'm On Fire

I have the plastic tub in one hand and the cup in the other. I bring the cup to my lips and in in it goes in one big gulp. At first I'm having a hard time trying to swish the liquid around my mouth because as I try to blow my cheeks out from side to side the air escapes through my nose and I'm not able to do it. I try again by tilting my head toward the left and I can feel the liquid move around, but just as I succeed in making the fluid spin around my mouth, it reaches the area of my former palate next to the Mack truck where my teeth used to be, and there is an explosion. Worse than an explosion. This is fire and brimstone. Nuclear. This is the Apocalypse and God is coming for his due. This is the time of punishment and time to pay the piper.

The pain is so intense that I can't get a breath out. I'm screaming in my mind, but no sound yet. I try to spit out what's in my mouth, but my mouth doesn't cooperate. There is some visceral sound coming from me and I see the nurse jump back as I throw up the little food I had in me along with the Peridex and spittle and blood and anything that was in me. I do a good job turning toward the nurse and getting throw up all over her. Well deserved because I think that the bitch is trying to poison me. I think she gave me nuclear waste.

She is saying something to me but I don't hear her because I'm on fire and I'm trying to jump out of bed. "Bruno, calm down. What's the matter?" I hear her say as she's trying to keep me down

I'm going to kill the fucking bitch. She lit me on fire and she is telling me to calm down. I want to say, "What the fuck have you given me?" But the most I can say is "Rrttz . . . rrttz." I need to get this fire in my mouth out and water is there on the table not too far. I just need to get to it. As I try to free my legs I find that I'm tangled in my sheets. I'm tugging and pulling at the sheets and I feel the tape that holds the IV needle on my wrist rip off. The clip monitor on my finger comes off and goes clunking on the floor. As the clip comes off my finger the monitor starts to beep! beep! beep!

I'm reaching for the table and the holy water on top of it that will redeem me. My finger-tips can feel the smoothness of the water pitcher, and the only thing I need to do is wrap my fingers around the little handle and salvation will be mine. I succeed in knocking it off the table and realize that for the second time today I knock down something filled with water as I hear the first of the river splashing down on to the floor.

My nurse gets the message and reaches behind her and takes my roommate's water pitcher and fills my water cup. I take a gulp and as I try to rinse my mouth water is spurting from my mouth, my nose and even my eyes. She's holding the little plastic tub under my mouth as I try to spit out as I rinse, but the most I can seem to do is to just spill everything down my chin.

I kept on trying, and after a few times of rinsing I succeed in calming down the fire in my mouth and throat. I lean my head back. My tears are mixing with throw up, Peridex, mucus, blood, and spittle, and I don't care. I lean my head back and make no effort to help my nurse clean me up and try to restore some order. I'm totally defeated. I want to die. Please, someone help me die.

I hate that fucking dentist for not doing his job.

"I think you had an allergic reaction to Peridex. I'll make a note of it on your chart," she says as I lie back. Only my eyes turn to look at her. I'm spent. I just want to wake up to my old life.

"Have you had a bowel movement?" The question brings me back.

What? A bowel movement? And what would I need to move as I haven't had any food since the day before my surgery? That makes it, what, four days? I just shake my head no.

"Okay, I want you to take your pain medication and I'll be back in a minute," she said as she held my little cup with liquid OxyContin.

"Yeah, now we're cooking!" I thought as the Oxy went down in one gulp. Sweet nectar. A few minutes later she is back with another little cup. "This is Colace, it will help your bowels." Another new friend, Mr. Colace, or is it Mrs. Colace? As the nurse is walking out of my room, I ask her to close the curtain around my side of the bed. I don't feel like having any contact with anyone even if it's just a wave.

I use the remote by my bed to lower the lights. I adjust the foot of the bed to take some pressure off my lower back and close my eyes as I feel my friend Oxy work his magic and sweet sleep embraces me. As I fall asleep I think that the best part of the day so far is that the nurse removed my IV that I had half pulled out. I fall asleep with my right hand draped over my left, holding on to the spot where the IV was inserted in it.

Next Day

I am far away someplace on a beach, and I know that soon lunch is going to be served to me. I am about to have a prosciutto panini and I'm drooling thinking about taking that first bite. The bread is crusty and as I watch it being sliced I know that it is still warm because I can see the heat rise from it.

I know that every layer of the crust that my teeth is going to cut through is going to feel like an explosion of bits of crust hitting every taste receptacle in my mouth. The Parma prosciutto is freshly sliced and the aroma is intoxicatingly wonderful. I have just somehow freshly picked tomatoes and basil from my back yard garden. Somehow I am able to do that even as I sit on a lounge chair on a beach on some far, far away island.

The roasted peppers and the slivers of pickled eggplant with a touch of parsley and just a bit of garlic are dripping with olive oil. In the strange way of dreams I am able to pick those olives on the trees of the farm that framed the home I had grown up in. I have those olives milled and I have first press oil. The mozzarella cheese is as white as the freshly fallen snow and that pinch of pink Himalayan salt is as pink as the lips of a newborn baby. What's that? Oh, my God! Is that a drizzle of balsamic vinegar with bits of oregano?

There is a small table next to my chair, and there is a Corona beer on top of it with a slice of lemon half inserted through the neck of the bottle waiting for me to push it down. I see myself pushing that slice of lemon in and flipping the bottle upside down. I watch the little bubbles rise as the lemon slice floats toward the bottom of the upside down bottle.

I know that the beer is ice cold because I can see the frost and the sweat around the bottle as the bubbles continue reaching toward the neck of the bottle away from the lemon. There is a little leather pouch next to my beer and the flap that closes the top of it is only closed halfway. I can't see the contents of the pouch but I know that there is a Padron 2000 Natural Cigar in it and my friend Joe left it there. I don't smoke but I know that the cigar is there for me. Just as I am about to take my first bite and sink my teeth into my sandwich I hear ...

" Bruno...BRUNO!"

It's Only a Dream

I open my eyes and there is a young lady by my side. "We need to take your vitals," she says, as she slips the pressure cuff around my arm. I sense another presence in the room, and as I turn to the other side of the bed I see my wife sitting there. God bless her, she's always there.

The moment of truth comes when my lunch arrives. The night before, sweet Bea came by and helped me with menu choices. As I laid back she said, "... mashed potatoes, roasted turkey , chocolate pudding, prune juice and cranberry juice." Sweet Bea came through again as the turkey was nice and tender. I lightly chewed through it, and swallowed it. The mashed potatoes kept on getting stuck between the Mack truck and the rest of the tunnel above my tongue, but I managed..

Meds seem to help numb the pain but every time I swallow, no matter how small a bit of food or how small a sip of liquid I take, the pain is stabbing. Prune juice or cranberry juice burn as they go down. I drink water at room temperature because the cold water or cold juices hurt just as much as anything hot does or as the swallowing of food does.

I love having my wife at my bedside, but I'm much company to her as I fade in and out because of my meds. Mid afternoon as my wife leaves to run some errands, I try to entertain myself by watching reruns of *Bonanza* and *The Rifleman*. For a change, I switch between FOX news and CNN but neither holds my attention too long, and thankfully soon I am back to sleep, tired of the politics.

Light or Bite, or Bright

AT about 5 pm I hear my name called again. Before I open my eyes I think it will be one of the people who came around to take vitals, but as I open my eyes I find myself looking up to someone who doesn't match any of the people who so far have taken a turn poking at me, feeling around at my face and neck, and being amazed at what they see as they look into my mouth.

She's either a doctor or an intern, I think to myself. She is wearing a stethoscope around her neck and a coat that all doctors wear, and she has a flashlight and a couple of pens peeking out of her pocket. Yeah, definitely a doctor, maybe a P.A. I have a feeling that I know her, but at this moment I can't seem to find a place in my memory for her.

She introduces herself and her name sounds like Light, Bite, or Bright, but maybe I'm still half asleep or I'm not paying attention. I don't catch her name but I hear her say Dr. L.'s name, and if she knows Dr. L. she must be part of the team .

"I would like to examine you, if it's okay."

My first reaction is that when these people come around they always bring some pain with them and I feel my back tense up, but her smile makes me listen to what she has to say. She is wearing a name badge along with the stethoscope around her neck. I try to read her name off her badge but I don't have my eyeglasses. But again, if she's part of Dr. L.'s team, I suppose she can examine me.

And then it dawns on me. She is Dr. L.'s P.A. and our first meeting was the same day that I met with Dr. L. Okay, I do know her, but still I can't figure her name out. Should I put on my eyeglasses and check the tag on her chest to see what it says? This being our second meeting, would it look like I'm checking out her chest if I look too closely at her name tag?

"If you don't mind I would like to ask you some questions as I go along."

"Okay," I answer. She has a pretty smile, nice haircut, very pleasant manners, and a pretty face. I don't let just anyone look into my mouth, but she's nice so I'll make an exception.

"Do you mind if I bring the back of the bed up?" she asks.

"Okay," I nod. After all, we haven't just met. I shouldn't be lying back in bed as she stands over me and by the time I think of it, the upper part of my bed is already moving up. As I come to a sitting position I find my nose level with her chest as she says, "Would you mind turning your head toward me?" As I do I find my nose an inch from her chest. I'm glad her doctor's jacket is buttoned all the way up and there is no cleavage showing.

"I'm going to feel the area around the back of your neck, your temples and around your chin and face," she says to me.

"Okay," I nod, as I start to relax my shoulders and allow my back to soften up against the pillow behind my neck and shoulders. She has my neck cupped in her hands with the tip of her fingers almost touching at the base of my neck and I can feel her fingers moving and probing. I close my eyes as she feels her way around my neck and all around under my ears.

Her hands are soft and have a warm touch. With my eyes closed, her fingers feel very long, almost like tentacles. I can now feel her hands around my neck almost in a chokehold. Her thumbs are under my Adam's apple and the rest of her fingers are beyond my neck as she asks, "Does this hurt if I apply pressure here?"

I want to say that my apple isn't doing much bobbing right now, but her hands feel great and I shake my head no.

She moves up toward the side of my forehead and probes, and every time she probes, she asks, "Does this hurt?" With my eyes still closed I think the question comes with such a husky voice that when I answer, "No," I do it with a voice that I feel I shouldn't. My God, I hope that didn't sound like I was moaning but this feels great. Where has she been the last three days? I hope I don't get excited, as I roll my knee caps up, just in case.

TENTACLES AND LIGHTNING BOLTS

AND now her hands move from my forehead lightly toward my cheek bone. Her finger-tips are still on my forehead but her thumbs are on the area just under my cheekbone. Almost like when you are about to give someone a kiss. Are my lips puckering up? No, just her squeezing my face. And this time when I hear. "Does this hurt?" It does!

I realize she has stabbed me. She has driven a knife right under my cheekbone, and I can feel the knife traveling to the Mack truck parked there and I think the explosion I just felt is that she stabbed one of those gigantic tires and it just exploded.

No-o-o! This can't be. Even before I open my eyes I know that what I thought to be her fingers are tentacles. Those tentacles are traveling like lightning bolts all through my face. I wasn't wrong to think that when she had my head cupped with her fingers behind my neck that they felt almost like they were tentacles. Well, they were tentacles, and now they are in my throat and into my brain. This is fucking Medusa trying to take over my face and suck my brain out.

I'm not going without a fight. I grab her by the neck and as I do I see Medusa's beautiful face turning ugly. I think she has fangs. I see tentacles with snake heads floating all around her head, but I have a firm hold on her neck as I punch her in the face. I get her right in the same cheekbone that she has stuck her tentacles in me.

As I punch her, I can feel her tentacles release my face but just for good measure I punch her right in one of her teats. Then for even better good measure I punch her on the other teat. I didn't want one of her teats to feel left out.

"There, bitch! How does that feel? Does that hurt?"

Then I realize that all of that is in my brain.

I don't know if it's a scream or a screech that comes out of me but the young lady jumps back. I see that it's her nice blond hair flying around her head and not a head of tentacles with snake heads. The look of surprise on her face is not a look of a mouthful of fangs. Her hands releasing my face are not tentacles releasing me.

"OH, MY GOD! OH, MY GOD!" she says as she jumps back a couple of feet from my bedside. She's trying to reach out to me but she's afraid. I'm not screaming anymore but I'm moaning, and these are not moans of pleasure. My hands are wet with tears as I'm cupping my face to bring some comfort to it.

"So sorry, so sorry," she says as she sees tears in my eyes, and by now I can see tears in hers.

"It's okay," I want to say, but it sounds like "Sokayey." No control as tears run down my face. Another lost battle.

I hate the fucking dentist! NO! I loathe that man.

RUN . . . BUT THERE'S NO PLACE TO HIDE

AFTER another clumsy apology and goodbye, the P.A. leaves the room and I'm alone again. I drift back to sleep and I dream again. I'm dreaming that I'm running. I don't know why I'm running but I know that I need to get away. Is it Medusa? I don't see the snakes but I know something is slithering behind me and I can feel that it is catching up to me. As I look down it has me by my ankle. I don't see or know what has me but I try to kick my leg free as I feel a hand on my leg, or tentacles. It's got me, and now it knows my name because I hear it calling me. I open my eyes, still trying to pull my leg away from the tentacles, but I see that it's a hand that's got me and not tentacles. I see the clock on the wall across my bed and it says 6:14, and I can now see that the hand holding my foot is attached to an arm and a body.

"Sorry, I didn't want to wake you up but you were kicking and thrashing and looked like you were trying to run away," my friend Peter says.

"Peter . . . sweet Peter," I cry as he reaches over and gives me a hug.

"How are you? How are you feeling?" he asks. "I spoke to your nurse, and she told me you had a busy couple of days. How is your pain? It's important to keep ahead of your pain."

I take a deep breath. I don't want to go too much into the last couple of days and I just say, "I'm okay."

As I speak, the sound of my voice is still foreign to my ears. To me it sounds like there is someone else speaking instead of me. During the day as I speak to the different people coming and going I start to realize that if I speak slowly I can actually hear some of the sound from my old voice, and also the words are distinguishable. But to me my voice still sounds like a squeaky toy that's in pain.

"But are you in pain? Are the meds helping you?" he asks.

"They help," I say, "but I hate the peaks and valleys. I'm either floating and I feel nothing, or I'm coming down from the high and each step I come down the pain increases and I'm begging for more drugs."

"They need to adjust the dose."

"They tried," I say, slowly so I can make myself understood.

"No, by adjusting it I mean to distribute the dosage differently." Peter picks up my chart and as he's looking through it I can hear him talking to himself, "10mg . . . changed to 5mg. That didn't work. Tylenol in between." Then after a small pause he says again, "I'll see what we can do to help you.

We're going to switch you back to 10mg dosage, but instead of the high dose of 10mg every three to four hours I'm going to ask them to switch you to a dose every hour, of two and a half to three mg. That should give you continuous control of your pain without the ups and downs. And in between you can still have your Tylenol. You'll be taking the same amount of pain medication, but you'll have more of a steady control of the pain."

"Would you talk to them?" I ask.

"Sure, don't worry. I'll talk to Dr. L. and I'll set it up. But tell me how you are doing?"

I shrug my shoulders as I say, "I don't know."

"It's okay. It's okay not to know how you feel. Drugs do funny things with our emotions and our mind. You just had a major surgery. Your body and mind need time to rest and recover. You are very lucky."

I listen to him but the only part I hear is when he says the word "lucky," and I want to ask, "How is it that I'm very lucky?" But I just look at him, waiting to find out why I'm so fucking lucky, as I'm the one with most of my mouth gone on a hospital bed with IVs and heart monitors on my chest and neck. And Peter helps me understand some things that I wasn't aware of. Sometimes we don't see in front of us because we're looking too far ahead.

You're Not Alone

"YOU are very lucky," he says again. "You have a support system around you that few people have. Your wife, your kids, friends, coworkers . . . me. All of us here," he continues as he points to the room in a circle that I think means the doctors and hospital. "All of us in your corner."

I feel the tears running down the side of my face and I make no effort to wipe them. Men are not supposed to be doing so much crying. Maybe Peter doesn't see them. Again as he points around he says, "All of us, we need your help to help us help you. You have cancer, but what I want you to know and understand is that you're not alone. We don't want you to feel that you're going to battle, or that you're going to kick cancer's butt, or that you'll fight cancer to your last breath, or give it hell. Your life is changed forever, but think of it as if you were embarking on a new journey. It's not a race and we are going to go slow and steady, and all of us, doctors, family, friends, we are all going to be in this journey. We will be there with you."

I'm wiping tears off my face again and maybe it's okay for men to cry. Just then my wife comes back from running her errands and sees me wiping tears from the side of my face. To her credit she doesn't panic or ask, "WHATS THE MATTER? WHY ARE YOU CRYING?"

I watch her and Peter hug, and then she comes to my side and with the most natural gesture she wipes the tears from my face as she says, "I just saw Dr. L. and he says that tomorrow morning you can go home."

"That's great!" Peter says.

Later that evening around 8pm, just as my drug stupor was taking over, Dr. L. came by. He looked in my mouth and told me that all looked good and that Dr J. was coming by in the morning . "…Rest now , and I'll see you next week in the office."

At one point I think I dreamed all of it.

Going Home

AT 11:30 the next morning I'm wheeled to the front door of M.E.E., where my wife's car is waiting. I'm happy to be going home, but I feel I'm not prepared to face my new life. My new normal is very scary.

I remember that Dr .J. or someone or other was supposed to stop by to show me how to use my obturator: how to insert it in place, how to remove it, and how to clean it. Nobody comes by. Maybe because of the hole opening up I don't need to wear it, or maybe I dreamed last night's meeting with Dr. L.

I haven't had a bowel movement in four days. The pain in my mouth is constant, but the meds every hour help to numb it. But for every bite of food or sip of water that I take, it feels like I'm swallowing hot coal. For the little drinking I do and the little bites of food I take, my two-year-old grandchild can take a bigger bite, or swallow better than I can.

Make Peace With Mr./Mrs. Peridex

THIS morning as the nurse was giving me instructions before I left the hospital, she told me that I needed again to try to rinse my mouth with the Peridex.

"NO! I'm not going through that pain again," was my firm answer to her.

"Bruno," she said to me, "I think I know what happened. The Peridex, at this point so close to your surgery, is too strong for you to be used as is. So we are going to dilute it with some warm water. I think that it might help do the trick. Before we let you go I need you to try because this is an important step to your healing. And don't swallow it."

She walked over with me to the sink by the bathroom. I don't know if she was helping me, or making sure that I did use the rinse. She filled a cup with about two ounces of water at the bathroom sink and poured the little tub of Peridex into it, gave it a swish, and handed it to me. I was holding the cup in my hands and looking at her. I didn't want a repeat of the previous time that I tried this, but with a smile she said, "I promise it won't be as bad." I was standing over the sink with one hand holding the cup and the other holding to the edge of the sink. "Go ahead, it won't be so bad."

She promised again that it wouldn't be so bad. I wanted to go home so I took a tentative sip and swished. After the initial touch of the liquid bouncing off the Mack truck, it wasn't that bad. The warm water that she mixed with the Peridex felt good but I couldn't make it move it around my mouth. The swishing had no swishing. Maybe I don't have enough liquid in my mouth. I tried to spit out what I had in my mouth, but it just spilled down my chin. I took a bigger gulp and swished. I felt it first and then I watched it spurt out of my nose, and the surprise of the liquid coming out of my nose made me take a breath in . . . and down the hatch went the Peridex.

Promptly I started to gag from it. I was coughing, gagging and spitting. Snot and blood were coming out of my mouth and nose. Tears were running down my face. "Spit it out," she said to me.

"Too late for that," I thought to myself. Just like I couldn't swish, I couldn't spit. I could feel some blobs of food or snot hanging in the cavern above my tongue. With the little sensation that my tongue still had, I could feel that it was gross.

As I looked in the mirror I saw that something was hanging from the side of my mouth on my beard. I leaned in over the sink and washed my face. I took a paper towel and as I was drying my face I saw the nurse looking at me. "The air in your mouth is escaping through the hole in your palate. That's why you can't puff out your cheeks and rinse. I want you to try something for me."

"Okay," I answered while thinking, "I'll try anything."

"After you take the liquid in your mouth, pinch your nose and that will prevent the air from escaping through your nose. That will allow you to puff your cheeks and swish and spit."

I gave it a try, leaning over the sink and pinching my nose and swishing. The rinsing part definitely worked. Why didn't she tell me this before all the shenanigans of drooling all over myself? The spitting I would need to work on it because it just dribbled out of my mouth. With a hand on my shoulder, the nurse said to me, "Your dismissal papers should be ready shortly."

Either by routine or I don't know why, as they wheeled me out the front door I stood up from the wheelchair and went to the driver side of my wife's car.

"What do you think you're doing? I'm driving," she said, as she directed me toward the other side of the car. As I walked around the other side, I heard the nurse say, "Men are all the same." She wheeled the chair away toward the hospital entrance. Not a "Good luck" or "Goodbye."

I hate the son of a bitch! That fucker! Why didn't he do his job?

Back Home

ONE good thing came of my time in the hospital. I had started to play with my new phone to fill some of the time and learned to text. I was feeling very self-conscious about the way my speech sounded, but my new phone made it easier for me to communicate with some friends and extended family.

I was enjoying FaceTime with my children and grandchildren but they seemed to do most of the talking. I learned to use YouTube for videos and music, and Google. Who knows, maybe Instagram will be next? As we were driving home from the hospital, just for the fun of it I put our home address in Google Maps, and the darn thing knew exactly where we lived.

I haven't taken a shower in five days and the first thing I want to do when I get home is to take one. The water feels good running over my body. I never knew it could feel so great to wear underwear again. Usually I can't wait to take them off.

Even the pajamas that my wife had waiting at the foot of our bed feels great, but above all it feels great to be back in my home with my family – my daughters and their husbands, my grandchildren, my son and his fiancé, and my wife.

I bask in their attentiveness and their love, as everyone is busy doing something for me or for each other.

We always have been close as a family, but as I watch everyone go about all that is going on and all that they are doing for me, I wonder if they think that they're going to lose me. My God, do they think that this cancer is going to kill me?

I'm still having a hard time swallowing. I sip liquid, and the food I eat needs to be liquefied before I can swallow it. The amount of food that I'm able to eat and swallow before I give up isn't much more than what you would give to a five-to-six-month-old baby when they start to take some cereal.

LIQUEFIED AND BLENDED

ALL that my wife cooked and blended for me needed to be very plain. Any kind of spices burned. Any liquid like Gatorade or juice, no matter what flavor, needed to be diluted with water, and I was only drinking it at room temperature. Two, three, four times a day my wife tried to do different combinations of food, but I just couldn't enjoy any of it. She made smoothies with blueberries, strawberries, cantaloupe, and any other items you can liquefy, but everything sat at my bedside table with a couple of sips gone. I tried to sip water as much as I could to keep hydrated, but I knew that what I was taking in wasn't enough. Every time I swallowed, it felt like I was being strangled. Just give me my friend Oxy and I'm happy. We tried some protein smoothies. Vanilla and strawberry made me gag. We finally settled on chocolate, but at room temperature and with no ice mixed in. On Friday afternoon after getting settled in from getting home from the hospital, as I took my dose of Oxy, I realized that I only had a few doses left in the bottle. "Honey, do we have a prescription for Oxy?"

It turned out we didn't. As we called the hospital for a refill, we were told that it couldn't be done by phone, and a family member would need to come in person and pick up the prescription. My wife enlisted my brother-in-law John to drive into the city. It took the poor man in rush hour traffic over four hours for the round trip that normally you can do in less then two hours. With the prescription in hand as he stopped at the drug store to have the script filled, he was told that they didn't have the liquid form of OxyContin but they hopefully would be able to get it in by tomorrow . . . maybe.

Saturday afternoon around four o'clock, I get my script filled. I had surgery on Tuesday. Today is Saturday, and the last time I remember having a bowel movement was either last Sunday or Monday. Probably Monday morning. My normal is two to three times a day. I start to think that if I don't eat, I don't need to go to the bathroom and I don't need to have a bowel movement. The little that I'm taking in is liquid, so my logic is that there isn't much there to pass. Late that afternoon at the suggestion of my friend Peter, I meet a new friend: Mr. Suppository.

Within minutes of making the acquaintance of Mr. Suppository, I feel like there is a volcano blowing up in my gut. The problem is that there isn't any place for it to go because of that ball of refuse sitting at the bottom of my bowel that blocks everything. I really wish that I could reach in and pull it out. I did, one nugget at the time.

When I get up during the night to take my OxyContin, and sometimes during the day, I don't use the little measuring spoon anymore. Just take a swig, and I think every swig gets a little bigger as I go along. Two, four, eight, twelve mg. What difference it will make? I just want to take the pain and make it go away.

It takes me about 20 minutes to sip about six to eight ounces of liquid. I sit at the edge of my bed and sip, sip, sip. No matter how hard I try to avoid it, some of it gets into my nose and chokes me, and what makes it down my throat takes my breath away. After every sip I need to stop and take a deep breath because I can't seem to draw a breath through my nose. Such a routine thing to do, to talk and to take a breath, or to be able to eat or drink and swallow and breathe at the same time. For me, those simple basic parts of life that we take for granted have become an adventure for every sip, swallow or breath of air.

Sunday morning after showering, I stepped on the scale in our bathroom. After the little digital numbers stopped bouncing around I focused on the numbers showing. I didn't have my eyeglasses on but these numbers are big enough for me to be able to see them without having my eyeglasses on. Something is wrong with the stupid thing. I stepped off and waited a couple of seconds for the scale to go back to a blank screen. I tapped the little circle that says "tap here," and waited for the numbers to show zeros.

I stepped on the scale and the same numbers appeared as before: 182 pounds. The previous Monday, the day before my surgery, my weight was 194 pounds. I lost 12 pounds in less than a week.

I wonder if I can market this new diet and make some money. As I stood on the scale I could see myself in the mirror. I never was a bundle of muscles, but always in decent shape. Maybe a couple or a few pounds overweight in the middle as I got older.

My arms looked thin, and as I looked down at my wrist, I saw my watch turned face down. I always wore it face up. I gave my wrist a side to side shake almost like when someone asks you, "How you're doing?" And you answer, "*Cosi'-cosi'*. So-so," with your hand palm down as you give it a back and forth shake. As I did that I saw my watch go for a spin around my wrist. My legs looked thin and almost too skinny.

I got dressed and as I buckled my belt I realized that I was two notches in from where I was before my surgery, as I can see from the line on my belt from the previous usage.

My days are a little bit foggy as the bliss of the drugs take over, and I'm staying ahead of the pain as I chug my OxyContin and Tylenol. I haven't spoken to anyone on the phone because most words beyond no and yes sound like air escaping from a balloon. With my family they seem to understand, especially when I take the time to speak slowly. With others it's embarrassing.

On Sunday the 12th of March, after my wife and I have a little argument about it – that I win – I make the decision that on Tuesday the 14th I am going to go back to work. She pleads that it's too soon. She enlists the kids to try to convince me that it's too soon. She even tries to use, "How are you going to communicate with people? You can't talk!"

"Nonsense," I think I say. "My clients, I don't need to communicate with them. I can read their minds . . . or I'll use sign language."

"Ha, ha. You don't know any sign language," she says with a victorious smile.

"Whatever," I think I say, and if you want to piss off a woman so she stops fighting you, the thing to say to them is, "Whatever."

"Fine!" And she walks out of the bedroom.

The sad part of all this is that after just one week out of work, our finances were being affected. Most of the little reserve we had saved had already had to be used to pay up front toward my MRI, CT scan, and doctor appointments. I always loved to be my own boss, and maybe it's the fact that we come from the generation that wanted the white picket fence, and to be your own boss. All of that is great for when you're young and stupid and you don't understand retirement or health care insurance.

My wife and I run a very small ma and pa business, and when I'm not able to be behind my chair to do my work, there is no pay. There is no vacation pay, there is no sick pay. There aren't any days that you can accumulate. You work, you get paid. You don't work, you don't get paid. But every single worker that works with me, within one year they get a full week of vacation pay. In the second year they get two weeks paid. For me and my wife, for the last 42, years we've never been able to take a paid vacation.

Over 40 years ago I was having a conversation with someone. I don't remember who it was, but during our conversation I had expressed my desire of opening my own business. He listened to me and all of my plans about how I was going to go about doing it. When he felt I was done explaining my grand plans he said to me, "That's great. You'll love being your own boss – but be careful of the curse of the small business."

"What curse? What are you talking about?" I asked him.

"Hey, I don't want to spoil the fun for you. In due time, you'll find out."

And I did find out.

When we say we own a small business, I mean a small business. There is a lot of noise around being an owner. Some people think that a small business is a place that employs under 50 people. Well, we are nothing more than ma and pa and few other people working together. I love the noise that our politicians make referring to the "small businesses" that employ 200 or 300 people. When it comes to our small business's place in the business world, we're what I like to refer to as a grain of sand on a beach.

You know that it's there, and all of those grains of sand make a beautiful beach. But you take that grain of sand individually and you realize that's only something that gets stuck between your toes or your ass crack and you just can't wait to get home to rinse it off. The small business is the backbone of our country. The motor in our vehicles. The soul in our bodies. But individually, for those who make rules and laws that don't apply to them, we are very, very disposable. No politicians knock on our doors, no lobbyists in Washington stand up for us. I've been a hair stylist for 44 years, and since the first day I became one, I found out that there was a movement to get all salons to be able to join together and be able to buy more affordable health care. You want to guess what we got? "No! You can't do that! You are individual corporations. We want to avoid a monopoly."

The Curse

I did find out what the curse of the small business was, and is. Very simply put: You're the business. You start with the dream of having your own business, but you never have enough money to have others do the needed work to get started. So when you find that perfect storefront and sign that five-year lease, you start to envision yourself standing in front of that door and seeing your thriving business come alive.

You roll up your sleeves and demolish, and rebuild, and paint and put down those floors. You enlist wife, kids, friends, in-laws and outlaws. It reminds me of growing up on the farm at harvest time. From two to 92, all hands on deck.

I have heard some politicians say that if you have a successful business "you didn't build it."

I didn't know if I was going to be successful, but I did build it with my own hands from every nail to every stud, to sheet rock, to every paint brush stroke and every floor tile. I got it all done.

Permit after permit, inspector after inspector, and finally the big day: I'm my own boss. Well not yet. I need a staff. I'm learning about payroll taxes and how to become a corporation. After all, you want to protect your new empire.

Six days a week, in at 6 am, out at 8 pm. Sunday morning's my day off. By 4:30 to 5 am, I'm always in the shop. I'm washing floors and windows. I'm on my hands and knees scrubbing the toilets. Every morning I dust and wipe counters and mirrors and chairs and anything that needs to be done. Wash and fold towels. Stock the shelves with products that we retail. Stop at the market as we need laundry detergent, paper towels, toilet paper, Kleenex, hand soap, napkins. Got to have candy for the front desk. Maybe it's time to buy in bulk. Someone at one point said to me, "Maybe you should hire a cleaning service to help you out."

Well, the budget wasn't there. After 42 years of being in business, I'm still the cleaning service. I have a great staff of people working with me, not *for* me, and they always do their part. My dad, God rest his soul, used say to me, "*li guai di la pignata li sa la cucchiare..* Only the spoon knows the trouble of the cooking pot." In the small business communities of America's Main Streets, every owner understands that they are the body and soul of their operation. They are the business.

Tuesday the 14th of March, barely a week removed from my surgery, I went back to work. I only had shared with my coworkers and few of my clients about my cancer. About 20 years earlier I had two surgeries to remove polyps from my sinuses, so I just told most people that I had sinus surgery again to avoid to having to explain to everyone about my cancer. But I wasn't so sure that was the reason, or why I was so reluctant to talk about cancer

As time went by, a little at a time I started to share with a few more people about the cancer I was dealing with. I wasn't trying to hide the fact that I had cancer, but it was because I found it hard to communicate and explain what A.C.C. was, due to my limited speech. Most people want an explanation of why you have cancer, and they'll ask question after question until they can point at something or someone to find the cause. As an example: "You must have done something for this kind of cancer to happen to you. Did you smoke?"

I try to talk as little and as slowly as I can, just enough to decide on what service needs to be done. All of my clients are clients of many years and we know each other well. Most times a "Hello!" is enough for me to know what they need. When I speak slowly I don't hear from my clients, "What did you say?" or "Can you say that again," or "What was that?" Every time I share with one of my clients that I have cancer, the response from them is always one of shock as I hear, "Oh, my God! Oh, my God!" Then the tears come from men or women.

That's when I break down, and it's very draining to spend most of the day wiping away tears every hour as my next appointment comes in, but at the same time there is nothing more genuine and fulfilling than those hugs that people that love you give, and to hear, "I love you."

I love all of the get-well cards, prayer cards, flowers, and candy. But I have to say those that I enjoyed the most were the homemade cards that the little kids made with a scribble or a handprint or a stick figure on them.

Many times over the next couple of months I was surprised as I shared my cancer story, how often I heard back, "Me too," or "I just finished my radiation treatments," or "Yeah, those few months we didn't see each other, I was recuperating from my cancer surgery."

I think of my clients as friends – grant you, not the kind of friends that you do every Saturday dinner out with, but nonetheless these are people that know every little detail of my life and my family, and me of theirs. I was surprised to find out how many people kept the fact that they had cancer private. But what surprised me the most was the times I heard a comment by some of my clients that were dealing or had dealt with cancer that made me sad. "Once people know that you have cancer, they seem to treat and look at you differently."

Was that why I had been so reluctant to talk about my cancer? Was I afraid that people would look and treat me differently because of cancer ?

Were people treating me differently and feeling pity toward me because of cancer?

I worked on Tuesday and Wednesday and booked way too many appointments. By Thursday I knew I had gone back too soon. I was very pale and the weight loss seemed to make it even more obvious. Most of my clothes hung on me like they were draped on me. I had taken to wearing my shirts untucked, hoping that they would fit better.

Both on Tuesday and Wednesday, my wife had my lunch bag filled with all sort of goodies: chocolate custard, jello, scrambled eggs, purée of veggies and spinach, candied peaches, bananas and anything soft that she could come up with.

At 10 am Tuesday, my first day back at work, my wife showed up with a protein drink in hand for me. (She did that every one of my workdays for over six months, coming by to drop off my protein drink so that it was freshly made. Drove half an hour each way from home and back, often with our two grandchildren in tow. And she did this after she had spent most of the morning cooking and blending.)

No matter how hard my wife tried, to me everything had no taste, and it took a great effort to swallow. Things that looked and smelled so delicious, lost all of it the moment it reached my mouth because anything with flavor burned and hurt and brought tears to my eyes. Most days my meals were scrambled eggs with no fixing or spices and a chocolate smoothie. Any kind of food I tried to eat got stuck near or around the Mack truck. On a positive note, I became very adept at rinsing my mouth and keeping the area that was surgically treated clean.

I HATE THAT DENTIST. I HOPE HE BURNS IN HELL.

THURSDAY afternoon, my third day back at work, around 2 pm, as I blew my nose, I saw blood on the Kleenex. I didn't think much of it because often this last week at one point or another I saw some blood discharge. Just as I disposed of the Kleenex I felt that coppery taste in my mouth that announces the arrival of a rivulet of blood sneaking down from my nostril to my mustache and just about touching my lip.

I was in our back room at work just finishing some scrambled eggs that my wife had made for me. I leaned back on one of the chairs and tried to put some pressure on the side of my nose, thinking that I have a bloody nose. In less than five minutes I had to take a roll of paper towels out of our dispensary because the Kleenex didn't seem to be doing the job anymore. Every few minutes I needed a new sheet and the wastebasket next to me with a white trash bag for lining was filled half way up. The bloody red Kleenex and paper towels made a stark contrast with the white lining of the basket.

I took a couple sheets of paper towel and rolled them in a ball and put them in the cavern where my palate used to be and bit down to apply some pressure, hoping to stanch the flow of blood. By now I felt blood dripping from my nose, my mouth and down my throat, and every time I took the paper towel ball out of my mouth, it was crimson red. I started to roll up Kleenex and make nose plugs out of it. About 2:30 my coworker Tiffany came in to let me know that my next appointment was here. She asked, "Are you all right?"

Even before she finished the sentence, I could see her horrified look as her eyes found the bucket full of bloody paper towels. She was looking at me pinching my nose with Kleenex sticking out of my nostrils and my mouth a quarter the way open biting on paper towels. I took the plug out of my mouth and asked her to cancel the rest of my appointments for the day.

I tried to figure out what to do for about another hour as I kept removing ball after ball of bloody paper towels. To get from the town of Randolph to M.E.E. in downtown Boston at this time of the day would take close to two hours because of traffic. Was something going on that meant I should go to the hospital? I looked at my watch and it was now about 3:30. Over an hour and a half of bleeding. Unknown to me, one of my coworkers texted my wife, and being one of the days that she sits with our grandchildren, she called my brother-in-law to come by the salon and take me to the emergency room.

Meanwhile I was tethering between getting in the car and driving myself to the emergency room or just keep pinching my nose and biting down on the paper towel plugs. I looked at the plugs I was taking out of my mouth and nose and I still saw blood, but it didn't seem to be as heavy as it was the last time I checked. Maybe I just needed to hang on a little longer and the bleeding would stop. Just then, the back room door opened again and my brother-in-law John walked in.

John is one of the kindest, most easygoing men that you can ever meet and he would do anything for anyone. He tells me that my wife called and asked him to come by and drive me to the hospital. As my coworker had done, he's looking at the bucket full of bloody Kleenex and paper towels.

"Let's wait a few minutes," I say to him as I take the plug out of my mouth and see that that there is a little less blood on it. "I think I'll go home," I say. "The bleeding seems to have slowed down. I should be okay." I thank him for offering to drive me to the hospital. He helps me dispose of the bloody Kleenex and towels around the area where I'm sitting, and few minutes later I drive home.

Next morning, Friday the 17th of March, I'm up by 4:30 am. My first appointment is scheduled at 6:15. I'm in the shower and again I get the coppery taste in my mouth. I turn my face up to the shower head and try to get a mouthful of water to swish around, but as I try most of it comes out of my nose and I'm not successful in getting a good swish because there just isn't any suction. As I try to spit out what's left in my mouth, what I get is a mix of blood and spit and mucus slobbering down my chin and mixing with the water coming down from my head. As the water reaches the drain and starts to spin around the mouth of the drain, I can't help thinking of a strawberry-vanilla swirl.

There's some light dribble, but there doesn't seem to be much blood dripping out anymore, so I continue with my preparation for work. I find a way to help me shave. Monday before I went back to work as I was shaving the right side of my face, I was okay, but as I tried to shave on the left I couldn't get my cheek to puff out and shave properly. I remembered what the nurse had said to me – that it would help me to pinch my nose, but it was kind of hard to do as I'm right handed and my left hand was in my way as I tried to shave the left side of my face. So I had the great idea to make nose plugs out of toilet paper, and voilà! They held and I was able to puff out my cheek and shave properly.

By 5:45 am I'm at work setting up my work station. I drive in with tissue paper stuffed in my nose because I'm still getting these little dribbles of blood, kind of oozing from my nostrils and down the back of my throat. By the time I'm done setting up, I feel blood going down my throat in a constant flow. I look up at the clock on wall above our reception desk and see that soon my first client will be here, and I'm hoping for the bleeding to stop so that I can work.

Before I left the house, my wife wanted to take me to the M.E.E. emergency room but I said no. Our finances being what they are, I need to work. But now, barely 6 o'clock, I know that I need to get to the hospital. I have Kleenex plugs in my nose and as I remove them they are saturated with blood. Within seconds of replacing them, I can feel – and as I look in the workstation mirror I can see – the little white tails sticking out of my nose turning red. I'm pushing them higher and higher in my nose to better absorb the blood. I have a ball of paper towels in my mouth.

I text my wife because I don't want to talk to her and hear "I told you so." I text to tell her to come by and pick me up to get to the hospital. Then I texted my 7 and 7:30 appointments to let them know I needed to cancel their appointments. The rest of the appointments will be taken care of when my coworkers come in. Just as I'm finishing texting, my 6:15 appointment comes through the door. I have plugs in my nose and my mouth. He's here, and I will need to cut his hair. With sign language I lead him to the shampoo area and shampoo and then cut his hair. As my client leaves, I go into the bathroom and change my nose and mouth plugs that by now are fully saturated with blood and as I look in the mirror I find myself asking my reflection, "What the fuck are you doing here? All of this for the miserable $25?" And the fucker in the mirror answers me. "Yeah. We need that 25 bucks."

Twenty minutes of seven my wife pulls up and we start our journey to town. I'm holding a bath towel against my mouth and nose (one of those towels you use at the beach), nose plugs in, and a ball of paper towels in my mouth, and still I can't seem to stop the bleeding. Now I'm in a hurry to get to the hospital and according to me, my wife doesn't drive fast enough. So as soon as she pulls up in front of the salon, through her protest I get behind the wheel and off we go.

Stubborn, stupid, foolish, moron. Call it whatever you want, but I'm driving. What a sight to see for anyone driving beside us: a bloody red towel against my mouth and nose plugs sticking out of my nose. As I se myself in the rearview mirror, I think of when our kids stuck straws in their nostrils to play monsters.

Thanks to the zipper lane for two people or more, we are making good time driving in and as I'm driving, my wife calls the emergency number that the nurse had given us when we left the hospital, in case when we got home there was an emergency. I guess this is an emergency.

She is told that they will be waiting for us. At 7:35 am we are in front of the hospital, and thank God for valet parking. The attendant that takes my car asks if I was in a car accident, but he is already talking to my back as he says it, because I'm feeling a sense of panic with all of this blood coming from my mouth and nose, and I kept going without answering.

The lady at the reception desk takes one look at the bloody towel I'm holding over my mouth as my wife gives her my name, and she points toward the double doors at the back of the room as she stands up and says, "Come right in, Mr. Di Carlo, the nurse is waiting for you."

She leads the way into one of the emergency room cubicles and sits me down. Within seconds another nurse comes in and she's pushing a table in front of her with scissors, gauze, tape, I.V. setups, and something that looks like a Q-tip. A big Q-tip, and only one side has the swab part of it. It's double the length of a normal Q-tip and the tip has a silvery color to it.

The room that we are in is very narrow and seems even smaller with the examining chair in the center of it. Around it is every piece of equipment that a hospital room may need, from monitors, pressure cuffs, a wash sink, computer and monitor, paper towel dispenser, and needle disposal box. The nurse that just came in is having a hard time fitting in between my chair and the rest of the equipment around the room. My wife is standing by the entrance to the little room as the nurse who just came in with the cart finds a stool to sit on and asks me, "So what's going on?"

I'm still holding the towel against my mouth as she takes it from me and puts it on the table. "Open wide," she says, and without waiting for my answer she takes a flashlight out of her pocket and shines the beam into my mouth, "Yeah! There is some big time bleeding in there. Name and date of birth?"

As I give her the information, she checks an ID bracelet that she's holding in her hands against my answers, and satisfied that it's me, she puts the bracelet around my wrist. She's sitting sideways to me but the tray cart that she pushed in with her is now behind her. We are leg to leg as she tries to reach the gauze on the table behind her, and finally she does get one package. I see her turning again toward the scissors on the tray behind her. I'm thinking that she wants them to cut the bag open. She finds that they are out of her reach, so she decides that she can just rip open the bag that the gauze is in.

She has a two-hand grip on the gauze bag and with all of her might she pulls in the two different directions. The bag rips open and her arms go flying straight out, doing a great impression of Christ on the cross. Her arms are spread-eagled, with each hand holding half of an empty bag, while for a moment the former contents of the bag seem to be floating on air.

At the same moment that her arms spread out and reach parallel with her body, there is an explosion as one of her hands hits the tray with the medical supplies on it. The tray tips over with everything on it splattering behind her.

"Oh, my!" she says.

From the corner of my eye I see my wife jump out of the way of flying tape, gauze, swabs and IV needles as they land by her feet. It is almost funny, if it wasn't for the fact that I am in pain.

The nurse makes no effort to collect the things scattered all over the floor, but turns toward a cabinet drawer beside her. After moving a few things around the drawers she takes out a clear bag with scissors, tape and many other things I can't distinguish. I guess this is a new setup for me. She rolls together few pieces of gauze about the size of a golf ball just like I had done with paper towels, and she asks me to open my mouth, "Bite down, but not too hard. You just want to put some pressure on the area that's bleeding, and I'm going to start an IV on you."

I nod my consent, knowing that I don't have much of a choice because my mouth is stuffed with gauze and I feel like I'm bleeding to death. By the time my IV is in, I feel blood in my mouth getting past the plug that the nurse had made for me with gauze. I point to my mouth to let the nurse know that I need a new golf ball. She takes another bag out of the new kit and this time she cuts the bag and unwraps a few more pieces of gauze to make a new plug. With one hand she takes out the bloody one and with the other hands me the new one.

Three times the process is repeated before one of the resident doctors comes in. Without a word, she goes to the sink to wash her hands. She washes and dries her hands and soon after, she puts on a pair of gloves. Through that process she's kept looking at me and at all that was scattered around the floor. But she doesn't make a comment about it and steps over the different items on the floor to get to my side. Maybe it happens often and this is not unusual.

As a person walking into this room, my first thought would be that they just had a life and death situation with doctors and nurses working on a patient. Someone is doing C.P.R. by banging on the patient's chest to start the heart, while another is trying to insert an IV into some elusive vein, and another is cutting the clothes off the traumatized body. A question from the doctor brings me back as I hear, "Name and birth date."

"MUMM ... MU ... MUMM ..."

I hear the question a second time as the doctor is looking at my bracelet. My wife steps in and answers all of the questions as my mouth is still stuffed with golf balls. And if I have that fucking bracelet on my wrist, how many times does it need to be confirmed?

"MUMUMUMUMUMMM ..."

"Let's take a look, Mr. Di Carlo."

Okay! Another one with good manners. As I open my mouth, she reaches in a drawer and takes out a pair of forceps that she uses to remove the gauze ball in my mouth. Without the pressure from the gauze ball, I again feel the blood oozing down my throat. She, like everyone else around, has a flashlight in her pocket. After a quick scan around the cavern and the Mack truck, she makes another plug to insert in my mouth. "How long has the area been bleeding?" she asks my wife, my advocate.

"Since yesterday afternoon," she answers. The doctor seems confused by my wife's answer as she repeats her words. "Did you say since yesterday?"

"Yes! Don't ask," my wife answers.

SILVER NITRATE—HOW FUN

"WE need to cauterize the area. That is the only way to stop the bleeding. Keep the pressure on, but not too much pressure," the doctor says, as she removes the plug from my mouth and sticks another fresh one in. She then walks out of the room. She comes back a few minutes later and in her hand she's holding what looks like an aerosol can. "I'm going to spray the area that I'm going to cauterize to numb it."

She removes the ball of gauze, sprays my mouth, and puts in a new gauze ball. With the taste and smell of the spray, I promptly gag into the plug that she has put back in my mouth. Thank God I don't have much in my stomach; nothing comes up. I'm leaning back in the chair as I start to feel the numbing sensation. I've never had the pleasure of having anything cauterized, so I don't know what to expect. I did know that they would use silver nitrate, but I had no idea how it was done. I soon find out as the doctor takes one of those long swabs, and I understand why the tip of it is silver. Ah. Silver nitrate.

I feel the nurse bumping her way behind my chair. For a brief moment she disappears but then as I look up behind me I see the top of her blonde hair. As I see the top of her head, I feel one of her hands on each side of my shoulders, and by the feel of her hands on my shoulders, she's not asking, "How are you doing?" Uh-oh, this can't be too good. I think she's back there to hold me down. My wife is still standing by the entrance of the room and she hasn't moved an inch. "Okay, here we go," the doctor says as she removes the gauze ball. I see the silver tip disappear into my mouth. At first touch I feel some burning, but not too bad. I think it takes my brain a moment to realize what is happening. Then the pain comes, and I don't see any others of the "we" in pain.

"HAAAA." That is the most I can get out of me as I start to slide down the chair, and almost immediately I feel the nurse getting a handful of my shirt to keep me from escaping.

Her hold on me keeps tightening as the pain in my mouth feels like an explosion in slow motion. The pain starts to travel from the epicenter that was the meeting place of the tip of the silver nitrate stick with the soft tissue around the area where my teeth used to be, to the top of the cave of what used to be the roof of my mouth, and into my nose.

"You need to keep still!" the doctor exclaims. She wants me to keep still as the pain is bouncing around in my mouth and in my head. "Fuck you and fuck your nurse." But all that comes out from me wis "MUMUMUM ..."

"It hurts!" I try to says as I am still squirming, but I stop trying to get away. The nurse lets go of my shirt and tries to have a calming hand on my shoulder. From the corner of my eye I can see my wife's horrified look as she's moved almost outside the room with her head peeking around the curtain. She has one of her hands around and over her mouth and nose. I would have liked to think that she was hiding a smile, but I can see the tears around her eyes. My body has slid halfway down the back of the chair and my shoulders are now where my ass should be.

"Take a deep breath," the doctor says.

I can't compose any words to say much as the pain is so intense. No, the pain is throbbing but doesn't seem to be increasing, as on cue the doctor says, "The pain should be diminishing about now." I look at the doctor by just turning my eyes toward her because I'm afraid that if I turn my head it will hurt even more. I don't know if it's because I see my wife's tears coming down her face that I feel tears coming down the side of my own face. She moves her hand and I can see her lips mouthing, "I'm sorry." And that just brings more tears for me and for her.

I feel so bad for my wife. This was almost our time. Our kids are grown up, two of them married with children. My son has a great woman in his life and they have plans to get married .

Mortgage almost paid off. Maybe we can even do a little travel in the next couple of years and use the few dollars we managed to put aside for rainy days. Boy, it's pouring now.

STORM BREWING

IN my childhood home, I loved to sit by our kitchen window. I learned to love sitting by that window from my paternal grandmother. As the first winter snow storm developed, my grandmother loved to sit by that kitchen window right next to our fireplace. She would stretch her legs over the hearth in front of the fireplace and lean back in her chair. She loved to watch as the trees and vineyards and the world outside our window started to color white. As the trees and vines bent under the weight of the fresh fallen snow, while sitting by that window she could see all the way down the hill that our home was built on and to the valley below and the Adriatic Sea in the distance. But soon with the swirling snow the horizon and the sea became one indistinguishable blur.

The view was spectacular down to the valley and our town across on the next hill. At the bottom of the valley in between the hill that my home was built on and the hill across where the town was located, there was a small river that ran like a ribbon all the way down to the Adriatic Sea.

As the trees became barren and winter set in with that first snow covering the valley, the river's tranquil flow to the sea was never interrupted. The moderate temperature of the Abruzzi region prevented the water from freezing. The blue of the water became even more noticeable, flowing along the now barren white banks all the way down to the sea in the distance.

As much as she loved this time of the year, she knew that as the snow started to build it would cause damage to the trees and vineyard. I was the youngest in my family and my grandmother was the one who took care of me. As the snow swirled and the wind howled outside, she would put another log on the fire and pull her shawl a little tighter around her shoulders. Then she would sit herself down in front of the fireplace and wave me over to her as she said, "*Vieni qua', siedi con me.* Come and sit with me."

As I sat on her lap, she would bring her shawl-wrapped arms around and engulf me in a warm embrace. I loved to sit on her lap on snowy days like these, with the back of my head nestled on her bosom and my legs stretched in front of me over hers. With her arms wrapped around me tightly to hold me against her she would rock back and forth, almost like she was trying to put me to sleep, and many times I did fall asleep. On many of those snowy days I remember her telling me stories of her younger days and our family, but at the end she always ended talking to me about the snow, and it seemed that she could have been talking to an audience, or anyone that was there or around the house.

Her voice is fresh and strong in my mind as I remember her saying, "*Quardi quant e bell la neve quanti cali, e come bell lu fiume . . . pero' lu problema e li uaai non e' quanda fa la neve ma quanti si squaie.* Look how beautiful the snow is while it's coming down and look how beautiful the river is . . . but the problems don't come with the fresh snowfall; they come as the snow melts."

A side note about that river, *Fiume Arielli.* My uncle, *Zio* Michele, served in the Italian army during WWII and he was stationed in Tobruk, Libya. In 1940 the English army fought the Italian army in the battle for control of Tobruk, and when the English won and took control, my uncle was one of the many thousands of Italian soldiers who became prisoners of war. As the war went on and the Allies were moving up the Italian peninsula and pushing the Germans back, the Abruzzi region was where many battles were fought. The Allied Command was looking for ways to access the mountainous Abruzzi region, and looking at maps they saw the river flowing by my town as a way in. They sought to interview prisoners that came from that area and my uncle was one of them. He was interrogated and asked questions about the river. The information they were seeking was whether the river was navigable.

After being taken prisoner in Tobruk, my uncle was transferred to England and by the time they came to interrogate him, he had been in England close to four years and had learned the English language well. But he used to say that he always held back from letting them know that he understood all of it. The questions about the river were asked by a sergeant of Italian descent. My uncle thought he had misunderstood and asked them to repeat the question. When they did, he laughed at them. That brought him a slap across the side of his head. For many years as he told the story, my uncle always clarified that he was never abused by the English and that light slap across his head was like the one you would give to someone when you wanted them to pay attention. "*Come faceva mamma.* The way our mother did," he would say.

As my uncle laughed the sergeant said. "*Che ridi? Respondi!* What are you laughing at? Answer the question!"

"*Scusate.* Sorry, I wasn't laughing at you, but at the question." The sergeant seemed confused by the answer as he asked, "Why does the question make you laugh?"

"Let me explain. You asked me if the river is navigable?" My uncle said as he paused.

"Yes!" The sergeant nodded as my uncle went on.

"This river is so big . . . " And when my uncle told this story he always stopped at this point to emphasize with his arms spread out the universal understanding of spreading your arms to demonstrate something that is very big, but he literally meant something as wide as his arm span.

"The river is so big and wide that as kids we stepped on a rock and jumped from one bank to the other. To answer your question, no! The river is not navigable."

AS the doctor and nurse bring me back to a sitting position, the doctor says, "Let's take a look." She's looking down at me, and I guess she wants me to open my mouth. As I do she says, "Looks good, but there are a couple more spots that we need to cauterize." And even before she's finished saying it, she has the swab in her hand. I nod my consent and close my eyes as I lean my head back and open my mouth.

The doctor cauterized five more spots before she could stop the bleeding. I'm spent and I have no will to fight when the doctor finally steps back. As she removes her gloves she sits down at the little desk to make some notes on the computer. Still typing, she said, "I'm going to admit you. Two days of bleeding is too much. You just had surgery, barely two weeks ago. We'll run some blood tests and in the meantime the IV will help you stay hydrated. We'll move you to the 11th floor. I don't think that you will need a blood transfusion, but we'll see what the blood tests tell us."

I didn't need a blood transfusion and they released me on Saturday around noon after one of Dr. L.'s associates came by to see me. He looked into my mouth and told me that all looked good.

"Do you have a follow up appointment with Dr. L ?" he asked.

"Yes," I nodded.

"Okay," was his answer.

I was glad to be going home and glad I didn't need to have a blood transfusion.

On Monday the following week I have my follow up appointment with Dr. L. Almost two weeks since surgery has gone by and we've made no call to find out if my biopsy results were in. We haven't received a call to tell us otherwise. Let sleeping dogs lie, don't talk about it.

Doctor L. had told me that when I woke up from surgery, the most important thing was that my cancer would be gone. Well if we don't talk about or ask, the cancer is gone.

At 9 am we are in Dr. L.'s office at M.E.E. I sit in the examining chair as my wife stands next to me. We are supposed to find out the results from my biopsy, but part of me is apprehensive about what we are going to find out. My mind seems to travel to places that it shouldn't, but I can't help it.

I don't feel well, but I have perfected my swig of OxyContin with Tylenol to prep me up. I don't feel the high that people that became addicted talk about. Maybe I'm stronger than them, but definitely constipation is a problem. After my suppository adventure and Colace and prune juice, nothing seems to work toward bringing me back to my normal.

Dr. L.

"GOOD morning, Mr. Di Carlo, Mrs. Di Carlo. You look great," Dr. L. says to me with a great smile on his face as he comes into the room. Following him there is the young man with the computer on a pedestal and then there is . . . "You remember my P.A.," I hear as he points at the young lady behind him.

Oh, my God! It's her! She's the one who stabbed me in the face. What was her name?

"How are you feeling?" Dr. L. asks, interrupting my thoughts .

"OKAY," I say slowly so that I can be understood. On our way to town, before we came into the hospital, my wife had a little talk with me as I had expressed some concern to her on how to communicate with the doctors. Since the surgery, outside of my family and those customers I had seen during the few days I worked, I hadn't spoken more than few words to anyone else. And as usual she had the answer as she said. "When you speak slowly as we are doing now I understand what you are communicating to me, and I'm sure the doctors will also understand."

"Remove the obturator. You must be a pro by now with taking it in and out. Let's take a look," Dr. L. says.

When I hesitate, Dr. L. asks, "Do you need help with it?"

The blank look on my face must be throwing everyone off because everything stops. The kid on the computer stops typing and is looking at me over his eyeglasses. The P.A. is looking over Dr. L.'s shoulder and Dr. L.is looking at me expectantly. *What obturator?* I think.

"I never had it in," I say as slowly as I can, but I feel some spittle shooting out of my mouth.

"What?" Dr. L. asks.

"I never . . ."

"What do you mean you never had it in?"

Then I feel the heat starting to flow from the pit of my stomach. I can't see my ears, but I know that they are turning red. I start to get frustrated as I adjust my body in the chair so that I can lean forward some and have my say. I point to the wrapped napkin that my wife is holding with the obturator in it.

Dr. L. looks at my wife's hands as she unwraps the obturator, but I'm not stopping. "I had no idea what to do with that fucking blob. Neither how to clean it, put it in, or take it off."

How much of it did I say? All of it. How much was understood by those present in the room ? I don't know.

Past the first fuck bomb, I don't think anyone understood anything. What I know is that I felt the reassuring hand of my wife on my shoulder as she pulled me back in the chair. She knew that no one could decipher what I was saying, so the fuck bombs couldn't be so bad. As normally as possible, she explained to Dr. L. and staff what the last ten days of my life had been.

She explained to Dr. L. that no one had come the morning of my release from the hospital, so we thought that I wasn't going to wear the obturator. And that's why nobody had taken the time to show or explain to me what to do or show me how and when to do it, and what to expect and how to respond to it.

"I saw you the night before your release...and I told you that Dr. J. was supposed to be there the next morning before you were released from the hospital and go over . . ." He stopped talking and I could see that something was not computing for him as he was looking at me.

"Yes," I answered him with a nod..

"We had Dr. J. scheduled to come in to see you," he said. Then to no one specifically he said, "Can you check with Dr. J. and see if we can get Mr. Di Carlo to see him this morning?"

The P.A. picked up the ball and said, "I'll go talk to him," as she walked out of the room.

"So you haven't used your obturator for what? Nine, ten days? How did you manage to eat or drink? Definitely I can see that your speech is being affected."

LIKE A SQUEAKY TOY

REALLY? What gave it away? That I sound like a squeaky toy? Or the spit flying everywhere when I try to speak? Or that I'm choking most of time when I eat, drink, or when I take a breath?

"Okay, let's take a look," Dr. L. said.

I leaned back and gingerly opened my mouth, as he took out a flashlight to look in the cave that was my mouth.

"Is that a truck parked in there?"

No, he didn't ask that, but I did. This morning as I had tried to brush my teeth, I took a flashlight into the bathroom, and for the first time since surgery I looked in my mouth.

Exactly ten days, and I hadn't had the courage to do that. I stood in front of the bathroom mirror, opened my mouth, and pointed the light at the inside. My mouth was reflected in the mirror and all I could see was black. I thought I wasn't getting the right angle and readjusted the beam of light closer to my mouth and moved my eyeglasses halfway down my nose to get a better view.

Still most of what I could see was black, but I also saw some wisps of red zigzagging along the black patches. I still couldn't see as well as I would have liked, so I lifted my chin a little higher and lowered my eyeglasses a little more so that they were sitting on the tip of my nose. I shined the light in. Nothing but blackness. Not because I didn't have enough light, but because all of it looked like it had been painted black, except . . .

"Wait! What's that? Are those little silvery stars on the roof of the dark cavern? Whoa . . . one, two, seven silvery stars. Maybe I can name them."

Still looking in the mirror, I started to get weak in my legs. I took hold of the side of the sink so as not to fall. As I was leaning over the sink I started to gag, and threw up the little I had in my stomach. Mostly liquid, and then nothing more than dry heaving and tears streaming down and mixing in with the vomit on my beard dripping toward my chin.

Every moment that passed, I hated that dentist more and more. I don't know how much hatred it can build in me, but I feel like it's a gigantic snowball rolling in my mind. I don't know how much space there is in my mind, but that ball is getting bigger and bigger.

Dr. L.'s voice brought me back when he said, "All looks good," just as the P.A. came back into the room.

"Did you talk to Dr. J.?" Dr. L. asked .

"Yes, and he will see Mr. Di Carlo when you're done." I like this. Even the P.A. now is referring to me as Mr.

"Did you ask why he didn't go to see Mr. Di Carlo?"

"Yes, I did."

"And why didn't he go?"

"He said that he was told that Mr. Di Carlo wouldn't be wearing the obturator."

"Who told him that?"

As my wife and I watched this back and forth, I could see that P.A. didn't want to throw anyone under the bus as she said, "Dr. J. was under the impression that Mr. Di Carlo wasn't going to wear the prosthetic, but he'll gladly see him after we're done and show him what to do and make any adjustments if needed."

Dr. L and P.A. were looking at each other and I could see that an understanding had been reached without putting blame on anyone. Dr. L. seemed to accept her answer as he said, "Okay. Then he looked at me as he sat down at his computer desk and said, "You look good. How have you been managing with food?"

"No good!" My wife answered for me.

"Fluids?" he asked.

"Not enough," my wife answered. Dr. L. was looking at my chart as he said to his P.A., "Was Mr. Di Carlo's weight taken this morning?"

"Yes," she said.

"Mr. Di Carlo, you have lost what? Close to 15 pounds?"

"Yes! I'm on this new fucking diet, and I'm trying to market it. Good opportunity, I need some investors." But my words were just meaningless, jumbled nonsense.

"What's that?" Dr. L. said as he looked up from my chart.

"He's just clowning around," my wife answered. She had became very adept at understanding my new lingo and how to clean it up. She continued on, "He's dropped about 15 pounds and still seems to be losing weight daily as he's not eating much solid food or taking that much liquid. He's very lethargic and the only bowel movement he's had was with the help of a suppository. And his urine looks like the color of an overripe banana, way too dark."

There take that! You asked, you fuckers. Well, that's my wife.

"Okay," Dr. L. said, as he turned his back to us and got busy entering a password on his computer. The room was quiet and there was nothing to do but watch him peck away at his keyboard. Soon I saw some charts pop up on the screen. Dr. L. scrolled down through them, and as he did that he made a comment that it seemed to me wasn't directed at anyone in particular because no one answered or questioned him. Maybe everyone understood what he said and I'm the only one left out. His back was still turned away from me so it's not my fault if I couldn't fully hear or understand him. Or maybe I didn't want to.

"OKAY, there it is! We have your reports," he says while his back is still turned. He stops talking and seems very immersed in what's in front of him. I know that soon the unspoken word will be spoken. I look at my watch. It is exactly 10 am.

Is it going to be up to me to ask? Maybe I'll let my wife ask. But maybe if left unspoken all will be okay. My wife is still standing at my side with her hand on my shoulder.

The king is naked.

"We have your biopsy results, and I'm sorry to say I don't have good news." I can feel my wife's hand tightening around my shoulder.

"I don't mean bad, but not good either."

I feel the heat coming up and the now familiar ball forming in my chest. I can feel a little trembling in my chin. I'll be damned if I cry, fuck this shit. I hold my feelings in check but I don't think I'm breathing. To top it all I'm getting a pain in my shoulder like I'm being squeezed in a vise. I'm getting a heart attack?

Thank God I realize that the vise is my wife's hand on my shoulder doing the squeezing and not the sign that I am getting a heart attack.

"The surgery was very successful . . ."

"*And the patient is going to die,*" I thought to myself.

" . . . but we still have microscopic cancer cells."

There it is. The unspoken word has been spoken. I want to say to him, "You promised me that when I woke up my cancer will be gone. Enough of this shit! I'm leaving."

There! I'm gone. I'm floating away and I don't know or recognize who the fuck all the people in that room under me are. As I'm floating away I see the door to the room that I was in magically opening and closing as I turn away from it, and I'm gone. I'm not turning back. Don't look and it will all go away and then when I wake up I'll realize that it's nothing more than a bad dream.

I don't want to, but my body and mind turn back toward that room and everyone is still there including me as Dr. L.'s voice brings me back to my nightmare.

"We will need to do another surgery." Here we go again with the "we" business, like I was given much of a choice.

"By the results of the biopsy we don't have clear margins."

"Can it be treated with radiation without another surgery?" my wife asks, interrupting Dr. L.

"No. Radiation treatments will be following surgery. After surgery you will meet Dr. B. He will be your radiologist/oncologist and he will decide the best course of action. You will also meet Dr. C. in case there is a chance that you need to also have a round of chemo. For now their job starts when I'm done with mine. I will meet with the cancer board to review your case. Overall you are in good health and you're just 60 years old. I think that their opinion, as is mine, will be that by doing a second surgery your odds of beating this goes up a least another 15%. Also, my opinion is that without that second surgery the chemo or radiation treatments will not be as effective in preventing the recurrence or spreading of the cancer."

As clearly as I could I say, "Dr. L., if I was your dad, or your son, or your brother, what would you recommend me to do?"

"I would tell them as I just told you. Have surgery again and then enjoy the rest of your life."

"Okay," I answer.

I know I have tears coming down the side of my face and I can feel some of my wife's tears dripping onto my shoulder. The P.A. is kind enough to hand my wife and me some Kleenex, but I'll be damned if I'll give anyone the satisfaction of watching me wipe them. But my wife as usual is on the job as I feel her wiping the side of my face. I want to say to her, "Fuck it, leave them. I'm paying the piper with them."

I'm thankful for her hand being there. I find myself leaning my face toward her hand as I think of some of Dr. L.'s words. He's talked about many things and I think that I got most of it, but my mind is stuck on one thing.

"What the fuck are clean, or was it clear, margins?"

But of course my wife is the one asking the questions with a more ladylike manner. Dr. L. proceeds to explain to us again what clear margins are. He brings his hand up in front of him toward me in the way you do when you look at someone and you give them the a-okay sign. For a moment I think he is going to say, "Just kidding, no cancer. All is good. Just pulling your leg, ha, ha, ha."

But as we are about to find out, nothing is okay. He's giving his okay sign with his left hand that now is about a foot from my face. He reached up with his right hand and used his index finger like a pointer to make a circle around the O of his okay sign.

"This is the tumor," he says while pointing at the circle that his index and thumb are making. "When a tumor is surgically removed we need to go beyond the tumor itself and try to get to healthy tissue. That's called achieving clear margins." He stops speaking for a moment but his index finger is still going around and around the empty area near the circle formed by his index and thumb. It seems to me he wants to make sure we are following his explanation, but he looks at my wife and not me.

Well, look at where we are now. She has become my spokesman -- man, lady, person, or whatever the fuck it's supposed to be. She's nodding to Dr. L.'s explanation and I follow her example like a puppet as the doctor continues on.

"In your case I was trying to save some of your teeth and the bone above in case someday you decided to get teeth implants. With the next surgery, and to get to what we hope will be our clear margins, more teeth will need to be removed and by the look of the biopsy . . .." He stops for a moment to look at the computer screen. "We will need to remove the bone because the bone is part of that area that is within your safe margins, and I'm very confident that when you wake up your cancer will be gone."

Where did I hear that before?

Everything is "we, we, we." Mr. D., pass the saw. I'm out, maybe Mrs. D. will get to assist.

"We want to schedule your surgery as soon as possible. Everything will be fine." Dr. L. says as he stands up and puts a hand on my shoulder. I have my wife's hand on one side and Dr. L.'s on the other.

"My secretary will set your appointment for surgery, and I think Dr. J. is ready to see you."

Dr. J.

A few minutes later, after introductions and apologies about the misunderstanding about him not seeing me at the hospital – and him making it clear that his impression was that his services were not needed, he says, "Let's take a look." As he's looking into my mouth he asks, "Have you got your biopsy results?"

"Yeah!" I answer, or make a noise that sounds like some kind of an answer as his fingers are still in my mouth. Dr. J. keeps looking at me and expecting a little more explanation. If you get your fucking fingers out of my mouth, maybe I can do a little better, I think, but my wife jumps in.

"He needs another surgery."

"Oh! I think you and I are going to have a long-term relationship," Dr. J. says, while laughing at his own joke.

"Where is the obturator?" Dr. J. asks.

My wife unwraps the piece of paper towel and hands the obturator to him. He takes it and goes to an area at the side of the room where a wash sink is located. His back is turned toward us but I can see that he is rinsing and brushing the blob.

He comes back and sits next to me. He has the obturator in his gloved hand extended toward me like he's making an offering. He then picks it up and says, "The hooks go around your teeth and they will hold the obturator in place. This is the way you pick it up and insert it in-to the area," he says, while demonstrating how to pick up the obturator so that it is between his thumb and index finger. He has the part of the obturator that would be against my front teeth with the rounded hooks facing toward the inside of his hand.

"When you get it inside your mouth, have your thumb in the center of the obturator and push up. That will help the hooks snap in place around your teeth."

I take the obturator and try to mimic what he has done. With Dr. J. looking on I open my mouth and try to insert the obturator.

Nothing. I pull it out and try to adjust my grip on it and try again. It doesn't fit, or I can't find the way to make it fit, and as I pull it out again Dr. J. says, "Let me do it for you so I can better show you how to do it. Lean your head back and open wide if you can."

THE BLOB'S COMING

HERE it comes. I saw the blob disappear past my nose into my mouth. I felt Dr. J's fingers around my mouth and then? Home run. He slammed the obturator in place and as he did I felt like he just hit me with a two by four across my mouth. My body jumped six inches off the chair and I don't know if it was because of the initial pain or that it surprised me by the way it snapped into place.

"Sorry! How does it feel?" he asked.

I could feel the hooks on the side of the obturator biting around my teeth right about my gum line. Strangely, after the initial shock and pain of him pushing the obturator in place, it didn't feel so bad anymore, but I couldn't fully close my mouth because my teeth were hitting some high spots, and I felt like that there was no place for my tongue to fit in.

"Like having a golf ball in my mouth," I answered. I never had a golf ball in my mouth but that was the first thing that came to mind to describe the way the obturator felt in my mouth. At the same moment, to my surprise, I almost heard my old voice back. Almost.

"Don't worry, I'll make some adjustments and it should fit fine."

After some grinding and filing, using a grinder that looks like the one I have in my garage, the blob, with Dr. J's help, had finally shaped and adjusted to a mold that will allow me to close my mouth, but my tongue still felts like it was being squeezed.

"Your tongue has been floating around for a couple of weeks unchecked in the space that the surgery has created. Give it a few days and you'll adapt to it," Dr. J. explained.

It took me a couple of days to learn how to maintain my new friend, the horned blob, including how to gently brush it to remove all food debris and how to rinse and soak it in mouthwash. Also within those couple of days I learned how to put it in and remove it without causing too much pain. I started to eat more and more soft-solid food, but still very bland. My mouth was still very sensitive to anything flavorful. Drinking was still sips, because if I didn't sip, it came out spurting out of my nose or choked me.

On Saturday, April 1st, my children, all of their better halves, and my grandchildren all came together at my house. My wife had said to me, "Choose any food that you would like and I'll make it for you."

My wife could or should be a gourmet cook. She is the Bill Belichick of wives in the kitchen. Give her chicken shit and she'll make chicken salad. Of all of the things I could have asked her to make for me, what did I ask for?

"Can I have pizza?" And after a couple of seconds of furrowed forehead she said, "Sure, we'll order out."

April Fool's Day was the first meal I had in close to a month that I would have to chew. I nibbled all the way down to the crust, and as my wife loves pizza crust, I passed the crust to her. I chewed my pizza very gingerly and took my time to savor every bite and enjoy everyone's comments of how good I was doing. I had two slices and a Bombay Sapphire gin and soda with a twist of lime. I could feel the gin burning as it went past the obturator and reached the soft tissue behind, but I enjoyed every burning moment of it.

As hard as it was, almost every day I felt a little improvement. Over the last month I had learned to take food or drinks in very small portions or sips. It took me some time to learn to chew my food only on the right side of my mouth. To try to chew food side to side as normally would be done put too much pressure on the obturator and it caused pain as it pushed up.

Also, the obturator has no teeth, just a flat surface, so if you chew against it nothing much happens.

By chewing slowly and in small amounts, I actually start to savor food again. Sleeping is still a problem. I have to prop myself up on four pillows. My nose is always clogged and as I lean back I'm not able to breathe through it. As I fall asleep and I'm only breathing through my mouth, within minutes I wake up choking as my mouth feels like parched sand paper. I'm cutting back on the use of OxyContin during the day and I try to control the pain by just using Tylenol. In the evenings before bed I do take a swig of my old friend OxyContin. With the help of a stool softener my bowels seem to be back to somewhat of a normal schedule and definitely the level of pain in my mouth and throat has gone down.

I'm trying to get myself ready to face surgery again. It's Sunday morning, and I'm sitting at the edge of my bed around 8 am sipping a chocolate smoothie that my wife made for me. It doesn't seem right that just as I'm getting better I have to go through the process all over again.

I have been working a few more hours a day and getting close to feeling like some normalcy is back in my life. I'm able to carry a conversation about my cancer without breaking down and became a blubbering idiot. But in three days it will be back to square one, back to zero. All the suffering of this past month will be replayed. I make no effort to wipe the tears as they stream down my face and drop into the glass with my smoothie that I'm holding on my lap.

I hate him.

GROUNDHOG DAY. ROUND TWO

WEDNESDAY, April 5th, I was back at the hospital in search of those elusive clear margins. It felt like the movie Groundhog Day. Same parking attendant, same receptionist that asked me to sign with my finger at check-in. Nurses remembered me from four weeks earlier, and the same anesthesiologist was there. Dr. L. had the same prep talk for me, "…and when you wake up your cancer will be gone." Same X on the right side of my face.

WHAT? You weren't paying attention to what you are reading.

It's on the left side of my face that the X was marked, followed by Dr. L.'s initials. Same hallway as I watched the overhead lights pass by one after another.

Will the light claim me this time?

"Bruno, this will help you relax," the nurse said to me as she inserted the tip of the needle into the IV port on the top of my hand. Then nothing. From one heart beat to another, sweet oblivion.

"Bruno. Bruno." I heard my name as I opened my eyes. I saw Peter smiling down at me. "Welcome back. How are you feeling?" I heard a chorus of voices asking.

I heard myself answer them and to my surprise, just like after my first surgery, my voice sounded almost like it did before they put me out. I moved my tongue around my mouth and all felt solid as I found the hard surface of the obturator. I was fading in and out as they told me that they were going to move me from the recovery room to my own room. I hoped that maybe the priest I saw after my first surgery would show up again. As the doors closed, the soft whirl of the moving elevator made me open my eyes. Instinctively I looked behind my head. The priest wasn't there, or if he was around I didn't see him.

As they brought me into my room I realized that I was on the opposite side of the hospital from my last surgery. I could see the Boston waterfront instead of the Longfellow Bridge and the Harvard Bridge and the CITGO sign by Fenway Park.

I saw planes come in and out of Logan Airport and to my left I saw the clock tower at Faneuil Hall marketplace. And then as I turned to my right I saw trees.

Trees?

I was supposed to be on the 11th floor. How can I see trees? And flowers and park benches. I could see them clearly, too clearly for me to be on the 11th floor. For a moment I think that they took me to a different hospital. Did something go wrong and they transferred me to a different hospital? Maybe it's the drugs and I'm imagining all of it. I leaned toward the window to get a better look and to my surprise I realized that what I was looking at was the top of some building, and what I was seeing must be one of those roof gardens.

The nurse must have been used to this look of confusion from patients, and even before I asked she said, "That's the Healing Garden, dedicated to all cancer patients. What you are looking at is the roof of the Yawkey building. That's part of Mass General Hospital. Maybe before you go home you should visit it."

I closed my eyes as soon as I settled into my bed. I went in and out for a while and in one of my "ins" I saw my wife's reassuring smile as she sat next to my bed looking down at me. As my eyes focused on her, she leaned in and gave me a kiss on my forehead. She was leaning on my pillow with her elbow as her hand rested on my forehead with her fingers lightly touching the front of my hair, while her other hand was searching for my fingertips, being careful of the IV on the top of my hand.

Her cheek was now resting on my forehead. With my eyes closed I felt the moment she let go of my hand, and moved hers on my face to the opposite side from my surgery. Her touch was as tender as if I was a newborn baby. My face is against her neck as I bring my arm up to hug her head to me.

Her lips felt very soothing as they moved from my forehead to my closed eyes, and as her lips lingered there, I took a deep breath in the hollow between her neck and shoulder and as I did, I was engulfed by her familiar scent reaching into my soul.

I feel a shudder breaking through me as I just let go and cried. I was shaking as my wife tried to pull back and see if I was okay, but I just hugged her even tighter and our tears mixed. At that moment our bodies and souls were connected in a way that we were as one.

The surgery had gone well and one more of my teeth had to be removed along with part of the bone above. Now there was the waiting game for the biopsy results. According to Dr. L., bone biopsies take longer than tissue biopsies, and it might be close to two weeks before we got any results.

Before I left the hospital there was an endless stream of people coming through to talk to me, from support groups to fundraisers. Medical students always came in a group. They formed a circle around my bed and asked the same question. "How do you feel?" And before I could even answer them I got the follow-up question, "Would you mind if we take a look?"

Most of the time I wanted to say, "Go fuck yourself." But I was being good and answered, "Sure." They pointed at my mouth with five different flashlights and talked as if I weren't there, but that's okay because at that point I didn't have any interest in anything.

I can usually read two or three books at the same time, but this surgery left me with no desire to read. Maybe it was the fog from the drugs I felt I was always in that didn't allow me to concentrate.

Three days later on a Saturday, I go home. I think I'm smarter this time about handling my medications, but the pain is just above anything I have ever experienced in my years. I thank God for my meds. The 10mg OxyContin is a normal dose. I try to follow what Peter taught me and divide the doses, but sometimes that just isn't enough. The new obturator seems to work well and I have become adept at what to do with it and how to take care of it. Sleep is still very elusive as I'm only able to breathe through my mouth. Four pillows are the norm anytime I decide to lie back.

The sleep that I get is drug induced, and when I sleep it is out of sheer tiredness and exhaustion. I'm up at all times of the night either to take a swig of OxyContin or just wandering around looking at my reflection in the dark windows. One thing I don't have to deal with after my second surgery is the constipation, because from day one after surgery I've been on the stool softeners, Dulcolax and Colace.

To eat and swallow is pain beyond pain. The doctors told me it's normal and that I need to keep on trying and force myself. Everything gets liquefied, but it's still hard to swallow. A sip of water or juice causes as much pain as food. The most I eat of solid food is some scrambled eggs and plain oatmeal. Anything with any flavor or spice burns. I have no strength or will to get out of bed and do anything. The weather is starting to change, and my wife and kids try to entice me to go out in the yard and enjoy some of the beautiful sunshine with the grandchildren. But after a few minutes I go back in and lie in bed. Even the little seedlings in my greenhouse don't seem to excite me.

Sunday morning I try to do some bookkeeping for our business. After a few minutes of it, I see the loss of income from me not being at work. Financially, we are starting to suffer. I go through the bills that have been accumulating. I choose the ones that I deem most important and ignore the others. Our finances are dwindling and to make matters worse just one week after I'm home I'm starting to receive bills from the hospital and doctors. My insurance re-ups every April 1st, and that means a new set of deductibles. My first and second surgeries were only one month apart, but my first surgery was in March, the second in April. Two different calendar years, and now I have a new set of deductibles. $3,400 in March, $3,400 in April, and that is in-network. Most of my cancer doctors are specialists and that will take me out-of-network with deductibles ranging around $6,400 to $13,000.

I'm not Einstein, but I know when I'm being screwed. M.I.T. Economist Jonathan Gruber, the so-called architect of the Affordable Care Act, said it best as he pointed out the stupidity of the American public for not holding Congress and the Senate accountable when they allowed that bill to pass and we the people didn't have any say in it. But as I said earlier in my story, before the changes my deductible was $500 for a family of five, and now it starts at $3,400 individually. There was room to fix the problem we had and still have. Change the water and don't throw the baby out with the bath water. As Oliver Hardy used to say, "Another nice mess you got us into, Stan."

On one of my past trips to visit my parents in Italy, I was sitting around the kitchen table with my dad discussing the results of one of the local elections. He wasn't too happy about the results, and his comment on the results were, "*Una volta un vecchietto mi a detto che ci sono coloro che si alzano al mattino per andare a lavorare. Poi ci sono coloro che si alzano per andare a pisciare sapendo che le regole per loro non sono le stesse che sono imposte al rest dei cittadini, e poi contenti tornano a letto.*" (A wise man once told me that there are those that get up in the morning and go to work. Then there are those that get up in the morning to just take a piss, knowing that the rules that they impose on others don't apply to them, and then, satisfied, they go back to sleep.)

Back to Work

WEDNESDAY the 12th of April I'm back to work. My speech is very limited. My mouth, my throat, my teeth, my tongue, everything hurts. I try to talk as little as possible and to communicate more with hand gestures. All of my coworkers are very helpful and have stepped up, but they have their own schedules to attend to. All of my clients are very understanding of appointment changes and of my farming some of my work out to someone else in the shop.

I hate to lose the income, but although the work needs to be done I just don't have the strength yet to do all of it. Now, after my second surgery I find it easier to share with people that I'm dealing with cancer, and I don't break down every time I talk about it. Also, as weird as it may sound, I don't have a sense of shame about it.

With almost everyone that I share my story with, they all seem to ask the same question, "Are you going to be suing him?" And my answer so far has been, "I don't want to invest my emotions into that for now." But every time someone asks me, I think of our medical expenses going up and my loss of wages as I'm not able to work like I used to.

A couple of times as I made some people aware of my cancer and the location of it, I got comments like, "You must be a smoker," or "You must have smoked for many years for that to happen."

In my younger years I did smoke. Truth be told at one point it was in my mind that maybe smoking had something to do with my cancer. I needed to know, so I asked both my surgeon Dr. L. and my oncologist Dr. B. about it. Both doctors had almost the same exact answer for me, "Your cancer has nothing to do with your smoking."

Maybe sometimes as people we need to point at something to justify what's happening, or maybe we just don't know what to say or how to respond when confronted by news of a loved one or friend or even a stranger dealing with cancer.

I'm working on the limited schedule of one hour to one and a half hour appointment slots, depending on the time needed for the service. My old normal was about every half hour to an hour. I just don't seem to have the strength to carry my normal schedule. Thank God for meds as they help with keeping my strength up, but at the end of the day I'm completely drained, drugs or not.

I have also started taking 50mg of Tramadol about every four hours to help with the pain. Tylenol and the occasional swig of OxyContin in between also seem to be a good cocktail. Tramadol is supposed to be a non-narcotic pain killer, but the only thing I care about is that it takes the pain away. Everyone tells me that one week was too soon to come back to work, but I didn't have much choice.

I felt very lethargic and have been getting heat waves and then chills. I took my temperature around one o'clock during my lunch time on Thursday. After looking at the number I waited a couple of minutes and took my temperature again. Same number, 101. Does fever mean an infection? Do I have an infection? I noticed that when I urinate I'm getting some burning and my urine has almost a pinkish shade to it.

At about three o'clock I texted my wife and asked her if she could call Dr. L.'s office to let them know that I was spiking a fewer and to see if I needed to go into the office. Maybe they'll say that after surgery temperature spiking is normal. She was told that they would see me the next day, Friday morning, or I could go to the emergency room. I choose the next day, Friday the 16th of April.

Before we leave the house, I take my temperature and it's still hovering around 101. To my wife's surprise I don't even attempt to get in the driver seat, and as I'm buckling myself in I hear, "Don't you want to drive?" My answer is as tired as my words. "No, I'm tired."

Tired of what?

Not working? Not been able to eat or drink? Not been able to take a full breath? Not been able to sleep? Tired of life? Maybe I shouldn't write that down.

As usual we arrive at the doctor's office by 7 am. At 9 am, the nurse takes us into the examining room and asks a string of the same questions. "Any changes to your health since your last visit? Any new medications?" But the one I love is always the last question that comes with every visit, and it doesn't matter which doctor I'm seeing. "You're allergic to Peridex?"

Well, let's see. Yes, there is a change in my health as there is this little issue with cancer and another surgery since the last month, and . . . no, I'm not allergic to fucking Peridex! But why bother, as that is a lifetime question now for every doctor appointment because nobody is going to remove that check mark next to my allergy status.

The P.A. comes in first and asks all the question and takes my temperature. A few minutes later Dr. L. and is his usual cheery self comes in. I'm not even done responding to his greeting as he tells me that I need to be admitted to the hospital. His P.A .must have given him a rundown.

"Why?" my wife and I seem to ask at the same time. Her "why" sounds better than mine.

"You are dehydrated, and I think that's why you're running a little fever and I want to have you on an IV for a least an overnight stay."

"Can I just drink more water?"

"It doesn't work like that. Sometimes the body needs a little extra help in getting rehydrated and by the time your body tells you that it need fluids, it's too late to do it by just drinking. Your body now needs help to be restored and when a person feels as sluggish as you do and the urine starts to turn dark, it means that the body is running out of fluids. Try to run a car without any engine oil in it. It might run for a while but then the engine will seize and die. You can go home if you like, but I can guarantee you that you'll be back before the weekend is over and probably by then you'll be coming back in by ambulance. Then instead of an overnight stay, you'll be spending a week."

And as usual my wife, the voice of reason, says, "You should stay honey. It's just an overnight."

I knew exactly where to go as this is my fourth admission into the hospital in the last four weeks. From one side of the 11th floor where Dr. L.'s office is located, we walk across to the other side of the 11th floor. No need to go to the admission office; all was nicely done by the receptionist at Dr. L.'s office. As I reach the nurses' desk, I am greeted with a nice, "Hello Bruno."

And as a welcome back the first thing they do is to stick an IV needle in me. But I get a promise that I will be allowed to go home the next day.

Saturday morning I feel great when a group of interns come by my room at about 7 am. I don't even mind when they ask, "Can we take a look?" I don't mind because before asking they tell me I look good and as soon as the paperwork is done, I will be able to go home. These guys are smart. Use a little cheese to get the patient to open his mouth. That's fine by me. I want out.

By 9:30 I'm dressed and ready to get out. I had asked my nurse what time I would be allowed to go home. She said soon, but that wasn't enough for me, "You mean soon as in now? I can call an Uber or a taxi and get out?"

"Not that soon, maybe at about 10:30," she says as she looks at the clock on the wall showing 9:30 am. I text my wife immediately. "Ready to go now. What time are you going to pick me up?"

"I'm working. I'll be there by 12 or 12:30."

"I'm ready now. I'll take a taxi or an Uber."

"NO!!! I'll be there soon. Wait for me."

"Okay."

Ten minutes later I text my wife again. "Are you almost done?" Wait ten more minutes for an answer and get nothing, so I text her again. "Are you on your way?"

"If you keep bothering me it will just take me longer to finish," I get as an answer.

At ten minutes after 10 am my nurse finishes with her paperwork. She tells me I can go and asks if my ride is here. "On the way," I say with a thumbs-up.

She smiles as she says, "You can wait here. To make it easier for you and your wife, just ask her to call you as soon as she's close to reaching the front entrance. We'll bring you down and she won't have to park her car."

10:20. I text her again. "Are you on your way? I'm ready." This time I get a call from her.

"Just left, I canceled my last appointment. I should be there in less than an hour."

"An hour? You should make it here in 25 minutes! Can you drive faster? I'm ready."

"Okay, I'll try."

"The nurse wants you to call when you get close to the hospital so they can bring me downstairs and you won't have to park the car."

"Okay."

"Where are you? How far did you get? Any traffic? Do you think you can make it here in less time?"

"I'm just getting on the highway; should be there shortly."

Ten minutes later I call her again, and I get her phone going to voice mail. 10:40. Twenty minutes since her last call. Should I call the nurse and tell her that I'm ready? I have a Shaw's shopping bag with my few things in it sitting on the bed next to me. I never had a chance to pack a bag because I was admitted from the doctor's office, so I don't have much with me. All that I needed was supplied by the hospital. I have my release papers, hospital-issued yellow socks with rubber grips, mini toothbrush, mini toothpaste, saline solution. Why not take the water pitcher also, as they just throw them away?

I'm sitting at the edge of my bed, with the bag on my lap looking at the airport just behind Boston Harbor in the distance, but not much registers in my focus. I just want to get out of here. Four admissions in less than five weeks. Enough! I want to go home.

Five minutes after 11 o'clock, I call my wife again and ask her, "Almost here?"

"Almost. I'm about to turn onto Blossom Street if this blessed traffic moves. I should be there in less than ten minutes."

"Great. See you soon," and without waiting for an answer from her I hang up as I'm walking down the hall to the nurses' station to tell them that my ride is a few minutes away and I'm ready to go down stairs. "Okay, I'll get someone to get the wheelchair to bring . . ."

"No! I want to walk down," I say, maybe with too much force.

"It's hospital policy that we take you to your car in a wheelchair and that one of the nurses or interns is with you."

"You can have someone with me, but I'm not sitting in a wheelchair." There, that's final.

"Okay, wait in your room and I'll have someone meet you there," she says as she goes to the phone on the desk to call someone.

A few minutes later I'm again sitting at the edge of my bed with my paper bag on my lap debating if I should call my wife again and see if she has arrived. Just then a man comes into my room wearing the garb that everyone wears, so I don't have any idea if he is a doctor, a nurse, or an intern. The only thing that matters to me is that he gets me out of here. "Ready?" he asks.

"Yes sir," I say as I put the paper bag under my arm and follow him out of my room. As we reach the hospital front entrance on Fruit Street, I don't see my wife's car, but I see stopped traffic up and down Fruit Street and spilling around the corner into Charles Street. We would need to take Charles Street to access the tunnel to exit the city. "Do you see your ride?" I hear my companion ask.

"Hmm. No," I say as I take another look at the unmoving cars. I'm dialing my wife's number as I speak. "Hi. Where are you?" I ask, even before she finishes saying hello.

"I think I'm still about ten minutes away. I'm stuck in traffic. I don't know if there is an accident or just traffic."

"Which street are you on?"

"I'm still about the same spot, turning into Blossom Street," she answers. And then I have the greatest idea as I say to her, "I'm going to walk to you because even here there is a lot of traffic."

"No, don't do that. I should be there soon . . ." I didn't hear the rest of what she said because I had hung up before she finished.

"My wife is stuck in traffic a few minutes away. I'm going to go and meet her," I say to my companion as I start to walk up Fruit Street without waiting for his permission or response.

I'm a man on a mission as I go up Fruit Street past the entrance of the Mass General Hospital and cross over to North Grove Street into Parkman Street. I can see Blossom Street a couple of hundred feet away. Almost home free.

As I'm walking, my companion is following me like a puppy and I can see that he is getting upset, or I should say I can hear it in the tone of his voice, as he says, "No! Stop, you can't be walking around like that! I need to be with you until you're in the car with your driver."

"You can follow me if you like." And I keep on going.

I hear him say something in what I think is Spanish and it doesn't sound like, "Have a good day." I keep going on Parkman Street and he still follows me, and in front of me nothing but stopped traffic. I'm moving with even more determination and my companion keeps on following. I still hear something coming from him, but I'm not turning or stopping to find out what he's saying.

Finally, as I am about to turn onto Blossom Street, after already traveling about a quarter of a mile away from the hospital, I finally see my wife's car.

I Just Wanted Out of There

FROM my wife's own words, the way she tells it, is that she saw this crazed man carrying a paper bag being chased by a hospital attendant coming up the street toward where she was stopped in traffic. As soon as she could get a little better visual and the crazy man got closer she realized it was me, her husband. At about the time that she recognized me, she realized that I had recognized her car and she noticed that my walking pace picked up.

I turned around and saw the attendant speed up to catch up to me. I tried to wave him off and yell, "My ride is here," while I pointed to my wife's car about two car lengths away from me. But the only thing I got was him throwing his arms up in exasperation as he sped up his pace.

He wasn't going to catch me. As I reached my wife's car I opened the back door and threw my bag over the seat, closed the door, opened the front door and jumped in all in one motion as I said to my wife even before I buckled in, "GO, GO. Turn left, the street is blocked, you can't get through there."

By now the attendant had caught up to our car and he was standing by the sidewalk as my wife was attempting to make the left turn. I opened the window and shouted, "THANK YOU," or something that sounded like it. As we drove away I could see my former companion in the side rearview mirror standing on the edge of the sidewalk shaking his head and looking down, and then I lost sight of him.

"WHAT HAPPENED? I told you to wait out front," my wife said, as she made a left turn into North Anderson Street and then to Cambridge Street and onto an open roadway. Not wall to wall traffic!

"What do you mean, what happened?" I answered, in the most indignant voice that I could muster, as if nothing unusual had just happened.

"Why are you running around the street with a paper bag under your arm?"

"Why am I running around with a paper bag under my arm? I don't know why I'm running around with a paper bag under my arm," I said as I leaned my head back against the headrest. The sun was on my side of the window and I could feel the warmth of it on my face.

I could see the clock tower at Faneuil Hall as we passed under it on our way to the entrance of the tunnel to the Leonard Zakim Bridge. With my head leaning against the headrest and the warm caress of the sun against the side of my face, I wanted to close my eyes and make it all go away. I wanted it to be just a dream. I was glad my wife hadn't asked again about my escaping with a paper bag under my arm.

Four admissions to the hospital in a month. My speech sounds like I have a mouth full of food that I can't chew anymore. A sip of water is nothing but pain. I never was a big drinker but I would love a glass of wine about now. My stomach is always in a ball. I hope that things work out better this time with Mr. Colace, but we'll see. My nose feels always stuffed and I can't breathe. I know that I won't be sleeping much because within minutes of falling asleep I wake up choking. The four pillows I use to prop my back up will help but the dryness will be awful.

"What happened?" my wife asks. And I don't know if she means today, or to our life.

I close my eyes for a moment. I don't know, but I wish I knew what happened. I try to generate some money to satisfy our financial commitments but I don't know how much more I can do than I've been doing. It seems that there is always another bill coming due. For every dollar I try to recoup by working an hour longer than I should, I seem to lose even more when I land back in the hospital. Each time it happens, it makes me feel that I'm taking two steps back for every step I take forward.

I turn toward my wife to answer her question and I see her profile as she is intent on her driving. I can see even under her well-applied makeup some dark circles under her eyes. This is part of the toll of me being sick being unloaded on her. I'm starting to believe what they say ab-out the caregivers -- that sometimes they are affected as much as those who are sick.

"I just wanted to get out of there," I say. Maybe it's the sound of my voice, or she just takes pity on me. She says "Okay, let's go home." She holds my hand all the way home. I know that she kept holding my hand even as I fell asleep with my head back against the headrest. I know it because in my ins and outs I could feel the reassuring presence of her fingers around mine.

One week later, Friday the 12th of May, we are back in Dr. L.'s office. Room #2, me in the examining chair, my wife in the corner seat across from me. My wife always sits with her back to the wall with her body facing toward me. Today I can see that her eyes are looking toward the Hancock Tower and the Prudential Building near it. From where she's sitting, a bit of the Golden Dome of our State House on Beacon Hill is visible.

From my seat facing her, to my left through the crystal clear windows, there is a spectacular view of the faithful Charles River that has greeted me for every one of my appointments with Dr. L. I feel that every time I sit in this chair, at about the same time of the day, between about 8:30 and 9:30, this is the perfect time of the day to see the sun on the water of the river. As the sun shines from beyond the Boston skyline, the reflection of the buildings in the shiny water seems to reach across the river. As the sun rises, the reflection shrinks moment by moment until it disappears. I can see the Longfellow Bridge with its one-way traffic, as the other half of the bridge seems to be wrapped in all kinds of construction activity. Not far beyond it, I see the Harvard Bridge with a little slower flow of morning commuters. Just beyond, at the bend of the river as it disappears behind Cambridge, I see the CITGO sign across Fenway Park and the Brookline skyline. Same over and over. Groundhog Day.

There are a couple of Regatta boats moving so smoothly across the surface of the water that at times it looks like they are only a shadow or a play of light as they go skimming across the water surface.

It's almost ironic as we sit here waiting for Dr. L. to come in and give us our verdict, or should I say my verdict, that we did the same thing we had about a month ago, while we were waiting for the results of the post-surgery biopsy after my first surgery.

What did we do? Nothing. Don't ask, and it will go away.

And this morning both my wife and I are sitting here looking outside our window like nothing is going on. We are looking outside at a normal world through eyes that don't know normal anymore.

I didn't want to call the office to see if the results of my second post-surgery biopsy were in. My wife didn't want to call to see if my results were in. I think that, like me, she is starting to follow my father's approach: Don't talk about it, don't look at it, and it's not there.

As we sit in this room we are making believe that by looking at normal things, such as the flow of a river or the morning rush hour, all is normal in our lives.

I keep on losing weight, and I'm now down a few ounces under 170 pounds. That makes me about 25 pounds lighter than my weight on the day of my first surgery, 194 pounds. My clothing floats on me, as I haven't had time, money or inclination to go and get few things that would fit me a little better than my present clothing.

CLEAR MARGINS—BUT!

"GOOD morning," Dr. L. says with a pleasant expression, as he enters the room followed by his P.A. and the kid – whose name I still don't know – who takes notes on his traveling computer. After the usual pleasantries are exchanged, and as usual I'm told, "You look great," I politely nod my "Thank you."

"Well, let's take a look," Dr. L. says as he hands me a little paper tray to put my obturator on. I remove the obturator and lean my head back as both Dr. L. and his P.A. shine their flashlights into my mouth.

"Looks great! You're doing a great job keeping the area clean and helping with the healing process," Dr. L. says as he sits at his desk. The P.A. takes another few moments to look and then says, "You can put your obturator back in."

" I see you've lost more weight. You are down what? 20 some pounds?" Dr. L. asks.

"Close to 25," my wife answers for me.

Dr. L. doesn't acknowledge my wife's answer to his question but gets busy typing on his computer. After a few key strokes, he stops and gets close to the computer screen for a better view. Maybe he needs eyeglasses. Or he's taking a second look.

My wife has moved next to me as Dr. L. gets busy on his computer. I find that I can't even take a breath, and from the stillness of my wife's hand on my shoulder I don't think she is breathing either. The same silence of a month ago. Everyone in the room is trying to do something, but the only thing to do is to look at Dr. L.'s back. Then slowly his body starts to turn on the swivel chair. He has a great smile on his face as the verdict arrives.

"Great news! Congratulations! We have clear margins."

I don't know if the noise I hear from my insides is a release or an intake of breath. My wife kisses my forehead and leaned in to hug me. Our tears mixed as one like so many other times this past month. Yet in the euphoria of the great news I hear, "But!"

What the fuck? Don't we get a minute to enjoy it before the monkey wrench gets thrown into it? There is always a but. This "but" is starting to feel like a butt. I wish sometimes that the butt would just butt out. I don't think we got even close to a minute to enjoy our euphoric moment before the "but!"

Even before my wife and I wiped off the tears of joy from our faces, I stopped breathing again. Dr. L. realized that he was the one that had thrown the monkey wrench into our little celebration and tried to bring back some of the party mood as he said. "This is great news that we have clear margins. But what we have are very narrow clear margins."

He was looking at us in the hope of seeing understanding on our faces, but he wasn't getting that from either of us. One moment you're telling me that we have found those elusive clear margins, and finally you live up to the promise that after surgery I would wake up and the cancer would be gone— and now you are saying that the margins are narrow.

Dr. L. leaned back on his chair and brought up the familiar okay sign with his thumb and index finger to make a circle for show and tell.

"By removing the extra teeth and the bone above it we were able to contain the cancer and to have clear, but narrow margins. What that means is that the tumor has been removed, but there is still a presence of microscopic cancer cells."

Take a breath, Bruno, and let this in. After all, even those microscopic cancer cells need to take a breath. Did I say that, or did I think it to myself?

Dr. L. was relentlessly plowing on. "You will need about 25 to 40 sessions of radiation treatments. There is a chance you might need some chemo treatments and there is a possibility you might need to have both. We will set up appointments with Dr. B. and Dr. C. They are the specialists in their field and after they review your case they'll advise what would be the best course for you. I feel that for you to get the best chance of success, my recommendation is that you will need to have the treatments. I think that Dr. B. and Dr. C. will agree with me. They are the top of their field and they'll do what is best for you. You still need time to heal before any treatments can begin, so as of now you are probably looking at about four to six weeks from now. That will take us to early to mid June for starting treatments."

Dr.'s B. & C.

SOUNDS like a law firm. Our first appointment was at the Yawkey building. The Yawkey is one of the dozen or more buildings of the Massachusetts General Hospital. The Wang, the White, the Lunder, the Bullfinch, the Ellison, the Cox and more make up the conglomerate that is the M.G.H. My friend, Dr. Peter Fredhenson, is with us. He has volunteered to accompany us for our first meeting with my radiologist. I'm very thankful for his being there because neither my wife nor I have any inkling what to ask about.

We meet a string of people who review, ask, look and poke. Finally we are told that the doctor will be with us shortly. When we are left alone, I ask Peter how he would like me to introduce him when the other doctors come into the room. With a smile he answers, "Just introduce me as your friend and if I need to bring up that I'm a physician, I will do it."

"Okay," I reply.

Just as I finish speaking, the door opens.

Two very distinguished gentlemen walked into the room. The first I would estimate at being in his mid to late sixties. He's about my height, around five feet ten inches, but his stately walk makes him look bigger than he is. Nice, full silvery hair with a decent haircut (though I could do better for him). He's wearing good dress shoes with navy dress pants, a nice crisp white shirt, and a bow tie. His hip-length white doctor's jacket complements the rest of his attire. He carries the garb nicely and looks elegant.

The other gentleman that just walked into the room would be a perfect fill-in for *Mister Roger's Neighborhood*. And yes, he's wearing a sweater.

"Hi, I'm Dr. B., and this is Dr C.," the first doctor says, as he introduces himself and then points to the other doctor with one hand, extending his other to me. We shake hands and I introduce my wife and my friend Peter to them. As Dr. B. shakes hands with Peter, almost instantly he seemed to sense that Peter isn't just a friend as I hear him say, "Are you a physician?" Was it intuition?

"Yes, I'm an E.N.T., but today I'm here as their friend," Peter answers while gesturing toward my wife and me. We shake hands all around, and when everyone is acquainted, Dr. B. asks me if I can remove my obturator so that he and Dr. C. can take a look.

They take turns peeking into my mouth, and both remark how well my mouth is healing. When they finish looking, they ask me to put my obturator back in. As I do, everyone takes a seat, forming a nice circle around me. Dr. B. takes the lead, explaining his role and Dr. C.'s.

"Dr C. and I have reviewed your case, and by the results of the biopsies you'll need to receive radiation treatments. In the notes on your chart I saw that Dr. L. also spoke to you about it. He did his part of the job, now it's our turn to help you get past this. The only way that we can make sure that all of the cancer is gone will be with radiation. A.C.C. likes to hide in the nerve linings. The radiation treatment will chase the cancer and take care of it. I'm going to recommend thirty-two treatments done every weekday over the course of about seven weeks. You'll have Saturday and Sunday off to allow you to recover. Your second surgery was in April, about four weeks ago. By the first week, or at the most, the beginning of the second week of June you should be ready to go. Dr. C. and I have decided that you'll have no need to go through chemo treatments because your cancer will not respond to chemotherapy treatment, and we both feel that your cancer is better treated with radiation treatments."

Dr. B. seems to take a pause to give us a chance to absorb all that he has put on our plate. Or I should say on my plate – a plate that's getting fuller and fuller with everything that's being piled on it. I'm at a buffet dinner with a full plate, but I wish I'd never been invited.

I find myself looking toward Dr. C., and he's agreeing with Dr. B's assessment, nodding yes. Peter also seems to be agreeing as I see him nod. My wife is nodding, and the kid typing on his portable computer is nodding. Everyone is nodding in unison. I am in a room filled with fucking bobbleheads. It's the fucking *Twilight Zone* again. Better start doing some nodding myself, if I don't want to be left out.

"Any questions?" Dr. B. asks as he looks around the room. Peter is the only one who has questions. At least he knows how to formulate a smart question and knows what to ask.

"What kind of radiation will he be receiving?" Peter asks.

"He'll be receiving proton radiation treatments," Dr. B. answers.

"Will he need to be tattooed?"

"No, but they'll do a mask for him."

"Is the radiation going to affect his gum and teeth?"

"There is always a possibility that the radiation will create some damage. I will do target-ed treatment to avoid hitting the neck and sinuses."

"What are the most common downsides of radiation treatments in that area of the head?"

"There are many things that can happen, and areas that can be affected. Teeth can get brittle and crack. At worst they would have to be pulled and he would have to wear a denture. Dry mouth is a very common side effect but there are mouth sprays that will help with that, if that's the case."

"What about the neck and throat area?" Peter asks, in full swing mode.

Dr. B. takes a moment to answer and then says "We never know how that area will respond, as it's a little different for everyone. There is a chance the throat area will be affected and it could become very difficult, if not impossible, to swallow food or liquid."

"Would he need to have a feeding tube?"

"I'm hoping that it doesn't come to that, but yes, there a strong chance that for three to six months he would need a feeding tube."

What's that pain in my shoulder again? It feels like my shoulder is again caught in a vise grip that keeps on squeezing. Hmm, look at this. It must be a new kind of vise they use, it comes with fingers and an arm. Oh, never mind, it's my wife squeezing my shoulder again.

I realize that my wife and I have become spectators to this back and forth between Peter and Dr. B.. I can't read my wife's mind but I know that just like me, she's heard the doctors talking about dry mouth and teeth being pulled, or the specter of a feeding tube.

Maybe if I just shut my eyes a little harder and keep them closed for a while, all will be gone. Or maybe I need to pray more, as I definitely haven't prayed hard enough. Oh God, I know that I have sinned and I'm not a perfect man, son, husband, father, friend, but I promise I'll try harder to pray more and come to visit your home more often, but please wake me up.

Maybe everyone is in on the joke. This can't be real. Can it be that I have fallen into one of those black holes and I just need to find my way out and all will be like it used to be?

"... so, yes, all of those things can happen, but I still feel that the radiation treatment will be the best course of action." Dr. B. concludes.

"I agree," Peter answers, as Dr. C. signals his agreement with a nod of his head. I see the three doctors turning expectantly toward my wife and me. It is Peter who speaks. "For now, it's the best course of action."

"Okay," I nod. Now I'm one of the bobbleheads.

"One last thing," Dr. B. says as he looks at me. "You need to see a dentist to have a full evaluation of your teeth and make sure that you don't have any cavities or cracks in your teeth."

"Okay," I say. Like I have a choice in anything that is about to happen in my life.

Lo odio quella bestia maledetta disgraziato figlio di puttana stronzo di dentista. I hate that damned beast son of a bitch piece of shit of a dentist.

Dr. C.

IN retrospect, I wished I had started to see Dr. C. a few years earlier. Dr. C. is married to one of my clients who I have known for over forty years. Another connection is that his dad belonged to the same *bocce* club that I played in. Immigrants tend to flock to one another, and I discovered that I had a lot in common with him, and along with talk of work and family, it came up that his daughter-in-law was one of my clients.

I had met Dr. C. years earlier. But when he found out that I played *bocce* with his dad on a weekly basis and had a similar immigrant background, we became a little more friendlier. On occasions when I could have gone to him as a patient I chose not to, so as not to seem that I would be looking for favoritism. Now that I needed a specialist the decision to take advantage of his expertise was an easy one.

Upon entering Dr. C's office for the first time I was made to feel at home by the receptionist, who introduced me to the office staff and the young woman that eventually would be my oral hygienist. When I called to set my appointment I had made them aware of what the technician would be faced with as they looked into my mouth. It was decided that Dr. C. should be the first to examine me and later have the hygienist look into my cave.

Dr. C. examined my mouth and deemed that I didn't have to go through a cleaning at this time. He took the time to examine every tooth that was left in my head. I could feel the pick that he was using moving expertly around every tooth and on top and around the gum area to search for hidden cavities or cracks.

"All looks good," he said, "but we'll take some X-rays to make sure nothing is hidden, and you should be good to go." He had a million-dollar smile on his face as he continued on. "You'll be able to start radiation without any problem, but there is something I would like you to do."

I found myself shaking my head yes because Dr. C's fingers and the little mirror were still in my mouth. "Radiation treatments can be very damaging to the area surrounding where the radiation is being directed. Your remaining teeth and gum line are directly in the line of fire of the area that will be radiated. I'm going to start you on fluoride treatments for your gums, and also I would like you to use Biotene toothpaste. It's very gentle and it will help with the dry mouth that you are probably going to get."

"Okay," I answered, and wished again that I had come to see him a couple of years sooner.

GENEROSITY

ON Saturday night the 3rd of June, my kids and grandkids came to visit us. They had decided that my wife and I needed some company, so they organized a dinner: "I'll bring the salad, you bring the pizza, and you bring the pastry." We had a nice dinner together, and after dinner as they were sipping some coffee and I was having a gin and soda, I noticed that next to the pastry dish there was a card with MOM & DAD printed across the envelope. Standing next to it there was a gift bag with colorful tissue paper coming out the top of it.

Whenever I get a card that is addressed to both my wife and me, I always defer to my wife to open the envelope. I was sitting next to her looking over her shoulder as she sliced open the top of the envelope. I have to admit that I was a little intrigued by this card as our birthdays and anniversary were not that day or anytime soon after. The card looked fat as my wife pulled it out of the envelope, and it had a big heart with "We love you" written across the front.

As my wife opened the card, I saw there was a bundle of hundred, fifty and twenty dollar bills nestled inside. The card also had a handwritten note from every one of our children, their spouses, and even some scribbles from our grandchildren.

"What's this?" my wife managed to say.

"Just a little something to help you guys pay some of your bills," they answered in unis-on.

"But you can't afford to do this. You have your own bills to pay. We can't take this," my wife said as she turned toward me to get some support. Needless to say, I was just sitting there with tears streaming down my face. I guess this is what family does. I had been the provider my all adult life, and I wasn't ready to relinquish that role yet, but you know what they say about making plans and God laughing.

Then my wife picked up the gift bag, and as she was about to open, it my son said, "Mom, let Dad open that." My wife passed the bag to me and I found it to be almost feather-light, as if it were empty. I pulled out the tissue paper and when I looked inside the bag I saw a collection of multi-colored construction paper circles about five inches wide. I picked one up to pull it out of the bag and realized that all of the circles were intertwined, and I could see that each circle has writing in the hidden inside part.

Just as I was ready to rip one of the rings off, one of my daughters yelled, "No, Dad! Don't break it apart yet. There are 32 rings to the kite, one for each day of your treatments. Each day after you finish your treatment you get to open one and read the message that all of us have written for you for that day. With each ring you open, it will give you a countdown toward your last day of treatment. The first one for you to open is the blue one. If you notice, there are a lot of double colors, but only one white one. Make sure you save the white ring for the last day."

Our three kids had put together $1,800 to help us pay some of our the bills that have been accumulating over the last few months. The previous day, Friday June 2nd, I had another surprise from one of my clients, a friend that we will call K. She doesn't want her name mentioned, but we know who she is.

K. was our last customer of the day on that Friday night. As usual, upon finishing the services to K's hair my wife and I spent a little time with her getting caught up on family news, and maybe setting a dinner date. We hugged and said goodbye, and then as she was walking out, she handed my wife a card as if it she had just remembered it. She said, "Oh, this is for you. Just a get-well card."

She hugged and kissed us again and left. My wife put the card in her handbag as we left the salon at the end of our work day. Later that night when we were sitting at our dinner table having a bite to eat, she said, "I forgot to open the card that K. gave us."

She reached over and took the card out of her bag. I was sitting next to her, and when she opened the envelope and took out the card I saw that this envelope, just like the one our children had given us, looked kind of fat. I keep gumming away at my sandwich as my wife was holding the open card in front of her. I was thinking that K. must have written down some very powerful words that were bringing her to tears. I couldn't see the inside of the card, but I saw her reach for something inside of it. I realized that she hadn't said anything, as I watched her wipe away the tears flowing down the side of her face. Our friend must have really, really put down some very, very heart-felt, strong words to make her cry.

"This is unbelievable," she said as she held the card forward to show me the contents. $1,000 dollars in crisp new $100 dollar bills. When we were done wiping our tears we realized that this gift wasn't such a surprise after all because K. was always very generous with us.

Another surprise came from my wife's sister Maria, and her husband John when they gave us $ 3.000 dollars. Another nice gesture: One of my nieces came to visit and left a nice get-well card on the vanity in our bathroom with $300 in cash and gift cards. We didn't even find it until after she left to go back home, out of state. Over the course of the next few months I had many of my clients give me get-well cards with twenty, fifties and even a $100 bill. Some of the people who were kind enough to give me that money were the ones that I would never have expected to be able to do that.

I wasn't asking anyone to give us money because in my mind I was just going to keep on borrowing on my house credit line. My thought was that you borrow when the need is there and if something bad were to happen to me, sell the house and pay off what is owed. I had my friend Franco offer to lend me $10,000, to pay back at whatever time I could. I thanked him and declined, but it made me feel good that he offered. Not long after that, I received a card for Christmas from Franco, addressed to me and my wife with a check for a thousand dollars as a gift.

One of my coworkers – who will remain unnamed because that's what she would want – approached me, saying she needed to talk to me. I followed her to our back room so that we could have some privacy. As I closed the door she said to me, "I want you to keep my vacation pay and use it to pay off some bills." I gave her a hug and a kiss. My "Thank you" came out between sobs and tears, because I could stop neither the sobs nor those tears.

SHARON, ATTORNEY AT LAW

ALSO that Saturday night, June the 3rd, after all our tears had been dried, I mentioned to my kids that a week earlier we had met with an attorney. We might be suing the dentist to try to recoup some of my medical expenses. They all agreed that I should do it as they were the ones who had been encouraging us to do it. We explained to them how it came to be that we had made the decision to pursue it through the courts. One of our friends had recommended a law firm in Boston specializing in medical litigation, and on that same day we had called to set up an appointment.

A week had passed after the initial call when we went to meet our lawyer. It took me a few passes to find the office located in the Boston financial district. As I drove around, I found myself thinking, "Expensive around here. I hope that if there's a case it will be on a contingency base because I can't even afford the parking rates in the city."

Our appointment was on a Friday. The next day, again we got together with our kids for pizza and drinks. I told them that as Mom and I walked into the lobby of the office building, we were greeted by a gentleman about six feet four, weighing 220 to 230 pounds. He was wearing a loose black suit jacket, shirt and tie, and jeans. The jacket moved well on his frame and there was a reason it was loose. As we approached, I could see a discreet bulge on his hip and I knew that it wasn't his wallet. The man was carrying. And I'm sure of that fact because I often carry a concealed weapon myself (fully licensed and legal), and that bulge is very distinctive. We came to a stop in front of him when he asked us if we had an appointment. "Yes, we have an appointment at 11 am," my wife answered. "And your name is?" he asked.

When we told him, he picked up the phone in front of him and punched in a number. We heard him announcing our name to the person on the line. After listening to the reply he said, "Okay," and walked us to the elevator. He used a key to open the doors. When the doors opened, he walked in and pushed a button with no number on it. He then stepped out of the elevator and stood in front of the doors as we walked in. As the doors started to close he said to us, "They are waiting for you."

He watched us the whole time as he disappeared between the closing doors. I didn't know if he stood in front of those doors just in case we changed our mind, or to prevent us from going anywhere else. The elevator felt like it went up one or two floors, but I'm not sure if it was more or less. As the doors opened silently, a young lady was there waiting for us. "Good morning, welcome. Follow me, please," she said cheerfully as she turned around, leading the way to a waiting area. "Make yourselves comfortable. They will be with you shortly."

We sat down as the receptionist went to sit at a desk no more than ten feet from us. My wife and I sat side by side with neither of us saying anything. The last time we were in a lawyer's office was about 38 years earlier as we passed papers on our first and only home, and that wasn't even our lawyer because we used the bank's lawyer.

"Good morning! Mr. and Mrs. Di Carlo?"

"Yes!" my wife and I answered in unison.

"Hi. I'm Sharon," she said as she extended her hand.

After introductions all around she said, "Follow me to my office." She closed her office door as she pointed us to two chairs in front of a beautiful cherrywood desk. She sat on the other side of the desk and reached into a drawer to take out a notepad and a pen. Our appointment was supposed to be with one of the lawyers and I thought Sharon was probably a paralegal who would take the information about the case.

I think she read my mind as she said, "I'm an attorney, not a paralegal. I want you to understand that we are going to give full attention to your case. I will conduct the initial interview and get all the facts together. I need you to give me the facts of your case as you know them, and I will ask questions if I feel I need you to clarify certain things. There will be an agreement you will sign for us to represent you if there is a lawsuit. I'll explain how it works if there is a settlement and what the firm will take from it. All of this is done on a contingency base. We'll do the work and research to get everything together so that you can concentrate on getting better."

"Okay," my wife and I said.

My wife is the note-taker and she did most of the talking, since my speech was still too jumbled. Sharon interrupted a couple of times over the 20 minutes or so that it took my wife to present our case, while Sharon diligently took notes of days, dates, and names. When we finished, Sharon took a couple of minutes to go over her notes, and then she said to us, "I have all that I need for now, but I have some forms for you to fill out and sign. We need those forms to obtain your medical records from all of your doctors, including the dentist. And talking about the dentist, have you had any contact with him since your surgery?"

"No! But I really would like to confront him, and maybe I'll bring a baseball bat with me," I think I said.

Sharon looked a little confused by my blowup, and as I got angry the words came out even more jumbled up. My wife intervened to say that I haven't seen him and I don't plan to because if I do see him I will probably kill him or hurt him very badly.

"Good! It's very important that you have no contact with him. Definitely don't try to talk to him. And further, only you, your wife, and I should know about this meeting. Not your friends, your clients, even your family. You shouldn't be talking to anyone about the fact that you're starting a lawsuit. If this goes to court, every person you talk to can potentially be called as a witness." Well, too late, our kids know about it as they were the ones who encouraged us to do it, I thought to myself.

"Once we collect your medical records we will have our medical team evaluate your case. They will let us know if they feel that there was negligence and if we should proceed with it or try to settle it out of court. This is a long process that can take one, maybe two years, and there are no guarantees of success. But for you, don't think about that. Just focus on getting well." She stood up. I guess that was our cue that this meeting was over. She reached again into one of the drawers on her side of the desk and came out with a business card. "This is my number and you can call anytime for updates, but probably it will be easier for me to let you know where we are as your records start to come in. Some doctor's offices are better than others in responding to a collection of patient records."

We shook hands, thanked her and got into the elevator with no number. As soon as we walked in, the doors closed and the elevator moved down. The big gentleman was waiting for us in the same spot we last saw him when the doors had closed. It's as if he never moved. "This way," he said as he directed us toward the front door.

I'M up 4:15 am, and my doctor's appointment is at 9 am. I didn't sleep much last night because the anticipation of this first day kept me awake and I'm a bit nervous. By 4:45 I'm in the car pulling out of my driveway. As I turn into the street I look at the kite that the kids had given me that is now draped between my elbow rest and the passenger seat. One ring for each day.

The trip to Mass General at this time of day shouldn't take much more than an hour, but I'm not taking any chances in case of some crazy construction, a flat tire, an earthquake, or a blizzard. Well, maybe not a blizzard; it *is* June 7th. The past couple of weeks everyone has been telling me that today is the beginning of the road that will lead me to my new normal.

Ten minutes later, at 4:55, I'm on Route 24 cruising toward the city and my new normal. I'm traveling at about 75 miles an hour. Maybe I should cut it back to about 70 and avoid getting pulled over and miss my appointment three hours from now and the beginning of my new normal.

There are three parking garages for me to choose from. The one that I choose is the Fruit Street garage directly across from the hospital's front entrance.

At orientation I had been told that on my first day of treatments I should inquire at the reception desk about the parking fees because patients receiving treatments are eligible to get a discount rate. In my previous appointments, I had to pay $18 for three hours of parking. Thirty-two visits at $18 a day would be a lot of money.

By 5:35 I'm pulling into the Fruit Street garage and as the gate opens I see that the third space on the left is available. Not a bad omen, because on previous hospital visits I found myself going up and down and around three floors before I could find a parking spot, and most times when I finally found parking, it would always be at the extreme opposite side from the elevator entrance.

As I nose my car into the parking space, I still can't believe what great luck it was to have found this parking space at ground level and less than a couple of hundred feet from the hospital entrance. Just as I'm about to put my car in park mode I see a sign on the wall in nice big block letters in front of the parking space that I'm in: COMPACT CARS ONLY. I can see that about a quarter of my car's rear end is out past the white lines of the parking spot.

Is my car a compact car? Well, a Chrysler 300 is not a compact car, but I decide that today my car is a compact car as I nudge it forward to make space for the car behind me to get by. And this may sound stereotypical, but there is this guy driving a Prius. As he slowly drives by, I see his eyes in my rearview mirror and I can't figure out if his eyes are saying, "What a lucky guy to find a parking space there" or "Look at that asshole taking a compact-car-only space with that tank of a car. Asshole, that parking is for my Prius."

Well, either way, fuck you! You should have gotten up earlier. Ever hear about the early bird and the worm and, FUCK YOU AND YOUR TOY CAR. Yeah, with all capital letters. I have cancer and I'm entitled to that parking space. In fact I should take down the "compact cars only" sign and put up "Bruno's parking. Stay the fuck out of it."

I edge my car forward with a tap-tap of the brakes until I get that gentle bump that tells me that my bumper has touched the garage walls. I put the car in park and get out to take a look at the parking line that runs beyond the parking spaces. And as I stand sideways, I see the trunk line nestled just inside the yellow line. I go around to the front of the car and I see my license plate touching against the wall.

As I look at my plate against the wall, this weird thought comes to mind as I remember the dances the nuns used to run for the school kids in the gym that turned into a dance hall. As we danced, the nuns would come around in between the dancing couples and separate those that seemed too close to each other. They would tell them to move back and "leave room for the Holy Ghost."

The Holy Ghost would look at this parking job and shake his head, or her head, or whatever other gender categories we now have.

As I walk up the ramp toward the parking garage exit facing the hospital entrance, I turn around to take another look at my car, and I am satisfied that it is in a safe place and I should find it there when I come back out. At the edge of the sidewalk in front of the garage exit, I stop to look at the circular drive in front of the hospital. I don't know for how long I stop on the edge of that sidewalk, but as I look at the entrance of the hospital I find myself looking up toward the first, second, and third floors, and then upward past the top of the building, until my neck is craned back so that I am looking up to the Heavens.

I don't know if it's just coincidence that I did that or whether I meant to look up. As I'm looking up to the Heavens, I cross myself and step off the sidewalk toward this journey that will bring me to the beginning of my new normal.

"Beep!" I heard a long screeching of tires as I step right in front of a cab coming around the corner. Well, I guess another good omen is that the cab stopped with just enough space for the Holy Ghost between my knee and his bumper.

The Lunder building is my destination. When I reach the front door of the M.G.H., I'm surprised that the door doesn't slide open for me, and then I see a sign on the door that says, "HELP US SAVE ENERGY. USE THE OTHER DOOR." And under the sign there is an arrow pointing to my left.

Instantly I feel the need to do my part in helping Mass General save energy, money and the planet by stepping up to the revolving door. Since being diagnosed with cancer, when I have an option I avoid touching things with my hands, especially in an area with a lot of people traffic. I use my elbows and shoulders a lot. It's now about five minutes of six. When I look around me, I don't see another soul coming up to the door, so no help is coming. With a full shoulder push I get the door to revolve, and I'm in.

There is a big lobby in front of me with an information desk and different seating areas. I'm standing just inside the revolving doors when I hear "Excuse us." I see a gurney with a man lying on it pushed by two EMTs pass by me. The man on the gurney seems to have some kind of face injuries as he holds an ice bag over his face. I step aside and watch them pass by as they head toward the sliding doors on the left of the lobby near an emergency entrance.

I look around and see various groups of people waiting. There is a young lady, a teenager probably, with one of those removable casts sitting down sideways with her leg elevated on the chair next to her. She's leaning her back against a lady in the next chair that is probably her mom. The young woman is using her phone to take a picture of her leg and in no time I hear a little beep as the picture is sent.

The mom seems to be engrossed in a *Cosmopolitan* magazine that she's holding close to her face and I can't see what she is looking at. The front page has a picture of Meghan Trainor standing with her hands over her hips and next to her head there is a big block headline that screams "OMG, SEX! This new (AND SO HOT) technique to deliver full-body bliss." Maybe she's found the article. Good for her.

There are a man and a woman sitting together, perhaps Chinese or Vietnamese, and they are having an animated discussion while the woman is pointing toward the door the EMTs had gone through, and he's pointing at what looks like an insurance card in his hand. I don't know from the sound of their voices if they are Vietnamese or Chinese – not that I know the difference between the Vietnamese and Chinese languages – but as I stand there listening to them I decide they are not Korean. I don't know why I decide they are not Korean or why I need to determine it, or even why it matters. I have a nephew-in-law who is Korean and these people don't look Korean.

Not knowing the English language when I first came to the States, it was difficult outside the family circle to communicate with others. So, I used to look at people and try to determine by their features whether they were of Italian heritage so that I could communicate with them. I guess wanting to know other people's ethnicity has remained with me. In another corner of the lobby I see a gentleman curled on a chair, and he seems to be wearing all of his wardrobe: boots with heavy socks tucked over sweat pants, heavy winter jacket, and a hat. I think the gentleman is using the lobby to get some rest and to get out of the chilly morning weather – just 58 degrees on this June 7th morning.

"Excuse me," I hear again, as I see the now empty gurney go by me again pushed by one of the EMTs I had seen earlier going the opposite way. I guess it's time to move out of the way and go find the Lunder building. I had an orientation day, but maybe I didn't pay too much attention to the instructions of the young lady as she handed me my new hospital I.D. that under no circumstances I should lose or come into the hospital without. And on a printed page she had the map of the hospital with directions for when and where to report for my treatments. Easier to go to the information desk and ask.

"Good morning," I say cheerfully to the nice young lady behind the front desk, and just as cheerfully, she answers, "Good morning! What can I help you with?"

Hey! She has an accent just like me. I wonder where she's from? Her hair pulled back in a bun gives her a sophisticated look. She's wearing a nice crisp white blouse over a pleated skirt. Maybe she's English. Nah, she doesn't have an English accent. She interrupts my thoughts with, "How may I be of assistance?"

"I'm looking for the Lunder building," I say, as I emerge from my trance.

"Do you have an appointment at Lunder?"

"Yes!"

"Right behind you," she says, pointing toward the area where the EMTs had gone in earlier. "There is a set of elevators on the right as you go around the corner that will take you to Lunder."

"Thank you," I said as I walk away, still wondering where she's from. I could have asked her. People with an accent never take offense if another with an accent asks them where they are from.

They say that it takes half a lifetime to know where you came from, and when you find out where you came from, you spend the other half of your lifetime trying to get back to it. Well, I guess for me there is no going back. I have no regrets.

America is my home and I would put my life up for her without a second thought. But sometimes what we miss is that childhood friend who you walked with to your first day of kindergarten, or the sound of that familiar tongue, or the music and sound of those folk songs that speak of love, *mamma*, and old friends. It can be the feel of that first flutter of love that touches your heart as you fall in love with your grade school classmate. Maybe it's the first time you get to hold hands with that special person and it feels like electricity is flowing through your body. Or the innocence of that first kiss that barely touches your lips.

I have, etched in my mind, a moment that was the goodbye between my dad, my brother and me on the day that I was leaving for the far-off shores of America. I was only 17 and a half years old when the three of us drove to Rome's Leonardo Da Vinci airport. We checked in my luggage and after hugging and kissing them goodbye, I couldn't wait to cross through the checkpoint, excited to go and start my new life in America, far away from the Navy.

"Why did you leave?" That is the most common question that I get the moment that comes up.

Sometimes, even after almost fifty years later from that day I first landed in the USA, I still ask myself that question. And of course I do know why I left for the street paved with gold.

When people think of immigrants, they imagine people with no home, or people who are oppressed and they don't have freedom of speech or religion. They think of people who are starving or are prosecuted, or people that will cross a desert , rivers or oceans to get to America.

Me? I didn't have any of those circumstances. I had food on my plate, clothing on my back and a roof over my head.

As I turned 17 years old, I was to register for Selective Service. Italy at that time had a mandatory requirement of one year of service. Except for the navy.

What branch I was assigned to? The Navy.

"Dad, I'm not going to serve in the navy!" I firmly said to my father after I found out of my assignment.

"*E perche'?* Why?" he asked.

"I can't even swim…I don't want to spend two years in the navy."

"You have to serve…there is no choice," he countered.

"There is a choice…" I answered.

"What?" my dad asked with a furrow on his eyebrow.

"I'll go to America and stay with my brother."

There were arguments, tears, promises and bribes, but nothing worked as I had made up my mind not to serve and to leave instead.

As I was about to disappear among the throngs of people, I turned around for one last wave. I saw my dad with his head down, wiping away tears as my brother Franco had his arm around his shoulders to comfort him. A dad shedding tears for his son.

You miss holding your mom or dad's hand as they take their last breath. You're too far away to comfort them and let them know that it's okay to let go and for one last time to tell them that you love them. And as they take their last breath and you're holding their hand to give them courage, you miss those tears dropping on your entwined hands.

LUNDER LL2

ABOUT 50 feet to my left around a corner of the room I saw the bank of elevators, and when I got there I saw on the wall to the left of the doors a directory of the underground floors. I saw the words "Radiation LL2." That must be my floor. I pushed the elevator call button and one of the doors opened almost at the moment I pushed the button. I was the only one there as I walked in and pushed the button marked LL2.

The doors closed with a very quiet swish. Boy, these elevators are great. I couldn't feel the motion at all. Again very softly the door opened, but I was still on the ground floor. The elevator hadn't moved. I pushed the button again, and as I did I put on my reading glasses. A new world appeared to me. I saw a little sign with words in very small print.

PUSH FLOOR BUTTON AND CLOSE BUTTON AT SAME TIME.

HOLD UNTIL ELEVATOR MOVES.

Well, there it was. I needed to hold both buttons at the same time for it to work.

I did, and still nothing happened. The darn thing refused to move. I looked at the little sign again and it still said that you needed to push both buttons at the same time for it to work. Did it again and still nothing happened. I looked around the elevator walls and ceiling expecting some divine intervention. I kept looking around and wondered if there was a camera someplace and someone was having a laugh at my expense. Maybe from one of the speakers in the ceiling I'm about hear, "Smile, you're on *Candid Camera.*"

I was tempted to put up my middle finger and do a spin around the elevator just in case my back was blocking someone watching. I didn't want them to miss my one-finger salute, or maybe even better I should do the two-finger horned salute. Then common sense prevailed and I used my middle finger to push the open door button. I stepped out of the elevator and looked around a bit to see if anyone was coming this way who could make this darn thing work.

It was about 6:15, and I saw a little more traffic through the lobby, but nobody was coming toward the elevators. I was standing in front of the elevator looking at it with my hands on my hips and my legs slightly apart, and that position made me think of Meghan Trainor on the cover of *Cosmopolitan.*

But as I stood there, I thought that I didn't look much like Meghan Trainor, but more like a picture that I remembered from my grade school books of Benito Mussolini standing on a balcony someplace in *Roma* with his fist on his hips and a look of defiance on his face. I could see the picture in my mind, but still something was missing and I realized that Mussolini in that picture had posed with his chin tilted up a bit more and his head turned to the right. As my head turned sideways and my chin tilted up, I saw the young woman at the reception desk. Maybe I should go back and see if she knows what to do and maybe I'll ask where she's from.

As I approached the desk I didn't see a sign of recognition from the nice young lady. I guessed I didn't make as much of an impression on her as she made on me, and she doesn't care to know where I come from.

"Good morning! How may I be of assistance?" she said with a great smile. I proceeded to explain my problems with the elevator, and again with a smile on her face she asked, "What floor are you trying to access?"

"LL2."

"Do you have a badge?"

"A badge?" I reply.

"Yes, at orientation you should have been issued an I.D. card."

But of course I had one. I reached into my shirt pocket, fished it out and handed it to her. In a moment she diagnosed what seemed to be my problem. On my badge that really is not a badge but an I.D. card, there was the logo of Massachusetts General Hospital on one side, and on the other, as big as day, there was "M.G.H. 1811." My name was under that, followed by my date of birth and a barcode.

The young woman by now was holding the I.D. card between her index finger and thumb, facing toward me. With her other index finger she was pointing under the barcode at two letters and a number as she said, "LL3. You need to go to LL3, that is your floor."

LUNDER LL3

A little laugh escaped me as I thanked her. I took my card back, and back to the elevators I went. Well, at least for now that solved my problem as I do know the right floor to go to. I should have paid more attention at orientation. It's not my fault, it's that fucking dentist's fault. I pressed the button to call the elevator and my hands went down at my side with my chin pointing down and my eyes looking at the floor for some lost dimes. No Mussolini stance here.

The elevator doors to my right opened up and the arrow was pointing down. Okay, time to start my journey. I walked in and pushed LL3. Well, this elevator was just as smooth as I still felt no motion. Are you fucking kidding me?

Now I was stabbing the call button for LL3 repeatedly and nothing happened. Again, I saw the little sign that said to hold both buttons at the same time. That explained it, LL3 and Close buttons. Nothing.

I thought that maybe I needed to hold the buttons a little longer as I did a mental count of one, one thousand, 2, 3, 4, 5, 6 one thousand.

Motherfucker, nothing happened. The fucking elevator refused to budge. Maybe if I stood on one foot and pushed both buttons at the same time it would work. I was looking around the elevator again and thinking this time to extend both of my middle fingers, but instead decided to exit the elevator. Just as the door opened, a young man with doctor's scrubs came in and as he looked at me he said, "What floor are you going down to?"

Finally someone to the rescue. I explained to him that I had been trying to get to LL3. Even before I was done explaining, he asked, "Are you a patient or do you work for the hospital? Do you have a hospital badge?" Here we go again with the fucking badge.

"Sure, I have a badge," I said as I showed him my little business card I.D. with a bar code. The man looked young, but he had a kind smile on his face that most people don't acquire until they are much older as he said, "No! You need one of these." And at the same time he picked up the badge that was hanging down from a string around his neck.

"I'm a patient, my first day here," I said.

The man looked at his watch and said," Well that explains it. It's now 6:35 and you can-not access the LL3 floor until 6:45." He gave a little pause to see If I understood what he meant, but I was like a statue. "Go and have some coffee, come back in a while," he said, as he held the door open for me to exit the elevator. Another exit with my head down.

I thought to myself that maybe I was supposed to have a badge instead of an I.D. card. I walked back to the front desk and I didn't see the young lady that was there earlier. But at this point, I would have taken anybody's advice. I saw another gentleman behind the counter.

"May I help you?" the older gentleman said.

"Yes, I have the wrong badge to access the Lunder building." I held my little card up.

"Let me see your I.D. card," he said. I handed him my card, and after one quick look he said, "Only medical personnel and staff can access those floors before 6:45. Patients have access after 6:45. There is a coffee shop down the hallway. Go have some coffee, come back in a while." He pointed behind him toward the back hallway. In less than five minutes I'd had two people tell me to go and have some coffee. I wondered if everyone who works for the hospital gets paid commission for coffee referral.

As I walk down the corridor, I notice that just about everyone who passes by me – men and women -- are wearing blue scrubs. There is a line of about 20 people ahead of me in front of a little alcove. That must be the coffee shop. Too many people, I decide, but just as I am about to turn away, I notice there are four people taking orders and the line seems to move along quickly. In less than five minutes I am next in line.

When my turn comes, I step up to the next server. I am greeted by a well-dressed man with creased pants and a spotless crisp shirt, wearing a tie with a tie pin. He has a nice, pleasant-accented voice. "Good morning, sir. How can I be of service?" Well, definitely this one speaks the queen's English. But his features are Indian, from India. So definitely, an English taught and learned from the colonial India and passed on. I order a cinnamon stick and a regular coffee.

Strangely, as I walk back to the elevator alcove I don't go to the doors and push the call button. I find myself stopping about ten feet away from the doors and looking at them. They are just doors. I don't know why I stop away from them.

Di cosa ai paura? What are you afraid of?

Do I want to cross those doors toward my new normal?

What is going to be my new normal?

Will the radiation kill the cancer that's hiding in the lining of my nerves?

Psalm 27

The lord is my salvation;

Whom should I fear?

Be stout-hearted and wait for the Lord.

Okay, I'll be stouthearted and trust in the Lord. I will enter through those doors and I won't be afraid. Today is the first day of the rest of my life. This is now. Everything else is all in the past. Start anew.

I'm leaning with one shoulder against one of the walls near the elevators. Each elevator door has a line of people in front of them, three to five people deep. I'm nibbling and choking on my dry cinnamon stick. Maybe a couple of sips of coffee will help to wash the dryness down, but the coffee has a burnt taste to it. I find myself leaning with both shoulders against the wall and that gives me a full view across the lobby. For a moment I feel like a pimp checking out his working ladies.

At 6:45 am on the dot, I dump my coffee and cinnamon stick in a trash barrel and get in the back of the line while watching the arrows on top of the elevator doors.

The lobby behind and around me is coming alive. Each elevator by now has close to ten people in an imaginary line. Green down arrow. I'm the fifth person in and as I look at the buttons, I see that LL3 is lighted. I move toward the back and stand against the wall. For a moment I think the elevator isn't moving, but after a couple of stops in between, bingo, the doors magically open. LL3.

I'm the last of the three people left in the elevator to exit. There is a reception desk to the left of the elevator doors, and as I approach, I see that there is a lady sitting behind the desk. Even before I reach the desk she bids me, "Good morning, sir."

"Good morning," I answer her. "It's my first day . . ."

"Oh! Welcome. Do you have your I.D. card? If not, your name and birth date."

"Yes!" I say as I take my card from my shirt pocket and hand it to her.

"Okay, Mr. Di Carlo," she says as she reads my name off my card. I see her type on her keyboard and I hear some whirring. Then she reaches under a part of the counter that I can't see and comes out with an I.D. bracelet. "Let me put this around your wrist." As she's snapping the bracelet in place she makes me aware that, "You are a little early, but there isn't a problem because we have some papers for you to fill out." I nod my consent as she continues on.

"So let's see. You'll have 32 visits. Did you drive in?"

"Yes," I answer.

"Okay. So let me guess, you have questions about the parking rates."

Well, a fucking mind reader. That was going to be my first question. What am I going to ask about now? She's looking up at me expectantly, and with a smile I answer, "Yes."

"Okay! There are discount rates for people like you coming for treatments every day. Your rates will be $6 for each day instead of $18. Every bit helps."

Lady, you can't even imagine the degree of help that break on parking fees will be for me, I think to myself as my overdue bills come to mind. At this point every dollar counts.

"I'm going to fill out an order slip for you. How many days would you like to buy to start with?"

"I'll do the 32."

She's looking up at me as she says, "You know you don't have to buy them all at once. It's okay to buy as you go along if you think it's too much money."

"It's okay. Last night I raided the Christmas fund. If you can I would like to do the whole amount."

And last night I did raid the Christmas fund – my work Christmas fund. As a rule, every week I try to put away few dollars toward my coworkers' Christmas presents. Well, now my funds are very low and I can use the few hundred dollars myself. An early Xmas present to myself: parking passes.

"Okay, just one more thing. Would you like to sign up for the highway?"

Not only is she a mind reader, but now she's offering employment. I wonder if it's the state D.P.W. or the town D.P.W. Either way, it will be great with five weeks of paid vacation and paid health care. Why do I need to be my own boss? The heck with it. Just not paying my $6,400 deductible will be a pay raise from where I'm now.

"... it's a new program that we have instituted, and as you get signed up for the program, it allows the doctors to have instant access to your records from different hospitals."

Darn it. It's not a job opportunity. Well, there goes my new job opportunity and pay increase.

I feel someone near me and when I turn around there is a guy standing by my shoulder. I give him one of those looks that say, "Move back."

As the lady keeps on explaining the program and how it works, I'm not paying too much attention because I can feel the guy's breath down my neck. Fuck this. I turn around and ask "Do you need something?" With a little too much edge in my voice.

"Yeah. I want to talk to her," he says with a tilt of his chin toward the receptionist.

"I'll be with you in a moment," the receptionist says, in a voice that implies, "Wait for your fucking turn!" This, as she says to me with a smile on her face, "You need to fill out the front and back of this form. Maybe you can have a seat in the reception area and bring it back to me."

"Okay," I say.

The reception area has about 30 seats in it with combinations of single seats, double-seat couches, and triple seats. I'm the only one there, so I choose a triple-seat couch. In front of the couch there is an oval-shaped coffee table centered between the three seats. Nobody is around, so I slide the coffee table toward the side of the couch where I'm sitting. I position the table so that I can put my feet up on it with the back of my legs on the table and my feet hanging from the side of the narrow oval to avoid putting my shoes on the table. I lean back and start to fill out the form that the receptionist has given me about joining this new highway. I'm barely past the first question when I feel the couch shift. Are you fucking kidding me? There are probably 29 empty seats out of 30 all around me, and the same guy that was breathing down my neck chooses to come and sit on my couch ... my fucking couch.

I finish filling out my form and then take a few minutes to read a pamphlet that came with it, that stated over and over that it was a secure website. I wonder if today there is any secure site that hackers can't get to, but I decide to sign up for the program, as I take the form back to the front desk. The receptionist takes the form and asks me again for my birth date. When she enters the information on her computer, I see a puzzled look on her face as she stops typing and says, "You're already signed up. Don't you remember doing it?"

I must have a puzzled look on my own face as I say to her, "I don't remember doing it. Maybe when I was under the influence of drugs?"

"Drugs?" she says.

"Well, drugs. You know, OxyContin, stuff like that after surgery."

"Ah, those kinds of drugs. Well, you are all set with this. You're in the highway," she says as she rips up the form I just filled out and disposes of it in a trash basket under her desk.

"One more thing. This is your slip for your parking passes," she says as she hands me a slip of paper with my name on it and the number of days that I wanted to pay for. "When you go back to your car, give them this at the pay station and they'll set up your parking pass. Soon, one of the technicians will come and meet you and take you in. Starting tomorrow you don't need to stop here. When you get off the elevator, just go down the hallway behind you and at the end, turn right. From there you'll see a set of double doors. Go through them. On the other side of the door, on the right you'll see a computer screen with a scanning station. Scan your card and your name will appear on the screen. That will let your team know you are here. This morning they'll go over with you all that you need to do when you arrive. That's all from me. Find a place to sit. You're a little early for your nine o'clock appointment."

The only part I hear of the whole speech is that I am "a little early for my appointment." Somehow I feel the need to explain to her that I came a long way and that I came from a far away place just like the three Kings had done to bring gifts to baby Jesus and that I prefer to wait here for a couple of hours instead of being stuck in traffic on the Expressway that I need to take to come into the city.

There is nothing express about the Route 3 Southeast Expressway that comes into Boston from the South Shore, and it doesn't make a difference what time of day or day of the week you choose. It probably was someone's idea of a joke to name it the Southeast Expressway.

The nice lady at the reception desk is probably wondering why I'm still standing in front of her desk. She says, "Good luck Mr. Di Carlo." And that is my hint to move on.

"Thank you," I say with a smile on my tightly closed lips as I turn toward the waiting area and ponder if I want to go back to my nest on the couch with the perfect setup for my feet to rest on the coffee table. Even ten feet away I can see the other guy still sitting there, but to add insult to injury he has pulled the coffee table toward the other side of the couch where he is sitting and he has his feet on the table.

Yeah. His shoes are on the table. That fucking moron. At least I had the decency to just rest my legs on it without my feet touching the table. Does that score points for me, or am I just as big of a moron for moving the table and putting my legs on it? I keep on walking toward the opposite side of the waiting area and find a one-chair seat and plop myself down.

There is a *Time* magazine from 2014 sitting on the table beside my chair. I put it on my lap just in case someone comes along and steals it from me like that guy stole my table. I see other magazines at different end tables around the room, but I don't want to get up to get them. They are probably the same as this *Time* magazine, three to five years old. A couple more years and they will be able to receive First Holy Communion, or maybe given time even get a Bar Mitzvah or a Bat Mitzvah.

I feel my phone in my pocket. Maybe I'll play one of the word games on it. As I dither between the three-year-old magazine on one hand and the phone on the other, the solution to my problem comes as I hear, "Bruno!" As I turn toward the voice I see a young woman standing a couple of feet away from me with a file in one hand, the other hand extended toward me. I stand up and as we shake hands she says, "Hi. I'm Lisa, one of the members of your team."

Play ball . . . we have a team, I want to say, but instead I just answer very shyly, "Hi.

"We have a seven o'clock cancellation and you are here early, so we can see you now."

"Okay," I say. Again I want and feel a need to explain why I'm here early, but I keep quiet and think that I'm being lucky to be seen two hours before my appointment, so definitely there is some truth to the early bird catching the worm.

"Follow me," she says as she turns toward the hallway that earlier I was told to follow. As we start down the hallway I see a sign on one of the walls that says "SELF CHECK IN" with an arrow under it pointing in front of us. As I walk next to Lisa, I realize that she's very young. Looking at her profile I think that she is in her early to mid twenties.

As we make the turn at the end of the hallway I see the double doors. About five feet in front of them Lisa stops. She points at the doors and says, "There are two ways to go in, and it's up to you which way you choose. You can go through the double doors in front of us, check in, and then change, or you can change and then check in by going in this way. While speaking, she's pointing at a side door that I haven't seen yet that's hidden in an alcove to the left of the double doors. As I follow her through the side doors I find myself in a room about 30 feet long and 10 feet wide.

One side of the room is lined with a series of changing rooms, and across from them there are two rows of lockers stacked one on top of the other. On the opposite side of the room from where we have come in I can see two bathrooms. Then Lisa points to an area next to the lockers with bins and another door.

"In those bins there are robes, one size fits all, men and women. When you come in, use any available changing room. You just need to remove your shirt and any jewelry that you have around your neck. After you change, take your personal belongings and lock them into any available locker and take the key with you. On that side of the room are bathrooms. And now please take one of the robes and I'll wait here while you change."

A few minutes later, coming out of the changing room with my shirt in hand, I see that locker number 17 is open and available. I put my car keys on the floor of the cabinet under my shirt, and close the door. I'm standing there in front of Lisa waiting to get my next step. She looks at me with a little smile on her face and says, "Lock it and take the key."

"Okay," I answer, thinking that I have already forgotten that she told me to lock the cabinet.

"Any questions so far?"

"No, no questions," I answer.

"Okay, follow me." As she opens the door near the bin filled with changing gowns, I can see that on the other side there is a kitchenette area and the room is just as long and wide as the changing and locker rooms combined. And both sides of this room are open to a hallway. As we enter the area, Lisa is pointing at different things. "The fridge is stocked with juices," she says as she opens the fridge door. "Here we have Saltines and Graham Crackers," she says as she opens another cabinet door next to the fridge. "And here we have an ice machine and water dispenser. Any time you think you need a drink or a snack, just help yourself. Do you have any questions?"

The only one I can think of is, "Is that a grand piano?" as I point to the left corner of the room.

"Well, yes that is a grand piano. We have volunteers that at different times of day or different days come in and play for the patients. If you see anyone at the piano and you have time, sit for a while and listen. They are very good. I heard that some of them played for the Boston Symphony. Now follow me because we are going to backtrack."

We walk back through the changing room and we come back out in front of the double doors. On the side of the wall just before the door there is a handicapped door button on the wall. As Lisa approaches, she pushes it and the double doors open up to another short hallway in front of us. Even before we enter the hallway I can hear the buzz of voices and other sounds. I can see part of a waiting area as the doors open, and with those doors opening I get my first peek of where I am going to be spending time five days a week for the next six to seven weeks.

As we cross through the double doors, Lisa stops by an alcove on our right. There is a desk with a computer monitor and scanner on top of it. "Do you have your I.D. card?" Lisa asks.

"Yes!" I answer. But the moment I answer yes, I find myself patting my invisible shirt pockets on the gown that don't have any chest pockets and remember that I left the card in my shirt pocket.

"No, sorry. I left it in the locker. I can go back and get it from my shirt," I say, as I start to go back toward the changing room.

"No, I have a mock one to show you what to do," Lisa says.

She takes a card out of her pocket and places it with the barcode under the scanner and magically a name appears on the screen. "When you scan your card you'll see your name on the screen. At the same time it tells us that you are here." She puts the card back in her pocket and moves forward in the hallway. She stops at the end of the hallway, and facing us on the left and right there are two waiting areas separated by a dividing wall. On both sides of the waiting areas there are similar setups of single seats and double couches, almost like the area I was in when I first came into LL3.

"You can wait in either side of these areas, because once you scan in we know you are here and we will find you." I follow her as she walks through the waiting areas to another hallway. At the back of that waiting area there is another hallway lined with a set of rooms numbered left to right from one to six. I stop next to Lisa at the edge of the hallway.

"You will be in room number four. Today we will do a dry run of what we will be doing for you for about seven weeks. If you follow me, we will go into the treatment room and you'll meet more members of your team."

As I walk into the room, the first thing I notice is the bed to my left. Behind the head of the bed is a machine that at first look makes me think of an Octopus. Then my eyes shift to a table next to the bed, and on the table I see a mask. My mask. I will say more about that mask later.

I stop for a moment to look at it and I think that the mask is laughing at me. But how can I see a laughing face if the mask has no face? And then I hear a voice that brings me back to reality.

"Hi, Bruno, I'm Kerry. I'm a member of your team."

Goodie! Another member of my team, and this one seems even younger than Lisa, I think, as I see a hand extended toward me. After we shake hands, she gently puts a hand on my shoulder to turn me toward a computer screen that also has a scanner.

"Do you have your I.D. card?" she asks.

Even as Kerry asks the question, Lisa comes to my rescue as she says "no" for me.

"Where is it?" she asks as she holds her hands palm up with a questioning look.

"Sorry," I say as I reach for my shirt pocket again, knowing that I have no front pocket on the hospital gown. I want to explain that I left my I.D. card in my shirt pocket in the locker room and so I say, "I left it in my shirt pocket." And for good measure this time I pat both sides of my chest looking for that elusive pocket again.

The next move surprises me, as Kerry reaches for my wrist and at the same time takes a pair of scissors from her pocket and cuts off the wrist band I was given up front when I checked in. I'm surprised that she cut my wrist band off, but I'm more surprised at how quickly she just pulled a pair of scissors from her pocket. It amazes me what these doctors and nurses and technicians can pull out of their pockets. So I don't have my little I.D. card and she cut my wrist band off. Am I being dismissed? "No more soup for you!" the Soup Nazi would say.

But instead she looks at my wrist band and says, "Can you tell me your name and birth date?"

Yeah! This is a test that I can pass, I think to myself. And then I wonder if I can fuck around with her by using the data from my European background by using my last name first and first last. I do give my last name first and she doesn't flinch. Okay, I'll get her with the birth date. This should throw her for a loop.

In Italy and most of Europe the birth date is given day first, and then month and year, instead of month, day and year. So, if you were born February 29, 2000, it would be 29-2-2000 instead of 2-29-2000, as is the American style.

So when I gave her my birth day first, it is higher than 12, more than the number of months in a year. There is no flinch as she says, "Oh, you must have grown up in *Italia*. My grandfather on my mother's side was Italian and he used to do the same thing to me as you just did with months and days to try to play a joke on me." I guess now the joke is on me.

She checks my answers against the data on my bracelet, and satisfied that it's me, she says, "It's very important that you make sure to have your card with you, as it gives us instant access to your records and facilitates your visit with us." I feel like I am being scolded by my first grade teacher when I didn't do my homework.

"Sorry. I'll make sure to have my card with me at all times."

"Come over to the bed," she says as she turns toward the bed in front of the Octopus machine.

Hey! Watch it! I'm a married man. What are we coming to, inviting me to bed just like that?" I didn't say it. It was only a thought. Keep on dreaming, buddy, to think that a young woman like that would look at an old man like you. As I turn, I see the mask again, and I think the mask is mocking me and I swear that it's facing at a different angle than last time I looked at it as I came into the room.

Some years ago, I took a few vacation days in Newport, R.I. with my wife and children. On a rainy day that we couldn't go to the beach, we visited a few of the mansions. I don't remember the specific one that we were in because after visiting the second one they all looked the same to me. I was in one of the rooms and as I walked around I felt this creepy feeling come over me, like someone was watching me. But I couldn't see anyone. Only by chance, I looked up and saw this painting of some lady hanging on one of the walls. The figure represented in the picture was a full-sized portrait of a middle-aged woman. I kept moving, still looking up at the painting, and her eyes followed me around the room for every step I took. I thought that I was imagining all of it, so I called to my 10-year-old son on the other side of the room to come over to where I was.

"Yeah, dad."

"Walk with me around the room and look up at that picture," I said as I pointed up and started to move, with my hand on his shoulder to encourage him to follow me.

"What's so spe . . . DA-A-AD! Her eyes are moving," he said as he wrapped his arms around my waist. "Dad, let's get out of here, that lady is following us around with her eyes."

At this moment I think the mask is following my movements and saying "Look at that fool. He forgot his I.D. card."

Kerry directs me to sit at the edge of the bed and reaches to the other side of the bed to get my mask.

"This is your personal mask that was custom made for you." She is holding it with the face toward her. The mask looks like a stiff hoodie that was made to fit around the oval of my face – over my chin, down toward the neck and around my shoulders to about the top of my nipples. Around the edges that would frame the top of my forehead, to down around my neck and shoulders. there are a series of snaps. As I sit at the edge of the bed, Lisa comes over with a small paper tray.

"Remove your obturator," she tells me. I start to comply, but then I think that before I remove my obturator, I should explain that once I do that I won't be able to communicate much beyond hand signals or the shake of my head. "No problem," she says.

Kerry is on one side of the bed and Lisa on the other as I remove the obturator. I look down, not wanting to meet their eyes as I do. I'm still self conscious about removing the obturator in front of others. Maybe even ashamed.

I told my wife that if I were to die before her, to have the "thing" removed from my mouth and not to bury me with it. When my resurrection comes I want my old palate back. I want to be whole again.

Kerry takes the paper tray with my obturator, and I think that she noticed that I'm embarrassed by it. "It will be safe here," she says as she puts the tray on the counter next to my mask.

I swear that the mask has moved again and now it's peeking inside the paper tray at my obturator and I can see what it's thinking. "What the fuck is that thing? Looks like the blob from the swamp with hooks on each side."

"Hi," I hear. Now the thing is talking to me. Shit, I really heard that. That was not my imagination.

"Hey, Bruno," I hear again, and when I turn around I see another young lady coming into the room. "I'm Amanda. I'm a member of your team."

"Hi," I reply.

"We have Pandora radio. Would you have any preference of music to listen to while you receive your treatments?"

"One of the sport channels would be great," I blabber, and to my surprise she understands.

"No, sorry, we just get music."

"Any music will be fine," I say.

Kerry instructs me to put my feet on the bed and to lie back. As I do, I see that Lisa has moved to on one side by my head and Kerry is on the other side. As the back of my head touches the table I feel a tightening in my chest and I can feel a tear trickling from my left eye down the side of my face.

I fake an itch as I scratch the side of my face and try to wipe the tear at the same time. There is a headrest where the back of my head touches the table and I'm asked to adjust my head to it. Lisa has moved directly behind me and she has my head cupped on her hands. She tells me to relax as she moves my head around.

"Don't try to help me," she says, as she moves my head side to side to align with some imaginary line I don't see.

"Scoot your body forward a bit." As I move my body forward I hear, "No, too far. Come back up some. Yeah, just like that. Is your neck comfortable? Relax your shoulders and let them touch the table."

I had my eyes closed for a moment, and as I open them I see the mask floating toward me. That fucking thing does move on its own and it's coming for me. Then I see that Lisa is carrying it. She stops beside the bed as she says, "We are going to try on the mask to make sure of the fit."

"Okay," I say, or something that sounds like it.

I close my eyes as the mask moves toward me and then engulfs me. Lisa is very gentle with the placing of the mask. I feel it around my forehead and neck and shoulders as I reopen my eyes. My eyes, nose and mouth are exposed through the opening at the front of the mask, but from just above my eyebrows, past my ears, down to my chest, and around my shoulders to my upper arms, the mask feels like a vise holding me down. And then I understand what those snaps on the side of the mask are for as I hear the first click. But it's not the sound of a click, but more like the sound that an open palm would make violently slapping the top of a counter. KLACK. KLACK. KLACK.

Every snap resonates doubly because Lisa and Kerry are now back on each side of my head and both of them snap one in place as the other does, and with every double snap I hear I feel my body getting closer to the table. Without realizing it my body is offering some resistance to each snap being closed in place. I don't know who does it, because my eyes are closed, but I feel a gentle but firm hand on my shoulders as I hear, "Relax, keep your shoulders flat."

I open my eyes when I don't hear any more snaps. Lisa and Kerry are like busy bees around me. Lisa disappears behind my line of view and in seconds I hear a whirr. The whirr is coming from what I'll to refer to as The Three-Headed Monster.

The first head appears about a foot above my face and it has a round shape that looks like a flying saucer with a shiny reflecting surface. It's not quite as clear as a mirror, but I can see myself in it. From the center of it I see a green light that I think is a laser. As I look at my reflection in the disk I see a grid of green lines crisscrossing my face. Where the lines intersect, they form squares of about two or three inches.

"Chin up. Shoulders back," someone from my team says. I haven't learned yet to distinguish Lisa's voice from Kerry's. In the reflection I see Lisa and Kerry apply what look like stickers at different places around the part of the mask that covers the area from the front of my ears to my chin.

The stickers seem to be applied along the grid created by the laser. I see Lisa and Kerry stand back to look at the work they have been doing and they seem satisfied with the location of the stickers.

I see Lisa take a marker from her pocket and draw some kind of mark on the stickers, but I can't distinguish what it is or whether it is just an X to mark the spot. Or maybe they are doing paint-by-numbers.

I close my eyes as I hear one of them saying, "Good on my side, all lined up. "Good on my side," the other responds. With my eyes still closed, an episode of *The Three Stooges* comes to mind. Larry, Moe and Curly are playing doctors.

"Calling Doctor Howard ... Doctor Fine ... Doctor Howard." I have no idea why that comes to mind, but maybe it will help me keep my mind off the vise that's pinning me to the table.

I keep my eyes closed as I hear a soft humming coming from the Three-Headed Monster above me. The sound is almost like the sound of a mosquito buzzing around your head. Then suddenly it's like someone steps on the accelerator. Startled by the sudden change I open my eyes and the noise continues to get louder and faster. It lasts for the duration of a count between one, one thousand to about three, one thousand. Then the noise cuts back to a soft whirr as the Three-Headed Monster retreats beyond my line of vision.

Lisa and Kerry are back at my sides as I hear the clasps being undone. They sound just as loud as when they were being fastened. As Lisa removes the mask, Kerry offers a helping hand to help me into a sitting position and says, "This is it for today. We have all your calibrations and tomorrow will be the first day of treatment. Sit for a moment to get your bearings. Sometimes people get a little light-headed when they sit up too quickly. Then you can put in your obturator and go and change."

I want to laugh because that's the same line I use with my elderly clients as they lie back at the shampoo bowls to get their hair shampooed before I cut their hair. Some people, mostly older ones, do get a little light-headed when they lie back and then come up to a sitting position, due to the scrambling of the inner ear crystals, and they walk like they had too much to drink. In my early days of being a stylist I had a lady land in a planter when she toppled over. I learned.

"I'm okay," I say, as I step off the table ignoring her helping hand. I see the blob from the swamp looking at me from the side table. With my back turned toward everyone in the room I put in my obturator. I should have rinsed it before putting it back in, but I just want to get out of there. Lisa walks with me toward the entrance of the changing room and stops at the door. "It was nice meeting you, Bruno," she says as we shake hands. "Please remember to have your I.D. card with you tomorrow. See you then." And she walks back toward the back hallway.

I stopped at the parking garage cashier and forked over $192 for 32 visits. The lady at the counter took a few minutes to enter some information on her desktop and handed me a nice shiny parking pass. She took the time to show me the proper way to run it through the scanner and told me a few times to make sure that the M.G.H. logo faces the inside of the scanner, because other-wise it will not scan. I had to pay an extra $6 for the day parking ticket above the $192.

I thanked her and a couple of minutes later I was back at my car. I was happy nobody realized that my car wasn't a compact car and had it towed away. For whatever reason, I pushed the door lock button down as soon as I sat in the car. I put my seat belt on but I didn't turn the car on. Just sat in my car doing nothing with my eyes fixed on the Compact Car Parking Only sign. I don't know if I sat for five minutes or 50 minutes. I sat with my hands cupped one into the other over my abdomen, and as weird it may sound my hands were cupped the same way as they would be if I was approaching the altar to receive the Eucharist at church. Beyond that I have no recollection of how long I sat there or what I was thinking about. At some point I remembered the ring kite that my children had given me sitting on the armrest next to me.

Okay, one ring a day. Was white the last one I should open? White, yes! They told me to save the white one for the last day. To make sure, I picked up the kite and held it stretched between my hands, and as I looked at all of the different colors, I saw that there was just one white one to distinguish itself as the last one to be opened. Just as I was about to separate the first ring, I realized that technically I haven't had any treatments yet. So the day didn't qualify for me to open one of the rings.

Leading to my first surgery – when finally my wife, my two daughters and their spouses, my son, his girlfriend and I all had cell phones – the kids decided to create a group. This way, if we had something going on like a dinner or a night out that everyone was going to attend, or a get-together for a game, instead of sending individual texts to everyone, we would send it to the group so that everyone would receive it at the same time. We named our group The Whole Crew. I took out my phone from my pocket and sent the first text of what would become my daily routine for the next seven weeks.

"Done. On my way home." I didn't know what else to say, and I didn't feel like explaining that today was just a dry run.

I arrive at the Fruit Street garage at 5:45 am. As I'm driving up to the scanner I can see into the first floor of the garage and I see that the second parking slot is open. I think to myself, "Not bad! Two days in a row I'm going to have front row parking. I offer my brand new parking pass to the scanner and…nothing. I scan it again and nothing happens. Okay! Maybe I'm not holding the pass close enough to the scanner. I turn around with half of my body hanging out of my car window. Only half because the rest is being held in place by the seat belt. I'm stretching to better reach and see what's happening, and I'm scanning and scanning.

There is a car stopped behind me and the man behind the wheel is watching me scan and scan. I see his eyes look at the next lane that now has nobody waiting, and then I hear a little screeching of tires as he backs into the next lane for the other access gate. He watches me as he passes by and I swear that he gives me a little head shake. "Well, fuck you, buddy, and you better not take my fucking parking space," I want to yell, but my seat belt is cutting off the sound coming out of my throat. I slap my car into park and try to open my door to get out of the car. My door opens about six inches and then "bang!" I hit the scanner because there isn't enough space for me to open the door. I slam the door shut, and now without a seat belt on, my whole upper body is hanging out the window. I give one big swipe past the scanner. Nothing. There are two cars stopped behind me and also two cars in the lane to the other access gate. I notice that there is a call button on the side of the scanner. I push it, and I think I held it a little too long.

" Sir, you can let go of the buzzer now. May I help you?"

"Yeah! I got this new parking pass yesterday and the f . . . darn thing doesn't work," I say as I'm waving the pass outside the window toward the camera that I can't see.

"Sir, turn the card around so that the M.G.H. logo is facing the scanner."

"I did . . . Oh!" And the fucking thing works at first try and grants me access.

"Thank you," I say, as I try to drive away as quickly as possible. I see the second parking space is still available. Well, I guess those cars that went by knew that I was there first and they were very thoughtful to leave the spot open for me.

I see the same sign as the day before that says the space is for compact cars only. Everyone who had gone by before me had bypassed it. Yeah, very thoughtful people. I edge my car in and stop when I hear the comforting soft tap as my bumper touches the wall.

Up the ramp I exit the parking area with my head down. I don't want those people behind that camera someplace to see me, but I guess after my experience at the entrance it's too late for that. Today I'm headed right for the coffee shop past the information area of M.G.H. But before I get in line for coffee I decide to use the men's room just past the coffee shop. Two stalls, very private bathroom. It's a long ride in and I need some relief.

There is a line at the coffee shop just like yesterday, and just like yesterday it seems to move along. The smile on the woman's face is very welcoming and I hear, "Good morning sir … help you?"

Her voice sounds foreign. Her skin coloration is dark and she has a head full of dreadlocks covered in hair netting. Her voice has the sound of the song *Je t'aime moi non plus*, without the sensuality.

"Hi, I'll have a blueberry muffin and a small dark no sugar," I answer.

As I walk away I wonder to myself who would have a French accent with a dark complexion. Someone from one of the former French colonies. Haiti. Yes, she's definitely from Haiti.

I'm back at the front reception area by 6:30 and I scout the area to find a place to spend the next 15 minutes and enjoy my muffin and coffee. In the corridor on the right of the front entrance that leads to the Wang building I see a set of three seats without armrests to divide them. I park myself in the middle seat and sit sideways so that I can put my knee on the seat on my right and rest my coffee and muffin on the seat to my left, so that now I occupy all three seats.

They have "Occupy Wall Street," I have occupy three seats, just in case someone gets the funny idea to sit next to me. I need space. My cancer needs space.

At 6:45 exactly the doors of the middle elevator ding open due to my calling of it at 6:44. I keep looking at my watch willing it to move faster, and I don't know why I need time to move faster because my appointment this morning is at 9:15 and I have over two hours to go.

When I call the elevator by pushing the down button, the up button is also on. I stand in front of the center elevator of the three doors in front of me. I wonder what would be the odds that the center elevator will be the one that will open up, and above the doors I will see an arrow pointing down. There is a group of young men and two women in their blue scrubs behind me as I stand with my legs slightly apart, about a foot from the elevator doors just in case someone cuts the line. And then look at that! Ding! And the middle door opens with the arrow pointing down. Maybe I should play the lottery.

Along with the hospital workers, a few other people who I think are patients pile into the elevator as the doors open. No one seems to have much to say or want to even make eye contact with anyone else. The few who are not staring down at the floor seem to be busy with their phones. The elevator hums down to LL2, a couple of people step off, and then we are off again. When I walked in and pushed the button for my floor, I moved toward the back of the elevator. As I look at the people standing shoulder to shoulder, I don't recognize anyone around me from the previous day.

The elevator stops almost at the same time as LL3 appears on the digital number display above the elevator door. I hear the chime of the doors opening and just about everyone in the elevator spills out. There is just me and another lady left in the back of the elevator. I motion with my hand for her to go out in front of me, but she shakes her head no. Well, the elevator doesn't go any further down, so maybe she meant to go up when she got into the down elevator.

Out of the elevator, I pause briefly, almost uncertain if I should stop again at the front desk to check in, but the receptionist doesn't pay any notice and yesterday she said to just go through. I follow the corridor to the left, as I had the day before, to my rendezvous with Mr. Radiation.

Coming out of the changing room I get a closer look at the two waiting areas as I stand in front of the wall that separates them. I realize that they are named waiting area A and B. Loo-king to the right I see that area B has few choices of seats, while area A has a much bigger array of couches, chairs and tables. As I stand at the entrance to the waiting area, I see that there are about 15 people scattered around the room in different seats. I scope both sides of the waiting areas and finally decide where I would like to sit.

In one corner of area A there is a reclining chair and nobody near it. That's the seat I want. I weave past the different seats and couches and people, and I can't believe my great luck as I take the seat. As I adjust myself in the chair I see buttons on the armrest. What do we have here? Controls for heat pads? And a back massager? Not bad!

I push both buttons simultaneously as I sit back and push the lever for the foot rest to come up. I'm all stretched out with my feet crossed one over the other as I start to feel the heat and the massager moving up and down my back. Not bad. Not bad at all.

Everyone around me has their eyes down looking at their phones and I get the feeling that most people around me want to keep to themselves. Well, maybe I'll look at my phone also.

Then I think, forget the stupid phone, and I just lean back and close my eyes to enjoy my massage .

As the heat intensifies on my back and the massager is doing its job up and down my back, I can feel a little smile creeping onto my face. This feels good.

"Hi, Bruno!"

"Did I hear my name?" I open my eyes and I can see the ceiling and I hear again the same voice. "Good morning." There is a child standing next to me. Not literally a child, but a very young woman. Do I know her?

"Hi," she says again. As she finishes speaking I realize that that's Amanda from my team.

By God, I think she looks even younger than yesterday. This is radiation, not kindergarten. I think that soon I'll need to ask to see their permission slips for them to be part of my team.

I'm still stretched out and when I try to push the footrest down, the chair isn't cooperating. And then this child points to the lever on the side of the chair that lowers the footrest. Why didn't I think of that? As I stand up and we shake hands I realize that this child is just as tall as me. "I noticed that you are very early, your appointment isn't until 9:15." Her voice is very kind, almost like a voice you would use with your elderly grandfather, as her hand rests on my arm.

I can explain one more time about the distance that I travel and that I prefer to sit here instead of in traffic, but I choose not to. Instead, I find myself bringing my chest up so I don't look like her grandfather, and as I do that, my white chest hair spills out of the loosening robe around my neck. Why doesn't the stupid thing stay closed? It seems that no matter how tight you tie the thing around your hips, it always comes loose and that makes everyone, whether sitting or walking around, need to hold the top corners under their chin.

"Just wanted you to know that we are aware that you are here and will see you shortly." She gives my arm a squeeze and walks away.

"Okay."

As I sit back down I realize again that everyone is addressed by their first name. No Mr. or Mrs., and everyone wears the same color gown. I'm still puzzled by the fact that these stupid gown don't have a second set of ties or a clasp near the neck so that people don't have to walk around holding the two pieces around their chest and neck.

I put my footrest up as I sit back down and look at some of the messages on my phone. Not much there. I take a peek at my watch and it's barely eight o'clock. Plenty of time. I lean back and in just a few minutes I doze off. Maybe it's the heat on my back or the massager that knocks me out. I fall asleep. I dream. I dream that I am a small child, no more than five or six years old. I am walking to church and I 'm late for services. I can see the church not far ahead in the town square, but I'm not making any headway getting to it. I can hear the church bells ringing and calling the faithful to services but the faster I walk, the further away the church gets. The bells keep on ringing with such urgency that it wakes me up, and as I open my eyes I can still hear bells ringing, but these bells were ringing with a different tone.

The distinct echo of a bell ringing is very clear, but the sound isn't one of a church bell but more like a marine bell that you hear on a boat. Then as the bell stops tolling, everyone around the room starts clapping.

I'm still trying to figure out if it was my dream or just my imagination hearing those bells and wondering why everyone is clapping. Not wanting to be left out, I started to clap and look around to see what we're clapping for, but I can't t see anything. I take another casual look around the room to see if anyone is looking at something or someone, but I don't see anything. I hear a lady behind me asking someone, "Do you know what those bells are and why people are clapping?"

I try to pay attention to the answer but one ever comes, or at least I don't hear one. Maybe they just shrugged their shoulders, and I didn't want to turn around and look or ask, but at least I know that it wasn't my imagination.

Around 8:45 Amanda comes for me, and as we walk down the hallway she stops at the front entrance of the radiation room. In front of us is a short hallway that leads into the treatment room. She's standing less than a foot in front of me. Her voice is soft and her tone is low. I feel she's given our conversation a sense of intimacy, almost sensuous, though not in the physical sense but more pleasing to the mind as she explains to me again about my treatment room and machine #4. All of my visits are going to be in the same room because the machines are calibrated a little differently and it's important to have the consistency of using the same machine. As she's talking to me, she takes a little pause. I see her pointing to the wall next to me where there is a painted #4 bigger than I am. I look at the #4 on the wall next to me and I think that I have been chosen to "Come on down-n-n . . . The price is right!" I'm all smiles. Whoa—I won! "You have won the prize behind door number 4."

As I stand at the entrance of my treatment room I can see on both my left and my right the big numbers in front of the respective rooms. I guess that's there to avoid confusion. Amanda takes me into the room and when I turn into the treatment room I see Lisa is there.

"Good morning, Bruno! Do you have your card?"

I'm ready for her as I have my card in hand. I want them to be proud of me. I look at the table near the treatment bed as Lisa scans my card. I don't see my mask. Maybe *it* went to take a shit. Crazy though. How can a mask go take a shit?

And then I see Kelly on the other side of the room and I notice something that I hadn't seen yesterday. There are about a dozen cubicles against the back wall of the room and each cubicle has a mask in it. They're all of the same color and shape, but the pieces of tape that make the X-marks-the-spot are in different areas of the masks. As Amanda reaches for mine and takes it out of the cubicle I can now see on the mask the pieces of tape or stickers that Lisa and Kelly had applied the day before when I was on the table. Amanda is walking toward me with the mask facing forward and I can't help looking at the mask and thinking that the darn thing got into a fight with the rest of the masks when we were gone overnight and then got bandaged up.

Maybe we can give it a flute or a drum, and it could look like one of those wounded drummer boys from a 1776 Revolutionary War painting, leading his regiment.

When Lisa is done checking me in, she puts my card on the table next to the scanner and as she look at me says, "You need to remove the chain around your neck." How did she see that chain around my neck? As I look down I see my gown is open almost down to my breast bone. How could she not see it?

I slip the chain over my head and Lisa puts her hand out and says, "I can put it with your card." I decline and slip the chain into my front pocket. As I put the chain in my pocket, I realize that I did something wrong. I broke protocol on how to remove my chain. When I was a young child, my grandmother taught me the proper way to remove a chain with Christ on the Cross, or a medallion of the Madonna, or a Saint, from around my neck. I learned it before I could read or write. I learned it before Catechism and Sunday school.

Even before I had my own chain with Christ on the Cross that I was given on the day of my First Holy Communion, my grandmother showed me how she did it. I shared a room with her and at night we shared the time of prayer. I was young and I could neither read nor write, but she would speak her prayers and I was to recite after her. We started and finished our prayers with the sign of the cross. After she closed her prayers with an *Amen* and crossed herself, she would go through the ritual of removing the chain from around her neck so that it wouldn't get tangled in her night garments and break.

She would be seated on a chair on the side of her bed, as I stood against her knees watching her brush her hair before getting into bed. She wore a beautiful medallion of the Virgin Mary that was given to her as a gift many, many years ago by my granddad on one of his visits from America.

When she was ready to remove the medallion she would say, "*Guarda e impara come si fa*. Look and learn how to do it." And this is how she showed me to do it: Her chain was long enough to slide over her head, so she would take the chain by both sides at about the area under her jaw and then with a back and forth motion from shoulder to shoulder she lifted the chain toward the top of her head. As the front of the chain with the medallion reached about the tip of her nose, she would slide the back of the chain over her head so she would have the chain extended between her two hands to prevent knotting. She would kiss the medallion with the Madonna's effigy in the palm of her hand and then put it down on the night table with the chain extended, creating a long oval.

But there is more to it.

My chain is also long enough to slide over the top of my head. I'm right-handed, so to remove the chain, I mimic the way my grandma used to do it. When the chain is over my head, the cross slides to the bottom of the loop. I place the cross in the palm of my left hand and then fold the chain over index, middle, ring and pinky fingers. At this point, this is the important part of this operation, as you have the cross in the palm of your hand. Pick up the cross between your thumb and index finger by the part of the cross that would be under the nailed feet of Christ on the Cross, bring it to your lips and with veneration kiss it, cross yourself and then put it away or down on the night table, making sure that the chain remains stretched out, to avoid tangles.

As my grandmother finished her ritual, she would put the medallion near my lips so that I could also kiss it and then place it on the night table next to her bed. For good measure, when she got into bed, just before shutting off the lights she would bring the tip of her fingers to her lips, kiss them, and then transfer the kiss to the medallion on the night table. When morning came and it was time to put the chain back on, she repeated the process in reverse.

I don't know why I didn't do that now. I just slipped the chain in my pocket. Am I embarrassed to show the ritual that I have been doing most of my life? Or am I intimidated to do it in front of this young woman for fear of her passing judgment? Am I being ashamed of my religion?

Lisa takes me back as she says, "Come to the table."

I hear those words and I want to cry because I know that it's a sign that I shouldn't be embarrassed by my religion. And I feel a moment of shame for having done that. The sign I perceived are the words, "Come to the table." Those words are familiar to Christians, as during our services when the time approaches to receive the sacraments, there is a song we sing that uses those exact same words. "Come to the table, to receive the body and blood of Christ."

I reach in my pocket and touch the chain and cross. Maybe this is another way as I get older, or as I'm experiencing sickness, that all at once I have become more aware of God in my time of need.

I had my years that I was too busy working, cutting the lawn, painting the deck, or just thinking that I didn't have to visit the house of God to be a good Christian. I could pray and ask for things I didn't need and I didn't realize weren't important. I could do it at any place, at any time, and it should be just has good as being in the house of God. Well, age and sickness have readjusted my way of thinking, and in many ways I'm starting to understand that God gives what you need, not what you want.

I'm told to lie back with my head on the headrest as Lisa and Kerry stand on each side of me. Lisa tells me to rest my shoulders down against the table and to relax my neck and head. Kerry moves my head around until she's satisfied that it aligns with the laser, and again like yesterday she tells me to stop helping them and just relax.

"Move your hips to the right. No, too far. Chin up, shoulders against the table. Scoot your hips a little more to the right."

What was that you said about not helping you? You want me to move my hips? Make up your mind if I should help or not, I think to myself. as I follow their directions.

After a few more adjustments they seem satisfied. From the corner of my eye I see Amanda coming toward the table. Is that a popsicle? Yes! She's holding a popsicle. Strange time for her to be having an ice cream. I want to ask, but without my obturator it would be almost impossible to formulate the words. Amanda is also a mind reader, as while holding the popsicle in front of her, she says, "This is a mouthpiece."

And I think again that she's reading my mind as she says "Yes, it looks like a popsicle, and we call it the popsicle. You're going to hold it between your teeth as your tongue remains flat under the popsicle."

She extends the popsicle toward me, and like a good boy I open my mouth and bite into it.

"Don't squeeze your jaw. Just bite lightly," Lisa says as she tries to pry the popsicle from my jaws.

Okay, I try to say, but without the obturator and with my tongue stuck under the popsicle in my mouth, I think it sounded more like a moan or a growl or a grunt or something guttural.

The mask comes from behind me and I can't see who's bringing it, but the fucking thing is laughing and mocking me as it says, "Good boy! Look at you with the lollipop."

I close my eyes as the mask engulfs my head and shoulders. "Chin up, shoulders down," I hear someone say. It seems to me that for every time they ask me not to help them, they are asking me to help after all. The johnny that I had held tight around my neck to prevent from opening up is now being pulled open around my shoulders to allow the mask to rest on my skin. I'm now exposed up to just about under my nipples. What a strange feeling. Just my chest is exposed, but I feel completely naked.

At this moment I can't explain why this feeling has come over me. I'm an adult and I've had plenty of occasions to be around others that were scantily clothed. Growing up in Europe, most men at the beach wear Speedo bathing suits no bigger than a bikini bottom, and most women go topless. As a boy in gym class we all stripped down in a big room with no partitions to change into our gym clothing. At this moment, I feel as naked as the day I was born, even with just my chest exposed.

The mask is now snugly against my upper body and head and I almost feel a sense of relief because it's covering me. I hear the snaps that connect the mask to the table being closed, and I try to count how many of them there are, but after eight I lose count because Lisa and Kerry seem to snap them in place at the same time and it's hard to distinguish if it's one or two that are being snapped in place.

With each snap that closes in place, the mask gets tighter around my face. Each one sounds like a hammer blow. Not too long ago, I watched again a movie from Leonardo DiCaprio's early career titled *The Man with the Iron Mask*. The story is set in medieval times and the hero played by DiCaprio finds himself locked away in a dungeon by his evil identical twin brother. The evil twin wants to take over the reins of the kingdom and etches a plot to make his brother disappear without killing him. He orders his henchmen to take his brother down to the dungeon and to have an iron mask made that would encircle his head and face so that nobody would know that he is a prisoner there. The hero is held down as the mask goes over his face and bolts are pounded in place to connect the part of the mask behind his head with the part of the mask that surrounds his face. Now, with each snap, I think of a hammer blow over an anvil.

With the last snap in place I feel that I'm now pinned to the table. I feel a little panicked as I try to move, almost like trying to fight against restraints. From my head to my shoulders and almost down to my elbow there isn't much movement that I can make. Maybe the technicians see the discomfort these restraints create every time a new person starts therapy, and they are prepared for it. Amanda has a reassuring hand on my chest almost like she is holding me in place, but without any pressure, as she says, "Take a deep breath and close your eyes. Listen to the music, it will help you relax." As I close my eyes, I think if that the rapture were to happen now like it happened in the show *The Walking Dead*, I would be in a similar situation to the one the character, Rick, found himself in after being shot at his job. He wakes hooked up to IVs and monitors in a hospital bed.

Rick was a police officer shot in the line of duty. Surgery is done and he is in the recovery room. During the time he's out, everything goes crazy and this strange virus kills most people around, just so they can come back as walking zombies or the walking dead. When he wakes hooked up to IVs and monitors, he gets no response to his calls for help. After a while he rips everything off and discovers that the world he knew has come to an end. Well, he is able to rip IVs and monitors off and walk away.

For me? I will have to spend eternity nailed to this table waiting for resurrection on Judgment Day, because now I have zero movement or mobility from my elbows up. My hands are stretched by my sides and I find my index finger touching the chain with Christ on the Cross through the fabric of my pants.

"Yeah, still there. J.C. *is* on the job."

I can feel a small smile on my face thinking of a show that my two grandchildren like to watch that has a slogan, "Chase's on the job. No job too small, no job too big."

"Okay," Amanda says, "We are going to leave the room during the treatment. We will be out of the room but we can see you. If you need us, just raise your hand and we will stop the treatment and come into the room. Any questions?"

"No," I say, as I try to raise my arm and attempt this new signal that is supposed to stop everything if needed. My arm only moves from the elbow up to my hand. That reminds me of some old newsreels from WWII that show Adolph Hitler coming into a room and everyone snapping to attention as they extend their arms in front of them at shoulder height for a Nazi salute. As Hitler proceeds into the room and walks by people, he gives this wimpy salute by just lifting his hand at the elbow.

I can only lift my arm up to the elbow, and if I try to do that I will look like I'm giving a fucking Nazi salute. Maybe I should just lift my hand with my index finger up, but would that be "wait a minute" or "I'm number one"? Or maybe my wave would look like I'm summoning a server at a restaurant. "Can we get some service around here?" "Can I get a hunting license?"

Swishhhhh.

Maybe I should spread my fingers out and wave as If I was leaving on a trip. Or maybe the best wave would be the one with my fingers lightly curled in and a discreet back and forth motion so that I would look like the Queen of England when she waves to her subjects. Or maybe even better with thumb, index and middle finger slightly curled and ring and pinky fingers all the way in, like some the effigies of saints that we see in paintings when they give the benediction.

Maybe if I need help I can try the time out sign. I try to reach across my stomach but my hands cannot reach each other. Well, that one is out.

I put my hands back down at my side as I hear footsteps receding from me. With each footstep fading away, I realize that the lights are dimming. There is quiet for a moment and then with finality I hear a door closing. The sound of the door closing feels like the clank of a vault being closed. Then I hear a soft swish of air escaping as the door separates me from the rest of the world. The sound reminds me of a big rig coming to a stop and the air brakes releasing air.

"Ding."

For a moment I think someone is calling for service because the ding sounds like the bell at a service desk, near that little, inviting sign in front of you that says, "Ring bell for service." Or maybe even like the show *The Price is Right*, as someone guesses the price of the item and you hear, "Ding, ding, ding." But this is just one ding.

I try to follow the footsteps by turning my head but my head doesn't turn. Only my eyes follow, and the door is too far behind my head for me to be able to see much.

The room is very quiet and I feel a familiar tightening around my chest. "Take a deep breath and close your eyes," someone said, but when I take a deep breath I find that my chest doesn't have much room for expansion. Maybe I'll just close my eyes without the deep breath.

I feel a tear coming down from the corner of my left eye and as it travels down my face it reaches the rim of my mask and starts to travel toward my lips. The slow-moving tear is waking up whatever sensory perception I have left on my face as I get the urge to wipe it or scratch at it. I try to reach up. My hand stops straight up above my belly. If I was standing up with my hand in that position I would be describing someone who was as tall as my waist line. Promptly I hear a voice I don't recognize, and I don't know if it belongs to someone on my team, because through the speaker the voice seems altered, almost robotic. "Are you okay?" it asks.

"I'm okay," I want to answer, and I think I do in my mind, but with the lollipop that I'm holding between my teeth, and not having my obturator in, the sound that I hear is complete gibberish. Now I feel tears on both sides of my face. If they can see me gesturing that I need help, can they see that I'm crying? I want to wipe away the tears. My hands involuntarily reach up and now they are across from each other over my stomach. I hear the voice of God come over the speaker again, "Bruno, are you okay?"

"Just an itch," I want to answer, but without my obturator while trying to hold the fucking lollipop in place between my teeth, speaking is almost impossible. I want to reach for the lollipop and remove it but I know that it's out of my hand's reach. I just lift my hand and form the okay sign.

"Okay! Here we go," the voice says.

This is it

THIS is it. I'm getting radiated. My life will never be the same again. A sad feeling engulfed me like a black blanket thrown over me. I close my eyes and total darkness takes over. The tears are still coming down the side of my face and my jaw is shaking. I don't know if my jaw is shaking because of my hold on the lollipop, but I know that it's shaking. I can feel the stick of the lollipop hitting my nose. I lighten the hold on the lollipop with my teeth and the shaking stop. Maybe I was biting down too hard. I wish I could have a good cry. I feel my chest trying to expand, but there's no room.

I feel alone. I am alone.

Through my two surgeries to achieve those clear margins, the waiting for results and the recovery following each, I never felt so hopeless and alone as I do at this moment. I want to look around to see if anyone is there, but I know that no one is because they told me that no one would be in the room. And I heard them leave the room, and I heard the door closing. The vise around my head is getting tighter. It seems to know that I want to look around or turn around, but it isn't having any of that.

My eyelids are closed but my eyeballs are moving side to side and around, only to find more darkness, but even in the darkness I see the room. I wish my wife was here to hold my hand. I wish Mr. C. never had said hello to me. I wish that the fucking dentist had done his job the proper way. Maybe he wasn't trained properly and never knew how to do the right thing.

"*Primum non nocere.*" First, do no harm.

The light humming of a machine coming alive brings me back to the quiet of the room as I open my eyes for a moment, but then I follow the advice: "Close your eyes. Relax."

The urgency of the sound increases by the moment and makes me think of the humming of thousands of bees buzzing around my head. I keep my eyes closed as the humming increases.

I'm not alone, not anymore.

With my eyes closed I listen to the humming and whirling of the machine as the tears keep on streaming down the side of my face and pooling where my face meets the mask. Take that deep breath. Relax, bring your mind somewhere else. And I finally do. I fall asleep for a moment or two, or longer. The humming of the machines is like a noisy car passing by and receding over the horizon as sleep takes over. Then, back to reality when the noise stops.

I don't know how to describe the sound of that door opening. The closest I can come to it is the sound of an airlock being released, but to me it is the sound of liberation. Liberation from my restraints. Well, I'll be released until tomorrow, and I'm glad I don't have to spend eternity bolted to this table. I find myself lifting my eyes to the side behind me as I hear the footsteps approaching. Soon the smiling faces of Lisa and Amanda appear in my peripheral vision. They both take one side of my head and go about unsnapping the bolts, and with each snap, liberation is closer.

"You did very well," Lisa says to me.

I nod back at them and as I look at Amanda I see her looking at the side of my face. Are the tears still there? I want to reach up and scratch my face and feel if there is any moisture there. Will that be too obvious? Amanda offers a hand to help me to a sitting position as she says, "Sit at the edge of the table for a minute. It will help you get your bearings."

I pull myself up, ignoring the helping hand, and step off the table the moment I'm in a sitting-up position. What? Who am I? A fucking old man that needs help getting off a table?

I'm at the side counter where my obturator sits, trying to get some of my dignity back. I rinse it, and as I lean forward to make it easier to snap it in place I can see Amanda and her smiling face going about preparing the room for the next patient. She doesn't seem to have taken offense from me not being receptive of her helping hand.

"Have a great day. We'll see you tomorrow," Lisa, Amanda and Kerry say in unison. I bid the same to them and walk out. Halfway to the changing room I realize I left my I.D. card on the counter by the computer. I retrace my steps but just as I make the turn down the hallway I see Lisa coming toward me. "You've forgotten your card," she says. I thank her and turn back toward the changing room with a spring in my step.

A man on a mission, I walk to the elevator, and impatiently I push the call button repeatedly. Even more impatiently, I do it again.

Why does it take so long? It's been already what? Three seconds.

I take a deep breath as I'm back in the garage and gain access to my car, lock the doors, and lean my head back against the headrest with my eyes closed. Like yesterday, I spend some time with complete blankness in my mind. Maybe a minute, or maybe ten, go by. Time to text my family and let them know I'm okay and done with my first session. The Whole Crew: One down ... 31 to go. Don't know what else to say.

I look at my kite sitting on the driver seat. Time to see that first ring. I try to open the staples without ripping the paper but my nails are too short to grasp the staple. As I pull the stapled sides apart, I'm glad that only a small cut by the staple opens up through the paper. The ring is only three-and-a-half inches by six, but it opens up to about a 12-inch-long banner to reveal the first of my 32 messages.

"Tough times never last, but tough people do!"

There are little star stickers all over the banner and in between the stickers there are two hand-drawn hearts. Between the two hearts is my youngest daughter's name, Chrissy.

Day 3, Friday June 9th, second treatment

NOT much change in today's routine, but this Friday morning offers a little lighter traffic as I find myself driving into the parking garage by 5:30. Even earlier than yesterday. Maybe people took this day off to have a long weekend to spend on Cape Cod. I take the same parking spot that tells me "compact cars only," which I ignore and tap-tap with my brakes and I'm in. A bathroom stop, and I'm in line for my muffin. This morning I choose a berry-berry muffin.

I sit in the same spot as yesterday so that I can have an all-around view of the lobby. My muffin doesn't have much taste. I eat the crown of it with a few sips of coffee and dump the rest of it in the trash receptacle. I spend some time with my phone, answering texts and messages and play some of my word puzzle.

By 6:45, I'm in the elevator going down to LL3 and I recognize some of the same faces from the previous couple of days. I was the last one walking into the elevator, but now I'm the first one walking out. I follow the hallway and instead of going to the changing room I go to the waiting area. I'm surprised to see some of the people that were in the elevator with me sitting there. If the doors for the floor don't open until 6:45, and I went down at 6:45, and these people were in the elevator with me, and when I walked down the corridor nobody passed me, how did they get ahead of me?

There must be a different entrance to the room. I walk back toward the elevator banks and just as I get there, one of the doors opens up and people spill out. I see a couple of faces that look familiar to me as they turn right instead of going across and down the hallway.

Hmmm. Well, just follow then. Just like that as they turn right, there is a set of double doors they go through, and as I also cross through the double doors I find myself by the entrance where the check-in station is. We had cut across instead of going around in a square and coming out at the same place. Good to know.

Today I choose locker #19. Always liked #19. Also, it is the only one still open with a key hanging from the door. As I come out of the locker room into the waiting area I see my recliner available and calling to me. I sit back, put my footrest up and set heat and massager on high. Not bad! Not bad at all.

From the corner of the room where I'm sitting I can view most of the room around me, and again I'm recognizing many of the faces from the last couple days. As every session is done by appointment only, it makes sense that I would run into the same group of people. I see an older couple – at least, I think that they are a couple – coming in. She's in a wheelchair being pushed by him. She looks Asian and he looks white. They both seem in their upper seventies. Probably they are a couple.

The man is wearing a hat with an Air Force emblem on it that says. "Korean War Veteran." By what I think his age is, it seems to me that he would have served in the Korean War. She was probably a civilian worker or a secretary employed in one of the American bases overseas. Maybe he was an officer with access to the civilians, and they met and fell in love. How stupid can I be? She could have been in the service herself. And since she looks of Korean descent, maybe she would have been someone of high value as a translator. Maybe she was an officer.

Looking at her again I decide that she is definitely of Korean descent. I solved another puzzle: definitely Korean. Just as the gentleman finds an open-ended seat so that he can park the wheelchair next to his chair, I see another couple coming in and she's also in a wheelchair that a man is pushing.

This lady has no hair; completely bald, and the pallor of her skin tells me that probably she's just finished chemo and now she's going through radiation, or maybe receiving both at the same time. They make their way around the room and they stop one chair away from me, about six feet away.

Now that I look at them I remember them from yesterday. I also remember that a while after I had taken my seat in the recliner they started having an animated discussion, and off and on they looked my way. They spoke in a language I couldn't distinguish, but for whatever reason I felt that I was part of that discussion. As they find an open-ended seat, the man does the same as the other gentleman did, lining up the wheelchair with the edge of the chair so they could sit side by side. As they settle in, I see that she's looking at me and she has a look on her face that people have when they are upset or disgusted by someone or something.

I'm puzzled because before yesterday I had never seen either one of them. I keep my eyes down on my phone pretending to scroll through my mail, but from the corner of my eye I can see her looking at me.

No, she's not looking at me. She's staring at me .

I try not to be too obvious as I do one look around the room trying not to linger on the stare that I'm getting from her. Yes! She's definitely staring at me.

Maybe she thinks that she knows me, or she recognizes me from yesterday. I do one more look around and I can't help looking at her because I see lightning bolts coming out of her eyes. Okay, be polite. I give a little nod and a small – very small – smile. I get no response to either my nod nor my half-smile. I'm back looking at my phone, but I hear the two of them talk to each other. I don't understand anything they are saying or hear anything in Italian, French, Latin, Spanish or Portuguese. Not that I speak all of those languages, but I studied Italian, French and Latin. Many Spanish and Portuguese words are similar to Italian or the other languages that I'm familiar with, or used to be. But then I hear some big word that I recognized.

"Nyet!" followed by a string of words that I don't understand.

"Da!" he answers, followed by a string of words that I don't understand.

I'm 100 percent sure I heard the words, "Nyet" and "Da," and even though I don't know Russian, I know these are Russian words that I have heard so many times from one of our Russian clients at the shop. Yes, definitely these two people across from me are Russian.

So? What the fuck is upsetting her so much that even though I don't understand what she's saying, I do know by her demeanor that for whatever reason she's upset by my presence or by something that I have done or I'm doing. The man is still trying to calm her down with words and with his hand on her arm as I see her slap his hand away and turn her wheel chair sideways from where I'm sitting so that now her back is to me. I guess by doing that she doesn't have to look at me.

Well, fuck you, lady. I don't know what I did to you, but fuck you.

I close my eyes and enjoy my heated back massage.

I keep my eyes closed for a few minutes, but even with my eyes closed I can't stop thinking about her stare and the reason for it. As I open my eyes, I notice a third party coming in pushing a wheelchair. There are three of them, two men and a woman. The older man is in the wheelchair pushed by the other man, and next to him is a lady. The two men are a picture of each other, not like twins but one as a younger version of the other. Father and son.

The two men are dressed almost alike with jeans and checkered shirts, and they both sport a beard. Those are not just any beards. Their facial hair reaches down to mid-chest. The dad's beard coloring reminds me of my goatee, almost all white. The son's is a dark brown color. Father and son's beards are the same shape and almost identical in length.

I'm sure that the last couple days I haven't seen these people, but why do I feel like I know them? I definitely know I didn't see them yesterday or before yesterday. Then it dawns on me why they look so familiar. I have seen them on TV. There is a TV show that portrays a family in which all of the men have these long beards. It was filmed down south some place. What the fuck was the name of that show? It was a bird name. Duck. Duck something. Hey, just use your new fancy phone with Google.

Duck. Duck Dynasty. Filmed in Louisiana. Robertson family, multi-millionaires, sporting empire – and there is a picture of them: Miss Kay, Phil, Willie, Si, Jase and Korie.

From the look of these two on the other side of the room they could be Phil and Willie. Can it be them? The lady with them doesn't look like Miss Kay. Well, maybe they are just relatives or lookalikes of the Robertson family.

I need some distraction so I decide to go across the room to a magazine rack. I leave my phone smack on the middle of my recliner seat just in case someone decides to take my seat while I'm away looking at books. I choose one titled *A Day in America*. That sounds to me like a good title for a book.

Back at my recliner I feel the Russian lady's eyes on me again, but I ignore her as she ignored me when I nodded at her.

Nyet! Da! to you too, lady.

Amanda calls my name at 8:45. I follow her into the room to the computer station. I have my I.D. in my hand as she says, "Name and birth date." I want to answer, "Same as yesterday." But I don't know them well enough to know if they will think I was joking or being an asshole. Lisa hands me the tray for my obturator as she says, "You need to remove the chain from around your neck. I follow her instructions and as I put the chain in my pocket, I realize that I had again strayed from my protocol of the last fifty-some years for the proper way to remove a chain with a religious effigy attached to it. "I tell you, this very night before the rooster crows, you will deny me three times . . ." Holy shit! Is that what I'm doing?

Lisa brings me to the table and after a few adjustments to my hips and shoulders, she's satisfied everything is aligned the proper way. I see Amanda coming with the mask and as it engulfs my head and upper body, I realize that I didn't close my eyes.

The mask knows that it has me.

Am I starting to accept the mask as part of me? After all, this is for my own good. The Stockholm Syndrome? You start to feel sympathetically aligned with your kidnappers. That must be it. The sound of the snaps as they secure me to the table don't seem as loud as yesterday. Lisa puts the lollipop in my mouth as she says, "See you shortly."

The footsteps recede and the lights dim as I hear the soft swish of the door and then the click of the airlock. "Ding." The sounds come and I know that it's game time. My team is on the field, and if my team is on the field I decide that I'm going to keep my eyes open. The thousands of bees come alive.

I see the three-headed monster adjust itself around my head. The first to stop above me is the disk section that to me looks like a UFO. The disk shines and reflects my image. A green dot comes out of the center. Is that the laser beam that's going to deliver the radiation treatment? As I take a closer look at my reflection in the disk above me, I realize that my face looks distorted and stretched to one side. As I swallow I feel my Adam's apple rubbing against the part of the mask that encircles my throat.

I have my lips closed around the lollipop while I'm biting down hard on it , and combined with the swallowing, there is no flow of air in my lungs. I close my eyes as I open my lips without letting go of the lollipop and feel the flow of air down to my lungs again.

Breathe. Breathe.

I feel my chest pushing against the mask as I try to take a deep breath. My eyes are open again as the three-headed monster comes alive with the soft whirl above me. The disk rotates from the front of my face toward the side of my head. I follow its progression with my eyes and I see that my image in the reflection starts to elongate. I feel my eyes stretch to the limit as they follow the disk until I think I'm going to get cross-eyed. As the disk disappears and the last of my image fades away, I can't help thinking that the image I have just seen has a sense of familiarity. Well, I know that it's my image, but it's that part of the elongated image that reminds me of something, and I can't put my finger on what it is.

The soft steps come into the room to release me.

Back in the safety of my car, I open the second ring from my kite. This one is from my granddaughter, Autumn, and it says "Autumn Lily loves you, nonno!" There are little star stickers around the words and something else that looks like an imprint of a little hand with another inscription. "Autumn's hand to hug you." I text my family. The Whole Crew: Two down ... 30 to go.

I'm glad it's Friday. It will be nice to have a couple of days off from radiation, and I won't have to drive into the city. Maybe I'll even sleep until 5 am.

Monday, June 12th. Day 4, 3rd treatment

IT'S starting to feel like Groundhog Day. Wake up and repeat the last day, and I'm only on my fourth day. Out of the changing room I make a beeline for my recliner. I think: How lucky can I be? Every day I seem to find the recliner waiting for me. As I sit down I realize that I need some Kleenex. I spot a box four chairs away on a side table and nobody is sitting there, or making use or in need of it. I guess I can go and take it back with me to my chair. Not many people around, but before I leave my chair, I put my phone on my seat, just in case.

I find that I'm breathing through my mouth more than my nose as the stuffiness in my head is getting worse. I don't know if it's the effects of radiation, or a cold, or allergies, or something else that's making it worse.

The side table with the Kleenex box is located on the opposite side of the room from the way I use to come into the waiting area. It's also opposite from the way I go into the treatment room and then back to the changing room. I take the box and as I turn around to walk back toward my chair, my recliner, I notice something that I haven't seen before.

My Recliner

AS I approach the chair with my prized box of Kleenex in hand, I notice there is a sign facing me, away from the chair. Not a little sign, a big sign. I would say about a foot and a half wide by two feet tall. Not enormous but big enough and very visible. The writing on it is in big block letters and I don't need to put on my eyeglasses to read it. These letters are big and you can't miss them.

THIS CHAIR GENEROUSLY DONATED BY MGH LADIES VISITING COMMITTEE FOR USE BY RADIATION ONCOLOGY PATIENTS UNDER TREATMENT

"Okay," I think to myself, that applies to me. But then I see there is more to the sign and that familiar ball in the pit of my stomach wakes up.

KINDLY LIMIT EACH USAGE OF THE CHAIR TO TEN MINUTES TO ALLOW OTHERS TO ENJOY

Holy shit. Shit. Fuck. Fuck.

Now I know why the Russian lady was looking at me the way she did. My phone is laughing at me from the recliner seat saying, "You fucking moron!" I think I also hear the masks laughing. A chorus.

I look around and I'm thankful that nobody is paying attention to me as I pick up my laughing phone and find another seat for myself. I'm keeping my eyes down as I scan to see if the Russian lady is anywhere around and I'm thankful I don't see her. Maybe today she's coming at a different time.

(I did seven weeks, five days a week, coming in for treatments with just the 4th of July as a day off with no treatments. I never sat in that chair again.)

I'm immersed in my phone playing a word game when I hear the bell again. Today I'm awake and I know I'm not dreaming. Very distinct: three bell tolls. The room comes alive as everyone is clapping and I join in. I decide to investigate as I walk toward where I hear the sound of the bells coming from. I don't have to go too far. As I reach the alcove that houses our check-in station I see a group of about ten people standing around a woman in a wheel chair.

I instantly recognize her as the Russian lady, and I see her husband standing behind her with both hands on her shoulders. There is another couple with two teenagers near them and four more people that I recognize as some of the personnel from the radiation center. Everyone in the group has tears streaming down their faces, but I also see that along with the tears there are many smiles on the faces of the small group. I'm about to turn away to give them some privacy when I see there is a bell hanging on the wall near where the group is gathered. This is my fourth day in this place and every morning I have walked by there. How come I didn't see that bell?

I resolve that as soon as things calm down some, and there aren't as many people around, I'm going to check out this bell and find out what's up with the tolling of it. I walk back toward the kitchenette area for a drink of water and a packet of crackers and from where I am standing I can see part of the alcove with the group of people. Even before I finish my water and crackers the group has dispersed. I take that as my chance to go and check out the bell.

The bell is of a gold color, about eight inches tall, and the bottom is about five inches wide. There is a shiny white pull cord hanging down on one side. For a moment, I wonder if the bell is just colored gold, or if it's made of gold. Next to the bell is a placard that reads:

MGH RADIATION ONCOLOGY GOOD LUCK BELL

Under the first line on the placard is an engraved bell just like the actual bell hanging besides it with the following lines under it:

RING THIS BELL
THREE TIMES WELL.
ITS TOLL WILL CLEARLY SAY,
MY TREATMENTS ARE DONE,
THIS COURSE HAS RUN!
AND NOW I'M ON MY WAY.

To close the quote, there is a date under the lines. I don't know if the date is the day the bell was hung or the date of the quote, but I can see that the quote has only a month and year and no day: 03/2012.

I feel tears coming to my eyes, and even now almost a year later as I put that moment into words, I can't help but well up because I think of that moment as the moment that gave me the strength to make it through. And the moment came through a complete stranger on the day before her last day of treatments. Or was it?

I was standing there looking at the bell and thinking: So this is the carrot? Go through your treatments and you get to ring that bell. This is the big reward? And I wiped a tear away.

I felt the presence of another as I heard some soft footsteps beyond me. At first I thought it was my imagination because it sounded like someone was floating toward me, or maybe it was like the sound a small child's feet make walking on carpet. I heard it, almost soundless. It felt as though the footsteps stopped behind me and I could feel this presence of another near me.

I didn't want to turn around because I didn't want whoever was there to see my eyes red with tears. I kept looking ahead pretending to still be reading the placard on the wall, as I heard a woman voice say to me.

"It had the same effect on me the first time I read it."

I still didn't turn around but her voice had a kind sound to it, almost like a mother speaking to a child. To me it sounded like her voice had a smile in it as she continued on. "Tomorrow is my last day, and yours will be here soon enough. Be strong."

With that, I felt her hand on my shoulder give me a gentle squeeze. Her hand felt small, almost as childlike as the sound of her footsteps, but I knew that it was an adult who had spoken to me. I turned around to look at her and return her kind words, but she had turned to walk toward the changing room. I saw a tall lady with blonde hair wearing a hospital gown like mine, and everyone else around the waiting area.

I never saw her face, and after a couple of moments of wondering whether or not I should, I decided to follow her to the changing room and speak to her. Of the six rooms, only one had the door closed so I deduced that she was using that room. I waited a couple of doors down from the closed door to give her privacy, and also I didn't want to intimidate her when she came out of the changing room and found me standing there.

I saw the door to the changing room open, and I put on my best smile and . . . a man came out of the room – an older gentleman with gray hair, who, upon looking at me with a smile frozen on my face said, "Well you must be having a great day with that smile on your face."

I just nodded as the gentleman walked toward the seating area. I walked the length of the changing rooms looking inside each of the six rooms, but all of them were empty.

The bathrooms! And even as the thought came to mind I saw that the two bathroom doors were open with lights off and I knew they were empty. I guess she was in a hurry, or maybe it took me longer than the few moments to search for her. Maybe I'll see her tomorrow when she gets to ring her bell, and maybe I could be one of the people congratulating her for finishing her treatments and thank her for the kind words.

I made sure to avoid the recliner with the massage and heated backrest. In fact, I sat on the complete opposite side of the room. I was feeling drained, and I don't know why. Maybe the radiation was starting to take effect. After only three treatments?

God knows they told me plenty of times that it would happen, and that there would be times that I would need someone to drive me to my treatments. "The best way is to set a schedule with family and friends to take turns with it. Plan ahead." Wise words.

"Bruno!"

That's my name, I think, as I hear a new voice calling my name. I see a new face, but as I look at him I know I have met him.

"Hi, I'm Frank. I'm a member of your team," he says. I'm about to extend my hand, but Frank doesn't offer his. Okay, another member of my team, and this one doesn't even want to shake hands. Soon I would need to ask them to start wearing name tags so I could remember everyone's name.

As we are walking down the corridor toward the treatment room, he tells me that it is nice to meet me and that the last couple days he had been on vacation, and he was sorry that he wasn't there for my first couple of days of treatments, but he'll see me through the rest of my treatments. As he speaks I remember that I had met him on my day of orientation. I told him about it and he said, "You're right. We probably did meet on that day. But sometimes we meet ten new people on orientation day, and the people we meet on those days don't always get assigned to the technicians they first meet."

Hmmm . . . Okay, I think to myself, you meet a lot of new people and you say, "It's so nice to meet you." But how come you didn't even shake my hand?

I find him a little cold compared to the rest of my team, or I should say the rest of the girls that I have met so far. But that's okay. They meet a lot of people and to be too emotionally involved with all of them would be too draining. Maybe this is what they mean when they say, "Take one for the team."

The patient is the one to take and absorb the lumps.

The mask is holding me firmly in place as I see my reflection above me. Then as the UFO rotates away and my face elongates I realize what the image brings to mind that I couldn't figure out yesterday. It's Mr. Conehead! When my head elongates, it looks exactly like the character played by Dan Aykroyd in the Saturday Night Live skits. And as the UFO turns away, it seems to say, "Good morning, Mr. Conehead." I watch my reflection on the disk as it passes by and turns.

The thousands of bees come alive as the rotation of the three-headed monster continues. When the buzzing recedes and the rotation stops, I see above my face what looks like a checkerboard – a square black-and-white checkerboard. There are 13 individual boxes, about one and a half inches square across, and 13 boxes down. My eyes scan the numbers of boxes again, and again I come up with 13 by 13. Isn't the number 13 bad luck?

As the checkerboard comes to a stop in front of my face it seems to say, "It's your move."

In the bottom corner of the checkerboard there is a little warning sticker with just an image with no words. The image shows the torso of a person in a halfway sitting position with a slash through it. Does that mean don't sit up? Is this their idea of a joke?.

Even if I wanted to sit up, I wouldn't be able to as I'm bolted to this table. Minimal time goes by as the monster comes alive and presents me the third head. What I see in front of me now is what looks like an over-sized football. When I say oversized I mean you would need both arms, not hands, to be able to get hold of it. There are two tubes and wires coming out the top part of it and what looks like a big suitcase handle.

Another day down. I'm back in the changing room in the privacy of my own cubicle with the door closed. I fish my Christ on the Cross and chain out of my pocket and place the cross in my open palm with the chain hanging over my cupped fingers. I kiss the Cross and slide the chain over my head, being careful to have Christ facing forward. I don't want to be the three-time denier. I had made sure to remember to take off my chain when I changed into my hospital gown before I went into the waiting room. Maybe I am a denier, as I'm ashamed to go through my protocol with the chain in front of others – yet.

My next ring says, "Almost time for the Cape. Love, Anthony."

My carrot on the string has been that upon finishing my treatments, my kids, their spouses, grandkids, my son's girlfriend, my wife, and I will be spending a week in a rented home on Cape Cod. At this moment, the six weeks remaining in front of me seem a long way off.

I wipe off a tear as I text my message to my family. The Whole Crew: 3 down, 29 to go.

TUESDAY, JUNE 13TH. DAY 5, 4TH TREATMENT

TODAY I'm up earlier than usual. By 4:30 I'm showered, dressed, had breakfast and I'm in my garage sitting in my antique car with the doors closed and light off. And no! I didn't have the car running. Today my car is being picked up as I have sold it. I wanted to have some time with my car before it was to be picked up.

Sounds crazy, doesn't it? Going into the garage to spend time with a car. Maybe it's a little crazy, but I wanted to feel one last time the contour of the vinyl seats and the smell of that carburetor when I start the car. I ran my fingertips over the dashboard and turned the key without turning the car on. The static of the AM radio is very comforting. Somehow I was never able to find the electric short that created that static.

About 15 minutes later I open the garage door and start the car. The roar of the engine coming alive feels good as I rev the car a couple of times just to feel the motor shake the body of the car. I back the car out of the garage into the street and then back the car into the driveway so that it's facing out. By previous arrangement, the car is going to be picked up at about eleven o'clock. Because of my ten o'clock treatment appointment, I'm not going to be there to see the car off, so it is left to my wife to sign papers when the car is picked up. Might as well.

This is hard for me because this isn't just a car. This car sat for about ten years in a relative's side yard, unused. When I removed the carpet, there was nothing there but daylight. Floors, running boards, quarter panels, all gone. I rescued this car from the junk pile, and it took seven years to bring it back to life. Along with me, my son put in some time to help.

Someday, I was hoping to say to him, "This is your car now, and maybe someday you can take your children for a ride in it, as I took you and your sisters . . . And if by then I'm gone, when you feel the breeze blowing through, maybe it will be me caressing you and yours."

My friend Marty is another reason that I wanted to keep this car. Marty put more time into this car than my son and I combined. Marty is that friend who when you call he doesn't ask "Why?" He just asks, "When? Where? Should I bring a shovel?" (Sorry, It needed to be said again.)

I'm not selling the car because I'm tired of it or because I want a different car or another one. I sold it simply because we need the money to pay the bills and mortgage. My kids at one point decided to name the car, and the name they chose was Rosie. Why Rosie? My kids had learned that the previous owner's wife had called it Rosie and they wanted to keep the name. I feel sad that today Rosie will be gone.

By six am, I'm at the hospital, following my coffee and muffin routine. A little while later, around 7:30, as I'm sitting in the waiting area, I hear, "Ding, ding, ding." Someone rang the bell.

I move to the hallway hoping to see the blonde lady and congratulate her, but to my disappointment it is a gentleman surrounded by family and technicians. I clap along with everyone else and go back to my seat.

Maybe her appointment is later in the morning A few minutes later, Amanda appears in front of me. "We have a cancellation," she says. Okay by me.

At about 8:30, as I am exiting the treatment room, I ask Amanda, "Do you know of an anyone who is finishing their treatment this morning?"

"I don't think so, but let me check." Amanda's fingers fly over the key board.

"We had a gentleman earlier this morning, but nobody else this morning. Are you looking for somebody specific?"

"Yes! Well, I don't know her and I don't have a name, but I ran into a lady yesterday that told me today was her last day, and I just wanted to wish her well."

"Can you describe her?"

"Yeah . . . well, maybe, not."

"She must really have made an impression on you if you can't even describe her."

"Well, I never saw her."

"So you are looking for someone that you don't know her name and you don't know what she looks like because you never saw her and you want to wish her well . . ."

"I did see her, but I just saw her from the back and she was tall and blonde. And when I went looking for her, she was gone . . ."

Amanda gives me a look that said, "Only four days and already he's lost some gray matter to radiation." After another look over the screen in front of her Amanda says again, " Sorry, we don't have anyone else finishing treatments this morning, and I know all of the people coming in because I'm here the whole day and I can tell you that there isn't a tall blonde lady among the patients. Maybe you misunderstood what she said and she was a companion to one of the patients."

"Yeah. You are right, I probably did. See you tomorrow," I say as I walk out.

I'm back in the dressing room. I take my gown off and I'm looking at my reflection in the mirror, which asks, "So, if she was a companion, why was she wearing one of the gowns?" Well, maybe she was wearing a gown for moral support of whoever she was with. It's a good explanation.

Not even nine o'clock and I'm done with my treatments. I don't have to be at work until 12:30, so I decide to ride home and make it easier for my wife with the car being picked up. Back in my car, I take out the next ring from my kite. I see that it's from one of my sons-in-law, and it says: "Your family will always be there for you." Tim 1.

The Whole Crew: 4 down, 28 to go.

I arrived at home at 10:30. After going in to say hello to my wife, I went back out and sat on my front steps. At exactly 11 am I watched as the 85-foot transport truck came and parked at the end of my driveway. The reason I knew the transport was 85 feet long was that the day before, the transport company representative called me to ask if an 85-foot long transport could make it down my street. I wanted to say "No!" But it was too late for that, because I had already received the money from the sale of the car.

The driver seemed like a nice person as he introduced himself with his first name. "I'm Ivan." Well, I guess that's a Russian name if I have ever heard one. He told me that he needed to take pictures of the car before it was loaded on the transport bed. He proceeded to go all around the car, and taking images of it as he went along. I stood to one side as he made some notes and pointed out to me a couple of spots where there were some light scratches. He said, "We document the car to make sure that there aren't any problems when the car is delivered. I need you to go over the notes that I made, and if you're okay with it I need you to sign here." He pointed to the bottom of the slip of paper. I took a moment to read through the notes he had made, and satisfied that it reflected the light damage on the car, I signed on the seller's name line. As I passed the papers back to Ivan he commented that I didn't look too happy and said, "It's going to a good home. Your car is going to be a California girl."

I smiled as Ivan gave me a copy of the papers I had just signed. I stood aside and watched the car being driven onto the bed of the transport. Within ten to maybe twelve minutes, the car was loaded and belts were placed in the front and rear ends of the car to hold it in place. Ivan walked the rim of the transport a couple of times and tugged at the straps holding the car in place. Satisfied that all was good, he came down from the upper deck of the transport bed to stand just above the driver's door. In one swift motion he opened the door of the cab and got in without touching the ground.

He gave a wave as he went into the cab without turning around. I waved back but I don't know if he could see me in his rearview mirror.

I had taken a couple of pictures as the car was driven onto the transport and then secured in place. I felt cold standing there, but I know it wasn't because of the day's temperature. I saw a black plume of smoke shoot up as Ivan started the diesel engine, and even before the smoke dissipated, the transport with my car on it was moving along.

As I walked back down my driveway I could see my wife's silhouette behind our front window. I gave her a wave and I got into my car. I didn't feel like talking, and I don't think that I could have, even if I wanted to, so I just left for work. As I was backing out of my driveway, I saw the transport coming back up the street and I was forced to let it go by. I followed it to the end of my street and I was thankful to see the driver put on his left directional as I put on my right directional. I slowly made my turn as I watched my rearview mirror, trying to hold on to one last moment, but with each foot I slowed down, it seemed that the transport sped up and went faster, almost trying to get away from me. After a few seconds the truck disappeared from view. I wiped away a few tears and cursed the man that I hold responsible for my situation and for not doing his job.

"I hate that fucking guy." And for those who by now don't know who I'm talking about, I'm not going to explain it.

WEDNESDAY JUNE 14TH DAY 6, 5TH TREATMENT

I'M starting to feel very familiar with the faces around me as I choose a seat in the waiting area. Most people seem to be involved with their phones, or reading material, or some quiet conversation with what seems to be either family or friends. But the common thread seems to be that people want to be on their own or with their own. Well, shit on that, we need to do something about that.

In the days before having our noses always stuck in our phones – when people talked to each other to fill the waiting time for an appointment, or while in line for a restaurant or a movie or a game – my wife would say that I could talk to a wall. Now, when you talk to another as they take their eyes off their phones, the response, or lack of response, is a look that says, "Are you talking to me? Can't you see that I'm busy looking at my phone!"

There are some people in the waiting area sitting back with their eyes closed, and some people who seem asleep with their head hanging to one side, or just staring down. Is that the look of defeat? For myself, I hope not.

I look around again to see if anyone makes eye contact, but everyone stays in a world of their own. I make a second sweep around hoping to see the blonde lady, but no luck there. I don't feel like reading, so I'll do as everyone else is and immerse myself in my phone. The first thing that I see when I enter my passcode on my phone and access Facebook is a posting from my nephew Sandro from Italy. The posting is a note wishing my dad happy birthday, and under the note there is a picture.

My dad has been gone three years now and the picture Sandro posted is one of my dad with my brother Franco (also gone about two and a half years ago), Sandro and myself. The picture was taken in front of my dad's home. Sandro and I had dragged a bridge table with four chairs from the den past the front door onto the little plaza in front of my parents' home so that we could play cards outside. It was a beautiful Saturday afternoon, with a soft breeze blowing through and the temperature in the lower 70s.

My niece Nicla had come outside with a bottle of Grappa and four glasses, and upon put-ting down the tray on the table, she immortalized that moment when she said, "*Quando siete belli tutti assieme, fate un brindisi e facciamo una foto*. Look how great you look together, make a toast and I'll take a picture."

I remember that Saturday because we were celebrating my dad's 90th birthday. As we finished our meal, sweets and coffee were served. Not a cake, but cookies and pies, and then we sang "Happy Birthday" to my dad. In Italian, of course. Another cup of espresso coffee as my dad got to cut his pie, and we all got what seems like a double slice of it.

My brother Franco loved to smoke a cigarette after coffee, and some years back, I did too. We moved outside to the table and chairs and cards so he could have a cigarette. As he lit his cigarette, I was assaulted by the aroma of the smoke flowing around the four of us. Even after so many years, there is nothing like the combination of the struck match and the aroma of a freshly lit cigarette, and anyone who's ever smoked will understand that. The temptation to have just one is always there. But for anyone who has smoked, there is no such thing as one cigarette. Maybe it's just the same as an alcoholic who can't have just one drink.

We played cards and as usual and always, there was the back and forth banter about one's skill or just plain luck. As the games proceeded to a conclusion, my dad and my brother won the games three-zip over my nephew and me. I think it was just luck on their side. This would be the last time I got to play cards with my dad. The next day Sunday, I left to come home to my family, and I never saw my dad alive again. I was happy that I had been there to celebrate his birthday.

My dad died the following May, two weeks shy of his 91st birthday. My brother, Vinnie, and I flew to Italy together to attend our dad's funeral. The day after the funeral, my brothers Vinnie and Franco and I locked the front door to the house and played cards and drank for over four hours. Mom sat on the couch by us and spent her time reciting prayers . But at one point we gave her some Grappa and the four of us toasted my dad. *"A la' salute di papa'."* To dad.

We became oblivious to knocks on the door, door bells, or phones ringing. With each drink we took, we toasted our dad over and over and told little anecdotes about him and our family. The following day as we said a tearful goodbye to my mom, sister, brother, nieces and nephews, my brother Vinnie and I flew home to Boston. My brother Vinnie is very conservative about drinking, but by the time we got off the plane we were both a little tipsy. We never saw our brother Franco again.

My dad had died in May, two weeks shy of his 91st birthday. My brother passed barely six months later, in December on Christmas Day morning, only 62 years old.

Merry Christmas.

Growing up in the old country my grandmother taught me that if you die on Christmas Day, your soul will be going directly to Heaven. I hope my brother is there with my grandparents, my dad and all of those we have loved. And I hope they are playing a *scopa* card game.

As I'm sitting waiting for my appointment, looking at the picture that my nephew has posted on Facebook, I feel the familiar tightening in my chest. Tears are streaming down my face. I don't want to look up. I think everyone is looking at me as I wipe the tears away. I decide that it would be best to make a bathroom trip to wash my face and take a breath.

My congestion from the treatments is getting worse, and with my emotions as they are at this moment, I feel like that I cannot breathe. There is a third bathroom located in a more reserved area of the changing room, and I am glad that the door is open. Maybe the blonde lady had been in the third room.

I rinse my face and dry off with some paper towels. I cry as I stand leaning forward on my hands over the side of the sink. I'm crying, and I don't know if I'm crying for the loss of my dad, for my brother or for myself and the changes that have taken over my life. I take a deep breath and try to blow my nose in the sink but nothing much happens because simply I cannot blow my nose anymore.

I curse the man I think is responsible for my predicament. I wash my face again and as I am done drying it, I look in the mirror and say, "Happy birthday, Dad. Miss you."

Today, after my treatment, I have an appointment scheduled with Dr. B. This will be a weekly meeting with him and his staff to see how I progress with my treatments and to remind me of the changes that might happen as the treatments intensifies.

As I'm waiting in the examining room there is a light knock on the door. "Yes!" I answer. The door opens and a young woman walks in. She's about mid to late twenties, or maybe very early thirties. "Hi, I'm Jen. I'm Dr. B.'s P.A. We will be meeting every week before you see Dr. B."

Her voice is kind and she has a demeanor that makes you want to put your head on her shoulder and let her give you a soothing pat on your back that says everything will be all right.

"How are you feeling?" she asks, while looking at the computer screen in front of her. "This is what, your fifth day?"

"Yes," I say.

"And?"

I shrug my shoulders as an answer. I don't really know how to answer "And?"

She gets up from her seat and comes to me, and as she stands in front of me, she puts her hand on my shoulder and says, "It's going to be all right. You'll be okay."

My God, I'm in love. Her voice is so soothing that I'm cured. I don't need any more radiation treatments.

"It's a long road and there will be times that will test your resolve, but Dr. B. will be here and I'll be here, and any time you need something or you have a question, we are all here with you to help you get through this. My promise to you is that you'll get through it." And she smiled the smile of an angel.

"Do you mind taking your obturator out so I can look in?"

Sure, no problem, I'll walk through fire and hot coals on bare feet. And obediently I remove the obturator, and as soon as I do, I became a blubbering idiot that can't even sound human anymore.

"Looks good! The healing process looks good and there doesn't seem to be any irritation from the radiation, but . . ."

Jen stops talking as she starts to feel around my cheekbone, and for a moment I have a flashback to this happening with Dr. L.'s P.A. after my first surgery, when she was doing the same as Jen is right now, and she stuck her thumb into the empty socket that is my upper palate. But the moment passes as Jen's fingers move gently from around my cheekbones, to the area around my jaw, to the back of my neck. Her fingers move around lightly and expertly probing every node along my face and neck.

"Your skin is looking great!" she says as she lightly touches the side of my face like a mom would with a child. As she finishes her examination, Jen sits down at the stool by her computer and continues on. "There are going to be changes starting to happen and I know that they talked to you about this at your orientation, but I want to go over few things so that you'll be better prepared."

I just shake my head yes because I don't want to use or have Jen hear my voice. She senses my uneasiness and says, "You can put your obturator back in."

As I did she continues on. "Soon you might start to experience mouth dryness or a foul taste in your mouth. If that happens there are some great sprays that we can recommend. There might be some sores that will develop in your mouth or throat. Your sinuses can get swollen and you can develop sores in your nostrils, and if that happens, breathing through your nose can get hard. If the sores in your throat get very bad you might not be able to swallow and we might have to put you on a feeding tube."

My face must have changed different shades like a chameleon because Jen stopped talking and found again her angelic smile as she said, "Look, all of this is possible, but it doesn't mean that it will happen. I need to prepare you for it. And it can happen. But for now don't focus on that. Think that what you are doing now will help you get rid of the cancer and this is just a little step in between now and the rest of your life that you need to take to get there. Okay?"

I nodded and as I did I saw her reach behind her in a drawer to take a few items out. "This is Biotene spray. It will help with mouth dryness if it happens," she said with a smile. "And this is also a sample of Biotene toothpaste. Save the spray for now but I want you to start to use this toothpaste. It's very gentle and you'll find it will help with the foul taste in your mouth."

Yippie! New friends to go along the good drugs and Colace and . . . "Okay," I said. Where is the fire? And then I remembered that Dr. C. had recommended the same toothpaste.

As I sat in my car, I thought of all that Jen gave me to think about. I didn't like that the specter of a feeding tube was popping up again. I took a deep breath and removed the next ring from my kite. This one was from one of my daughters, and as I read it, I realized that these were the right words for my mood at that moment: "Every day may not be good, but there is something good in every day. Love, Chrissy."

The Whole Crew: Five down, 27 to go.

TODAY starts on a sober note as there was a shooting in Washington, D.C. US Congressman Steve Scalise and three others got shot in a park while preparing for a charity ball game. Scalise is in critical condition and they don't know if he'll make it.

The election is still a big divider among most people, but to start shooting people doesn't seem to be right and it only succeeds in dividing people even more. I miss the days of President Ronald Reagan and House Speaker Tip O'Neil. They always seemed to understand that they might have had different views, but at the end of the day they found common ground as they worked for the common good of the people and the country and settled things over a scotch and a cigar.

I hear different conversations around the waiting room, but still I haven't met anyone yet as I sit around waiting for my turn. Not much more than a polite nod as I pass people in the hallway or in the dressing room. The seat I took this morning is back to back with the Korean War veteran and his wife. They are talking in a low tone but I can detect some excitement in their voices.

"Can't believe it. Just another day to go," I hear her say.

"You did well, my . . . " And he follows with a word that I can't distinguish or understand. Maybe it was an endearing term that they use for each other and maybe it was a Korean word. For a moment I want to put my hand on her shoulder and to say to them, "Congratulations." Instead I turn away, feeling I am invading their privacy.

The next ring on my kite is from my son-in-law, Tim 2, and as I read it, it brings a smirk to my face: "CANCER = The New York Jets. YOU = The New England Patriots. T 2."

My family we are all crazy Patriots fans.

The Whole Crew: Six down, 26 to go.

CONGRESSMAN Scalise is still in critical condition. The charity game was still played last night and the Democrats won 11-2. As a gesture of solidarity, a group of Democrat and Republican congressmen decide to place the trophy from the game in Congressman Scalise's office until he returns.

My routine is to recite my morning prayers as I drive to work. This morning as I drive toward the city for my treatments, I include Mr. Scalise in my prayers. As I don't know the names of all the other people that got hurt along with Mr. Scalise, I use the pronoun "*loro*" (them), along with the names of those I love and pray for every day. And I ask God to give them strength and to watch over them. I finish my prayers asking God to grant entrance to Paradise to those who have passed on that I loved and love.

The solitude of the morning as I travel into the city for my treatments is starting to wear on me. There are thousands of cars around me and thousands of people, but I always feel alone.

This morning as the three-headed monster comes alive with the buzzing of the thousands of bees, I realized that there is background music. I hear the Beatles coming on, and the pleasant sound of them singing *Hey Jude* flows through the speakers. I try to follow the words in my mind and sing along. The sound is so soothing that I don't even hear the thousands of bees anymore.

My next ring is from my son and it says: "Few more weeks and you can enjoy a fine cigar and a nice whiskey! Anthony."

Wishful thinking.

The Whole Crew: Seven down, 25 to go.

AS I sat and waited for my treatment, I looked at my phone and couldn't help getting a good laugh. I must have been so loud that one lady said to me, "You need to share that."

As I opened my group text, I saw a picture that my daughters Elisa sent to our group link. The picture showed her in her classroom at her desk, and it focused on her feet; specifically her shoes. Her shoes were one blue, one black, and she hadn't realized until she was at work that she had two different shoes on. I was tempted to show the lady the picture, but then I decided against it. Would have been a nice opener to meet some of the people. Well, maybe I'm becoming just like everyone else and want to be on my own.

Something happened today that made me think that sometimes there is something at work in and around and beyond us. Nothing earth-shattering, but something that made me think about the blonde lady and the coincidence of what happened today.

I was in the treatment room with my friend, the mask, over me, and as everyone was leaving the room, I heard the "DING!" that lets me know the treatment is about to start. I closed my eyes and the music came on, and like yesterday I focused on it to help me relax. The voice that I heard was one you cannot confuse with anyone else's.

It was Louis, as in Louis Armstrong. Satchmo, singing *What a Wonderful World.*

I could feel the smile on my face as the raspy voice sang the wonderful lyrics. The timeline of listening and falling asleep is one that I can't define, because the next thing I heard was Amanda saying, "Okay, Bruno, you're done."

You can say, "So? It's a beautiful song with wonderful lyrics and a pleasant sound that appeals to one and all." But! When I got back to my car I opened my next ring and it was from my daughter Elisa, and this is the message I found: "What a Wonderful World. (Our song!) 4/18/09."

As soon as I read the words I knew the meaning. The date was that of her wedding day, and the song that we had chosen for us to have for our father and daughter dance was *What a Wonderful World*. Tears came to my eyes as I read her message. Coincidence? Sure, everything is possible. But in my mind, there was more to it. I think of the blonde lady. Why didn't I turn around so I could see her face? Maybe I wasn't supposed to see her face.

The Whole Crew: Eight down, 24 to go.

TUESDAY, JUNE 20TH. DAY 10, 9TH TREATMENT

I'M starting to feel some burning around my face and it feels as though I have spent too much time in the sun without sunscreen. My cheeks have taken on a rosy color.

I stop at a convenience shop and invest two dollars in a newspaper to take in with me and read while I wait. Among the local headlines, there is an article about a special election in the state of Georgia. The article shows that over $50 million was spent, between the Democrat and Republican candidates.

We hear so much talk about free education. Imagine how many kids could go to college for free with that kind of money? And that's only one election. What potential the money that's spent nationally could have toward education, or work programs, or homelessness, soup kitchens, special needs programs, and on and on. Some third-world countries don't even have a national budget of $50 million.

My next ring is unsigned but I recognize my wife's handwriting: "Strongest person I know. You got this."

The Whole Crew: Nine down, 23 to go.

FIRST day of summer and it's a wonderful day in Boston -- sunny and clear, blue skies. Today after treatment I have my weekly meeting with Dr. B. to evaluate my progress. Jen the N.P. is first in the room as she was last week, and I love to see her. Not that kind of love.

She has the kindest eyes and her demeanor is one of kindness. There are plenty of kind people, but with Jen it seems to pour out of her. Her hands are soft on my face as she examines my cheeks and her fingers make her way down to the area around my neck and throat. "How are you feeling?" she asks.

"Okay," I say, without much conviction, just as I did last Wednesday. She's looking at me and I can see concern in her face, but it's only for a moment as she says, "Can you remove the obturator so that I can take a look?"

I gingerly remove my obturator as the last couple of days my throat seemed to be on fire. And the area where the edge of the obturator touches what's left of my palate has become so sensitive, that just moving the obturator in and out brings shards of pain. As I tilt my head back Jen uses a tongue suppresser to look at the back of my throat.

"Yeah! There is irritation. It looks like a gigantic cold sore."

Well, Einstein, I knew that! What the fuck are you going to do about it? No, I didn't say that, but I thought about it. And even if I tried to say it without my obturator in, it would have sounded like Curly of the Three Stooges with his "Nyuk-nyuk-nyuk." And Jen is too much of a nice person for me to use those words.

" Does it feel very sensitive? Have you been having problems swallowing?" Jen asks with a caring voice.

"Some. Not too bad," I answer with a back and forth shake of my hand.

"Have you been using the mouth sprays – I think I gave you Biotene – or anything else?"

"No, nothing yet," I answer with a shake of my head.

"I'll have Dr. B. look at the back of your throat and your mouth and see what he'll suggest to help you with the pain. I have to say that you look great. And look at the skin on your face! It feels so soft and even your coloring is good," Jen says as she touches the side of my face.

Dr. B. doesn't seem too concerned with my mouth or throat and says some soreness is going to be part of the radiation treatments.

As I walk back to my car I love the touch of the sun on my face and I can feel the heat of the day starting to build around my body. I stop for a moment, leaning against a stop sign at the edge of the sidewalk before crossing the road to access the parking garage. It feels good . . . and then I realize that I'm not supposed to be in the sun without sunscreen on. I had been told, "With radiation treatments it's very important that you avoid direct sun exposure. If you do go out, make sure you use sunscreen with the highest protection. Neutrogena is a good one, but make sure you get something with a sun protection factor of 60 or above." And that was one of the first recommendations made by the nurse who interviewed me on orientation day before I started my radiation treatments.

I never was one of those beach bunnies who could spend the day in the sun with coconut oil smeared all over and a reflector in hand to intensify the effect of the sun. But I do enjoy the outdoors.

"Nyet sun for you-u-u-u!" the Russian lady would say to me.

"THIS SUCKS."

Back at my car I opened my daily piece of kite and as I read the words I could feel a smirk come onto on my face. "FUCK CANCER 101!!! TOGETHER WE'LL DO THIS."

It was unsigned, but again I recognized my wife's handwriting. The reason it made me smile is that it brought to mind an episode that started on Sunday February 19th. That was two weeks before my first surgery. On that Sunday morning at about 6:30 am, with the yard still covered in darkness, I decided I wanted to get going with some starter seeds for my vegetable garden. At the back edge of our property, I built a small seven foot by seven foot greenhouse that I use to get a jump on the spring planting season by growing my own vegetable and flower plants. And I also save some money in the process. Of course, the money I spent to build the greenhouse will take a lifetime to recoup and be ahead of the cost I incur yearly to buy plants for my garden.

As I walked from my back door to the greenhouse I felt a sense in me that I can't explain. I don't know if it was sadness or depression. The news that cancer had entered my life, the realization that I would need surgery to remove it, and the hope that the treatments would work and I'd be cured – it was all still too fresh in my mind. Sometimes I still wondered if it was just a bad dream.

Rejuvenation

THE morning air was cold but not frigid, and as I walked into the greenhouse it felt just as cold in there as outside. I could see my breath as I plugged in the heater for the greenhouse. The soft humming of the fan from it felt very reassuring as the heater came alive, starting to push warm air in and around the room. In a short time, I was able to remove my gloves and jacket. The heat spread quickly through the small space.

As much enjoyment as I get from being with my family, I was starting to feel I needed some time to learn how to deal with the changes that were sure to happen and to learn how to accept those changes on my own. And some of this alone time helped me think. My garden, my yard, my little greenhouse – I referred to them as "my brain food." And definitely that morning I felt that spending some time playing in the dirt would do me good.

For every day that passed I knew the countdown was on, and for each day that passed I knew I was getting closer to the day that was going to be the one that was the last of a normal life. I can't describe what normal is, but definitely that morning I felt the weight of those big changes coming into my life. And the fact that cancer had entered my life definitely contributed to the feeling of sadness I was experiencing. Cancer was something they made movies about, and it was always somebody else. Shed few tears, send a donation and move on with your life. Now the chickens had come home to roost. In my body. In my temple.

As I filled my trays with soil and patted them down to receive the little seeds, I stopped and looked across the garden area of my yard. There was some snow in some areas still clinging on, but most of the ground was visible. In one corner of the garden I noticed some green sprouts, and I realized that those little sprouts were the garlic cloves that I had planted in the fall.

Rejuvenation.

I finished filling my trays with soil, chose the seeds that I wanted to start and lined up the seeds in each pod one by one, like little soldiers. Then I put about a half inch of water in the bottom of the trays, followed by the clear plastic domes over the top of the trays so as the heat built up it would create its own little greenhouse and maintain the moisture in the soil and the seeds would germinate. I set the heater on 68 degrees, took one last look around, and went back in the house.

New life

THAT day, March the 5th, the day before my surgery, was two weeks to the day from when I started my seedlings and in those two weeks I hadn't bothered to go down to the greenhouse to check on the progress of the seeds. That morning I felt that need again to hang on to some sense of normalcy. As I walked down to the greenhouse at about 7 am, there was still a chill in the air, as there was two weeks ago. But when I opened the door, I was greeted by the smell of moist soil and the embrace of warm air. Even before I closed the door, I could see through the transparent domes that all of the seeds had sprouted and as I removed the domes, some of the seedlings had started to grow sideways.

It brought a smile to my face as I stood there looking down at these beautiful, light green sprouts. Some were no bigger than a blade of grass. I decided to take a picture of the trays to share with my friend Eddy Rubin, also an avid and enthusiastic gardener.

As I took the pictures, I decided to do a selfie with the trays of new life in the background. I sent the selfie to my friend Eddy and then decided to also send it to my group, The Whole Crew. In the little box, I decided to express my feeling of the moment about how to beat cancer.

My 101 suggestion was to maintain as normal a moment I could, so on my selfie I gave the big finger to cancer. My wife had just reminded me to keep on doing that.

"FUCK CANCER"

I still don't know whether, when I took that selfie and shared it, if I was doing it to give my family a sense of reassurance I was okay, or if I was trying to convince myself that I was okay and that everything was going to be okay.

The Whole Crew: Ten down, 22 to go.

THURSDAY, JUNE 22ND. DAY 12, 11TH TREATMENT

MY routine is set, and I follow as best as I can the recommendations everyone seems to make to help me deal with the changes that are happening. I can't seem to be able to drink anything without it coming out of my nose. It's embarrassing, but most people seem to try to ignore it by turning away or making believe that nothing is happening.

I am having a few sips of coffee and a muffin in the lobby of MGH while waiting for my appointment. I don't pay too much attention until two different people in a row seem to take a second look at me as they walk by me. And then I saw them speed up their steps.

As I reach up with a napkin and wipe under my nose, I look at the napkin and I can see it has turned black with a mix of coffee and muffin that looks like snots. Even though I just wiped, I can feel rivulets of black fluid streaming toward my lips. I look around trying to find the nearest trash can to throw away both my coffee and muffin, and I walk away with my head down without looking back. For the rest of my treatments, almost another five weeks, I won't buy another breakfast.

My next ring is one of hope and wishful thinking, and it's from my son in law T2: "You have AT LEAST 5 more Super Bowls left in you! T.2"

I sat in my car thinking that the way the New England Patriots have been going about it, they could win those five in the next five years. Does that mean that's it? Just another five years? Maybe they can win one every other year, so that will give me another ten years.

The Whole Crew: 11 down, 21 to go.

FRIDAY, JUNE 23RD. DAY 13, 12TH TREATMENT

I have a sleepless night. The pain in my throat seems to be increasing, along with the fact that I can't breathe through my nose and I'm forced to breathe through my mouth. There seems to be a complete blockage of my nostrils, and it doesn't help to blow my nose because nothing comes out. During the day I'm okay with it, but at night within minutes of falling asleep, just breathing through the mouth creates dryness in my mouth and throat, causing me to wake up choking – not choking so that you can cough it up, but choking like having a mouth full of sand and razor blades. Maybe the gigantic cold sore that my mouth has become is truly becoming GIGANTIC.

Friday morning the traffic, like most Fridays, seems light and I'm in Boston before 6 am. Amanda makes a comment about my skin looking good when I take my obturator out to prepare for my treatment.

I say "Thank you," but as I lie down on the table I'm almost annoyed by that comment. The room seems cold, but I think it's my body more than the room. On my way out, I run into Lisa. She is coming in late.

"Good morning, Bruno!" she says cheerfully.

"Hi, Lisa."

"I'm running a little late. I see that you're done. See you tomorrow," she says as she continues on.

"Yes, see you tomorrow," I answer.

And as I say "See you tomorrow," I think: In your dreams, young lady! I'm not coming in on a Saturday.

"You look great. Keep up the good work," Lisa says as she rounds the corner.

"Thanks," I say as I keep walking away. I think we are speaking to each other's back and neither one of us wants to be there.

Later that morning, when I get back to work, I am working on a client who I haven't seen in a while, and she isn't aware of my cancer. She makes a comment to me that almost sends me over the edge. "Bruno, you look great! Good to see you, have you been on vacation? And look at that sunburn. Soon you'll have a nice tan. And your skin is so smooth!"

That's not a fucking sunburn! I'm getting radiated and from my teeth to my eyes I feel like a fucking French fry that has been fried too long. But with a smile I say, "Yeah, I'm doing okay." In my mind I want to say, "Fuck you." But it's not her fault that she doesn't know about my predicament.

Before leaving Boston for work I read my daily kite ring. "This time next year, this will all be behind you. Only good times ahead! Love Anthony!"

The Whole Crew: 12 down, 30 to go.

MONDAY, JUNE 26TH. DAY 14, 13TH TREATMENT

ANOTHER angel.

I didn't shave over the weekend. The skin on my face seems very sensitive, so I decide to give it a couple days of rest. As I'm looking in the mirror Monday morning I realize that I'm starting to show a decent beard growth. But strangely, it looks like I shaved and made a perfect line from the bottom of my ear to about the midpoint between my nostrils and my lips.

This morning as I come into the kitchenette area for my glass of water, the lady volunteers are on the job, as usual, making sure everyone has a glass of water or crackers or a magazine to read. Or just a good word. There are always two of them around, but it feels like that there are 22 of them because they seem to be everywhere and doing everything for everyone.

This morning I see that there is something different as soon I come out into the waiting area after changing into my hospital gown. Or I should say that I hear something different.

I hear piano music, and as I turn toward the sound I see the usually empty bench in front of the piano in the side alcove is occupied by a lady. I walk toward her, fascinated by the sound. I'm afraid to make too much noise as I walk. Her back is to me as I sit in one of the four chairs behind her, and I don't know if she's aware of my presence there. The sound of the music is very soothing, even though I don't recognize the tunes that she's playing. At the same time, I think that even the piano is aware of the pain in the souls around this place.

When I had seen the piano previously, the cover of the keyboard was closed. But now with her playing, the cover is open. I see that the inside of the keyboard cover and the side panels are decorated with the view of a field covered in daisies and roses. The prevalent color in the field and the flowers is yellow.

Isn't that the color that represents hope?

Listening to the notes flowing around me, and looking at those painted fields covered in flowers, makes me want to stay there forever. I realize I am the only one sitting there having my own private concert, so I decide to turn one of the chairs in front of me to accommodate my stretched legs. I fold my arms in front of me, lean back with my feet up, and close my eyes.

I feel tears coming down that I can't explain, but in the recess of my mind I do know why those tears come: I recognize the tune. She's playing an *Ave Maria*. I love that song because it makes me think of a bride walking down the aisle on her wedding day. But as soon as I see that bride walking down the aisle, the picture switches to a casket being pushed down the same aisle by a group of pallbearers, as the *Ave Maria* plays in the background. I think of those who I would like to be my pallbearers .

Do I think that I'm going to die?

We all die .

My mental picture is still there as I see me in that coffin being pushed down the aisle as the *Ave Maria* is playing. I stifle a sob as my tears keep on coming down, but at the same time I feel anger coming up from the pit of my stomach. Anger toward that dentist? Or God? Or at my stupidity for not taking matters into my own hands and not questioning the "Don't worry, it's nothing"? Or maybe I'm in the stage of "Why me?" Maybe I'm feeling the loss of that part of life that you always hear about happening to other people. Usually, after that moment of "Oh, it's too bad," we move on with our lives, too busy to think of anyone else, or maybe just thankful that it was them and not us.

I try silently to wipe away the tears, but either because of my sobs or the sniffle or because I can't take a breath, I must have made noises. It seems to me that for a moment I sense I caused a little hesitation in her playing, but only momentarily.

Then it's like someone turned the volume down, as I can hear the sound or the loudness of her playing changing to a softer tone. Then I hear her voice come lightly over her music. "I have been where you are," she says. "Twenty years and counting. You'll be okay." And the volume of the music seems to rise again.

I close my eyes and I can feel a smile on my face. I think I fell asleep for a few moments, because the next thing I remember is my name being called. When I open my eyes, I see Frank on the other side of the room looking for me. I wave at him as I collect my phone and locker key and I.D. card. As I pass by the lady at the piano I lightly touch the back of her shoulder and just whisper to her, "Thank you." I don't know if I'm thanking her for the music or for the kind words to bring a little sanity back to me.

She nods without turning around or stopping her playing as I walk by. As I reach where Frank is and we turn the corner, I realized I never saw her face.

Another angel?

As I am following Frank walking toward my treatment room, I decide that I'm going to go back and thank the piano lady in a proper way for her music playing, and to wish her another 20 years and more of being cancer-free.

I make believe that I'm feeling around my pockets for something as I say to Frank, "I left my keys on the chair back there." I turn to walk back and hear Frank say, "Okay."

Even before I turn the corner, I realize the piano music has stopped and I know she isn't going to be there. But I still turn the corner. What I see is the piano as it stood silently with the flowered keyboard cover down. That week I didn't see her again, and the following week I was going to be starting with the new time slot of 12 o'clock. I never saw the lady piano player again.

"The Whole Crew: 12 down, 19 to go. I think I heard an angel."

To which I get a flurry of "?,?,?,?,?,?,?." I don't know what to answer. Her words were real, and I know that she was real, and I heard her playing the piano, so I feel that angels don't necessarily need to have wings and be invisible or fly around. So I just don't answer.

The next ring on my kite is from my daughter Elisa. "Remember November 4th? You got to hold your first grandbaby!"

Yes, I do remember, as I wipe tears from my face.

TUESDAY, JUNE 27TH. DAY 15, 14TH TREATMENT

TODAY is the fourth day I haven't shaved, and as I put on my gown before my treatment I happen to look up in the mirror that is in the back of the changing room and I notice some good growth to my beard. It looks like I'm growing this gigantic goatee that goes from under my earlobe all the way down my neck past the Adam's apple.

I can see the perfect line that goes from the bottom part of my earlobe to the midpoint of my nostrils and mouth being very noticeable. The little redness on my face makes it stand out even more. I turn my face from one side to the other so that I can see both sides and realize that when in the past I purposely did grow a beard I was never able to achieve such perfect contours to it. I feel the side of my face above the line, and my skin is as smooth as smooth can be. I feel no trace of hair anywhere.

As I'm looking in the mirror there is something that bothers me about the way I look, but I just can't put my finger on it. Then, "Bang!" The light goes on and I realize what's bothering me about my new look. I notice that my mustache has also taken a different look from what I normally have. I have been wearing a full mustache with a round shape that contours my lips and continues under my chin to form a goatee that I usually keep trimmed close to my face.

Now as I look at my mustache, I see, instead of the curved look around my lips, this straight line running across the top of my lip and the first thing that comes to mind is Charlie Chaplin and Adolph Hitler having had the same mustache.

JOHN...BUT MY FRIENDS CALL ME DICK

WHEN I stepped out of the changing room, at that moment a friendship started that I hope would last for many, many years to come. So far, over the past two weeks the most I got from anyone around was a polite "Hi" or "Good morning," or a nod with a very subdued smile.

I was at the water station drinking a cup of water, and as I finished my first cup I was in the process of refilling another to take it with me into the waiting area. The way I was standing I was blocking the bin that contained the robes everyone took with them into the changing room. Just as I was about to take a sip of water I felt a presence near me that for whatever reason took me by surprise.

I was in la-la land, and as I turned, there was a gentleman a little older than me standing there, pointing at the bin to let me know that he was trying to reach for one of the gowns. I said "Sorry," and started to move over for him. Of course in trying to move out of the way and doing it too quickly, I didn't look behind me and bumped into another gentleman who was there. I spilled most of the water on myself and the floor. The man looking for the gown was very apologetic as he handed me a bunch of Kleenex to wipe the water off my gown and proceeded to put some on the floors to absorb the water. He kept saying "I'm sorry. So sorry. I didn't mean to make you jump like that."

"No, no problem. I was in your way," I said, as I picked a gown out of the bin and passed it to him.

"Thanks," he said, as he took the gown and went into the changing room. I filled another cup with water and took a few sips. Just as I was ready to go find a place to sit, the door to the changing room opened and the older gentleman came out. As he saw me he extended his hand toward me.

"Hi, I'm John...My friends call me Dick. Again, I'm sorry about the spillage."

"Hi, I'm Bruno. Don't worry. I was in the way."

"This is my first day in. How about you?" Dick asked.

"I'm in my second week. In fact, today will make it two weeks."

"How many treatments are you having?" Dick asked.

"I'm supposed to have 32 treatments. What about you?"

"Twenty-six, a little less than you. Where is your cancer?"

"I have ACC—Adenoid Cystic Carcinoma."

I saw a little confused look in Dick's face as he asked, "I know that the adenoid is part of the sinus/nose area. Is that where your cancer is?"

"Yes, and no . . . " I proceeded to explain to Dick about my surgeries. I could feel my speech impediment getting in the way at times when I started to speak too fast. I was learning to make myself slow down when I was trying to communicate something. When I slowed down, my words came out a little more clearly. As I gave the details of my surgeries and treatments, I could see his face turning down and sad. I honestly felt that he was in pain for me.

"Oh, my God, the pain that you must have endured." And by now he had his hand on my shoulder, just like an old friend would do. For someone I had just met, it felt good to talk to him. And his hand was reassuring as he gave my upper arm a squeeze and said, "You must be a very strong man to go through what you're going through."

"Thanks, Dick, but look around us. I don't think that there is anyone around here that is not going through something similar, and all of them have their own story. What about you, Dick?"

"I'm in for prostate cancer – and talking about that, I also need to drink some water." He filled a cup and took a swig from it. After he finished his first cup he said, "I have to have a full bladder before they do my treatments and I need to drink at least four cups . . . So, cheers." He lifted his cup and took another drink.

We sat in the waiting area like two old friends catching up on the weather, sports, the shooting in Washington, a little politics, and our families, until my name was called. We shook hands as we parted and promised to see each other tomorrow.

As I opened my ring, I saw a bunch of scribbles and heart stickers, and my granddaughter's name.

The Whole crew: 14 down, 18 to go.

Wednesday, June 28th. Day 16, 15th treatment

WHEN I walk in through the double doors to check myself in, I'm greeted by the sight of the man with the long beard, his son and his wife. Along with his team from radiation, they are there all together around the bell. He rings the bell, sitting down on his wheelchair. There's applause and smiles all around as everyone closes in on him with kisses, hugs and pats on his back. I politely applaud as I skirt around the little group and go into the changing room. I guess the people from Duck Dynasty are going home.

The hospital temperature feels like ice cubes as I change into my gown. The long-sleeved johnny feels good, almost like a warm embrace as I wrap it around my chest and try to tie the two strings together, and . . . What the fuck? Where is it? There is one of the strings to tie at the side of my chest, but I can't find the second one. I feel around with my hand but I can't locate the string, and finally I look in the mirror and see that where there was supposed to be a string about ten inches long there is a little nob of a piece about one inch long. Well not much there to tie a bow with. I go back outside and find another gown. I'm nice and warm and I don't want to take my johnny off, so I just put the second one over the first one.

As I come out of the dressing room, for whatever reason I decide I want locker number one to put my clothes and wallet in. Today I want to be *numero uno*. No luck. Number one is locked and taken. Maybe I'll settle for number two, *numero due*. Taken. All right, let's take number three. *Numero tre'*. Yeah, that's available. Not so bad to settle for number three or to finish in third place. Or maybe not so great – third out of three.

As I walk to the waiting area, I feel very snug with the two johnnies on, and I feel that I might do this more often if the place stays as cold as it feels like now. I smile as I see Dick's raised arm waving at me from the other side of the room.

Back in my car after treatments I open my next ring. "Wake up every day and *bitch slap* that cancer 'til it's gone. Love, Chrissy."

I would like to use a baseball bat on cancer and on that fucking dentist.

The Whole Crew: 15 down, 17 to go.

THURSDAY, JUNE 29TH. DAY 17, 16TH TREATMENT

THIS morning, when I was on the table, Amanda told me that it might be a couple of minutes before we got started because they were running late and they needed time to finish getting the room ready. So why bring me in? I could have waited outside and spent more time with Dick.

To fill some of the time, I asked about the machine with the thousands of bees and how it worked and if anyone could explain the process. I described the three pieces of the machine as they looked to me: the checkered board, the football and the UFO.

"That's good," Amanda said with a smile, "I have heard people calling those machines everything from the Devil to their Savior. I have had people give them their ex-spouse's name and their lover's name, but you have opened a new level of names. In simple words, the football and the checkered board are mini CT SCAN machines that talk to the computer, and after revolving couple times, the spaceship delivers the beam of radiation."

"Okay," I said, as closed my eyes waiting for the thousands of bees.

Back in my car as I read my next ring, the message brought tears in to my eyes. But lately it seemed that everything brought tears to my eyes. "We all love you."

Around the inscription there were hearts and stars, x's and o's, and there were a lot of little hands reaching for those hearts. I counted nine hands. I guessed each hand was one of my kids, their mates, my grandchildren, and my wife.

The Whole Crew: 16 down, 16 to go. Halfway. Love you.

FRIDAY, JUNE 30TH. DAY 18, 17TH TREATMENT

I'M glad another week has gone by, and I'm looking forward to the weekend. With the 4th of July holiday on a Tuesday, it would have been nice to get a long weekend, but I will be coming in on Monday. I would love a three-day weekend; I think I need very badly for some rest and also to just get away from the hours of sitting in traffic in and out of the city. Maybe Monday the traffic will be light as many people will have the day before the holiday off. I feel good that I'm halfway done with my treatments, but I fear that the worst is still to come, as my mouth, nose and throat feel like they are on fire.

The quote on my next ring seems to have read my mind, as it says, "Dad, we don't know who wrote this quote, but here it is: 'I'm trying to see the top of the mountain, but there are still too many trees in the way . . . And yes, fuck cancer.'"

And that's exactly the way I feel.

The Whole Crew: 17 down, 15 to go.

TODAY, my friend Dick introduces me to another newcomer to our club. Yesterday after I went in for my treatment, Dick noticed a gentleman standing by the entrance to the waiting room, looking lost. Dick went up to him, introduced himself, and as he had with me a few days earlier, he found out that this was this gentleman's first day. His name is John. But he's just in a new time slot, not a newcomer.

I've met two people in four days named John, but one of them prefers to be called Dick. Go figure. The three of us form a little gang as we sit in a corner and talk and tell jokes, and it feels like we could be at a bar having a drink, or in our family room with friends talking about old times, or just enjoying the contact with other human beings and sharing a laugh.

I see some of the other people around starting to pay attention while discreetly looking down at their phones, books or magazines. But I see that from the corner of their eyes, they are looking and wondering what this little group has going on.

On the other side of the room, I see a lady I have seen over the last couple of weeks around the waiting room. But we've never exchanged any words, and I think she's making eye contact with me and moving toward us like she is going to engage us in conversation. John and Dick's backs are turned toward her and they don't realize our visual exchange. Just as she gets about two feet away from us, John says something to Dick that I can't hear too well, but Dick gets a good belly laugh out of it.

My attention to what John is saying is diverted by the approach of the lady, as I'm facing toward her with a smile, ready to greet her. At the same time that Dick's laugh sounds, she stops in her tracks. I think she feels she will be intruding.

I can see the look of hesitation come over her face as she turns away from us. Well, maybe she changed her mind. Who knows, maybe tomorrow this will encourage more people to talk to others and help some of them understand that they are not alone on this journey.

As I sit in my car to open my next ring, I get a sharp pain in my nose. I use some Kleenex to do some poking around and realize that there is a crust that has formed on both sides of my nostrils. I try to lightly blow my nose but the only thing that I succeed in doing is creating more pain. My tongue feels numb and my throat hurts. I think that at this point instead of one Mack truck being parked where my palate used to be, there are two of them parked there.

Happy 4th of July.

"Get well so you can help me with my yard work. Tim 1!" The words are followed by a smiley face.

The Whole Crew: 18 down, 14 to go.

WEDNESDAY, JULY 5TH. DAY 20, 19TH TREATMENT

MY wife took the ride in with me for today's session so she could be there for my aftertreatment weekly meeting with Dr. B. As I came out of the changing room and met up with my wife, I saw Dick and John at the water fountain. I did an introduction all around for my wife, and our little group was now four people talking and joking and laughing. We talked family, the 4th of July holiday, and hope. After a few minutes, my wife excused herself and we three boys were left alone. The next day, my new schedule would start with an afternoon time slot. Dick, John, and I exchanged phone numbers and promised to keep in touch. Then Dick put his hand on my shoulder like he did the first time we met and said something that I will treasure for as long as I live.

"Promise me that you will keep in touch . . ." I started to open my mouth to say, "I will," but he stopped me as he went on. "I want to know that you are okay. Promise me that you'll do that."

"I will," I said. We gave each other a hug just as my name got called for my treatment.

We saw Dr. B. after the treatment, but the highlight of the visit is always that I get to see Jen. The room lights up as she walks in, and from that moment on she's comforting and caring. My wife loves her just as much as I do. As we sit in the examining room, Jen always sits at a wall bench placed between the patient's chair and the chair of the accompanying party so as to give full attention to everyone in the room. She asks her questions with so much care and compassion, that as I answer I feel as if I'm the only patient that she has to give her time to. Her laugh is contagious, and it's impossible not to respond to her energy.

Today to combat my nose sores and dryness I meet a new friend, Mupirocin ointment.

Back in the car I open my next ring as my wife looks on with me.

"Drinks on the beach watching sunsets." How appropriate that the message is from my wife and she's there as I open that ring. I'm starting to believe that there isn't such think as coincidence. We smile at each other, and as we exchange a kiss, I say, "I'll drink to that."

The Whole Crew: 19 down, 13 to go.

THURSDAY, JULY 6TH. DAY 21, 20TH TREATMENT.

TODAY is the first day of a new time for my treatments. I wish that my appointments were still in the morning so that I could be with my friends. My friend Peter and Dr. B. felt that as the treatment progressed, there would be times that I might get too weak to drive and it would be easier to have a midday appointment in case I needed to find a driver. "Why do you need to be up so early? Take your time in the morning. Your body needs time to recover. Take the late appointments. It will be best," Dr. B. said at the time of our first meeting. Peter and my wife nodded their heads in approval of the suggestion.

My afternoon appointments driving into the city aren't much different from the early morning. In a way, I think the morning traffic was easier to deal with because I had the option to drive in earlier and avoid the worst of it. It's been taking me about 45 minutes to drive from the junction of old Route 128 and Route 3 to my exit just before the Zakim

Bridge, approximately eight miles away. The first day I thought that maybe there was an accident along the route, so I switched my radio to a local station that gives traffic reports every ten minutes. No accidents up ahead, just plain old traffic.

When the change from morning appointments to afternoons started, it didn't hit me until I came out of the changing room how much I would miss my new friends. I filled my water cup to take with me to help me combat my dry mouth and walked around the corner from the changing room into the waiting area. For a moment I did a look around to find my little group, but all I saw was new faces.

Faces of strangers. At that moment I wished that someone had come up to me and said, "Hey, come in. Is this your first day? Let me introduce you to some of the others."

But nothing happened. Everyone kept their eyes down to their phones, magazines and books. Or, they looked down, defeated, clearly not wanting to have to listen to another sob story by a newcomer.

Only one day, and I missed Dick and John. Once again I was a stranger among strangers.

"You have got this down!!! Love you" The message from today's ring, like yesterday's, was from my wife. The way I feel this afternoon, it gave me strength. When I got home and told my wife about feeling like a stranger when I walked into the waiting room, she reminded me that when we meet new people we are only strangers for a moment. I resolved that the next day I would make an effort to meet and talk to some of the new people I saw today.

The Whole Crew: 20 down, 12 to go.

FRIDAY, JULY 7TH. DAY 22, 21ST TREATMENTS

AS tired and weak as I felt, I was still trying to hold on to a work schedule to help us keep up with our financial commitments of mortgage, car payment and all of those other bills that never stop coming. They are part of owning a home or running a small business. The medical bills kept on piling up, but I was doing my best to make some minimum payments toward them.

I was getting to work by 6 am, and booking my first appointment at 6:30. I was taking appointments until 10 am so that I could be out of the shop by 10:30. That allowed me one and a half hours to get to my 12 noon appointment for my treatment. Some days I barely made it in time.

One morning, an episode happened that for a moment or two made me lose a little faith in my fellow human beings.

It started when one of my clients called at about ten minutes of nine to let me know that she wasn't feeling too well and she needed to reschedule her appointment. "I waited to the last moment to call you because I wanted to see if I felt better, but I don't think I can come in," she said to me.

I did reschedule her appointment for the following week, wished her to get better soon, and I told her, "See you next week." I hated the last-minute loss of income the cancelation would create, but at the same time the way I felt physically, I welcomed the half hour to sit back.

Even before I leaned back in my chair, though, I realized that the opening that was created between 9 and 9:30 would be a good opportunity to do some work that I had been putting aside. My business at that time was going through the yearly insurance audit that every corporation goes through to establish the cost of workman's compensation insurance to be paid by the business.

In order for the insurance company to establish the dollar amount to be paid by the business for workman's compensation, the corporation needs to present the insurance company the quarterly earnings of the business and the workers that work for the corporation. I had all of the papers ready to fax, but as I don't have a fax machine I had been procrastinating. I saw this cancelation and this half hour of time as the perfect occasion to go to a local mailbox store that is located about a hundred yards from my shop's front door and send the fax.

It's a beautiful morning and I am enjoying the short walk across the mall parking lot. I'm in front of their door at five minutes of nine. I look through the front door and see that the store is dark. At the same time, I notice the little sticker by the door handle that announces the store hours. I realize they are open from 9 am to 6 pm.

I look at my watch and see that nine o'clock is only a couple of minutes away, so I decide I can wait a few minutes for the store to open. As I'm standing on the sidewalk, I find myself gravitating toward a corner of the sidewalk with sun. At 5:30 this morning as I was driving in to work, my car thermometer was showing a temperature of 65 degrees, and I drove all the way in with the heat on, and now I want the feel of the sun on my face. Cool summer so far.

I know I should have sunscreen on, but another thing that I was told at orientation to do, or not to do, was not to put sunscreen on before treatments. And this morning, knowing I was going to be inside at work, I didn't put on sunscreen, opting to do it after I came out of my treatment.

It is now about five minutes after nine and the store is still closed. As I look at my watch, I think I still should have plenty of time to do my errand and get back to work by 9:30.

From the corner of my eye I see a big trailer truck on the street that skirts the mall parking lot. It's slowing down and it pulls over a couple of hundred yards before the entrance of the mall parking lot.

Looking at the truck, I think: A delivery coming to the supermarket. I can tell this driver probably has never delivered to this supermarket, because the loading dock is on the side of the mall facing him and he's coming from the opposite side of the street that he should be on.

On the opposite side he would be able to pull into the lot and then back the rig to the dock. My business has been in this mall for 41 years, and for eight of them it was located in the very same store that is now the mailbox store. I have seen drivers do this maneuver hundreds of times, and I definitely know that he's coming in the wrong way.

I can see the driver, but I can't really see his face. But I can see his head turning toward the parking lot where I'm standing and doing a look-around, and reaching the conclusion that he will do a U-turn from the street into the parking lot. I can see that his approach will work, because the traffic is very light and there are no cars in the lot area that will block the space that he'll need to accomplish his maneuver. The side street that the truck is on is only a two-lane, and to allow him to make the turn into the lot he will need to cross over the opposite lane and take a wide turn into the lot. The driver allows a couple of cars to go past him on the other side of the street, and when he sees the road is clear, the big rig starts to make a wide sweep across the road to make the turn into the parking lot.

There are a couple of cars behind the rear of the trailer, but everyone seems to be patient and willing to allow this driver to do his job.

The truck and trailer takes almost an L-shape as it slowly makes the turn into the parking lot, effectively blocking both sides of the street as it tries to complete the turn.

I can see that this driver has experience, because he is making a perfectly smooth turn, and just about as the nose of the truck is getting past the mouth of the entrance to the lot and entering the parking area, I see a small SUV pull into one of the parking spots in front of the store.

Nothing wrong with that. But there are about 100 parking spaces in front of the store, and not one single parking space is taken. There are about 100 spaces available that this driver could have taken, but instead the parking space that the driver chooses to take is the last spot at the edge of the parking area on the street side, about ten feet from the nose of the truck, effectively blocking this truck from finishing his turn into the lot.

I hear a little screech and release of air as the truck driver applies his air brakes, followed by a couple of brake screeches from the six cars by now lined up behind the truck.

Standing at the edge of the sidewalk, I do one of those things you do that makes sense when you are with another person or near another human being: You put your hands palm up in front of you and say, referring of course to the car driver, "What the fuck is the moron doing?" But I'm by myself and it doesn't make any sense. I take another look around me and I am glad nobody is there to see the look on my face.

The truck is now a big L, stopped between the two sides of street and the lot with traffic blocked on both side of the road. Maybe a minute has passed since this started, but already there are about a dozen cars behind the truck, and a few on the opposite side. Now I can fully see the truck driver's face and I can see that he's saying the same as I did few minutes earlier: "What the fuck!!!"

I hear a discreet tap, tap of the horn. Not a prolonged one that says, "GET THE FUCK OUT THE WAY!!!!" No, it's just a polite two taps that say, "Can you please move. Thank you."

I can't see the driver of the SUV as the windows are darkened, but there doesn't seem to be any response from the car or the owner. I see the truck driver take a look behind him and beside him, maybe considering how to back the truck out, but I can see that he dismisses the idea very quickly because now there are lines to the front, side, and behind his truck. Again I hear a soft tatap of the horn.

By now, the SUV driver should have seen this truck that towers 10 feet above the nose of his car. The front grille of the truck is about six feet away from the nose of the SUV. Maybe the driver of the SUV has the windows closed and the radio on and he's not aware of the dilemma the truck driver is in.

For whatever reason, I decide to be the Good Samaritan and get involved. I step off the sidewalk and signal to the truckdriver by waving my arm with my index finger up to show not that I was number one or wanted service at our table, but to tell him, "Hold on a minute and I'll go and talk to that driver."

He nods to me as I walk wide around the nose of the SUV so that I can approach the car from the front. This way, I won't catch the driver by surprise. As I'm going around to the front of the SUV, I have heard at least four different cars blowing their horns, and the driver of this SUV must be either deaf, or maybe dead, not to hear what's going on.

I approach the car's driver side and gently tap the side window. As I tap on the window I see this "lady" sitting in the driver's seat. She turns toward me but makes no attempt to open the window. Standing a couple of feet away from the window, I make a rolling motion with my hand and arm, and finally the window slides down.

My first reaction at seeing her is, "She's a big motherfucker." She could be a football player. And soon I find out that her mouth is as big as her body, when she says, "WHATAFUCKUWANT." Just like that, one big word. I'm taken aback by her response, not because of what she said, but by her accent and by the sound of her voice. Her voice is big and she has an accent like me. Mine is the kind you hear in some of those mob movies, hers has a Caribbean sound to it. Maybe Jamaican.

With my best smile on my face I say to her, "Sorry to bother you, ma'am, but would you mind just moving your car over a couple of spots?"

"Why should I move?" Is her response.

I do my best to use my hand and fingers to point at the truck and make a half circle with my hand to show the truck making the turn and point at the truck again in case she hasn't seen the truck shiny grille in front of her.

"What he do if I wasn't in my car?" Well, at least I know that she has seen the truck.

"He's just trying to make a living. Do him a favor, just move your car over a few spaces."

You'd think I had said to her, "Go fuck yourself in Hell, lady . . . and stay there." She turns her body toward me and her chest is as big as the rest of her body. As she turns, one of her breasts is stuck against the steering wheel and the motion pulls on her blouse revealing a cleavage big enough to park the same Mack truck that usually is parked where my palate used to be.

In the center of her cleavage I see a Crucifix hanging there that's about double the size of the one I wear. I swear that my hand went up to my chest to make sure that my Crucifix is not hanging out of my shirt as I'm leaning forward, because at this moment I want to hide that I'm a Christian like her as I'm witness to her ignorance.

I just hope it's not my third denial.

"I NO MOVE!" She says again.

I lose it. In the next moment, I rip the car door open and reach for her head. I'm rewarded with two handfuls of dreadlocks that my hands grab on the sides of her head. I have her now. As I drag her out of the car I'm surprised at how light she is and how easily she tumbles out of the car. She is too stunned to scream and I wouldn't care if she was screaming. As she hits the ground her Crucifix bounces up and in one motion I grab it and yank it. The chain breaks and I have the Crucifix in my hand with pieces of the chain hanging down, "You don't deserve to wear this," I say as I get into her car, put it in drive and move it about four spaces over. I put the car in park, shut it off, and take the keys out.

The woman is still on the ground, too stunned to do anything, and as I'm walking toward her still holding a couple of dreadlocks in one of my hands, she is trying to crawl away from me because by now she knows that she has a crazy man in front of her. She stops moving as I get close to her, but she's reaching up around her neck trying to find her necklace and asks for HIS help. "Sorry, lady, you have lost the privilege to look for HIS help," I say as I drop her keys in her lap. "You have a great day now." And I walk away.

Are those sirens that I hear in the distance?

And then the moment passes. No, I didn't drag her out of the car.

I stand back and say to her, "Sorry to have bothered you, ma'am." I still have a smile on my face as I'm starting to walk away. But then the feeling comes back that I want to drag her out of her car, and I can't just walk away without saying anything. I still have my best smile on my face as I approach her car and lean my arm across her open window, and with an almost suave voice I said, "I hope that you have a great day—as great as the day you making for that man." I say this as I point toward the tuck.

I walk past the front of her car toward the truck and as I make eye contact with the truckdriver, I put my hands arms up to my sides with my fingers lightly curled in. Strangely, at this moment what comes to my mind is the moment in church during services when we recite the Our Father prayer and we hold our hands out in supplication to ask forgiveness for our sins.

I stop for a moment as I pass by the front of the truck, and as I look up at the driver, I mouth, "Sorry man. I tried." I don't know if he hears my words, but I'm sure he understands what I tried to do. I turn and walk back toward the sidewalk.

I barely make it past the front grille of the truck when I heard the SUV start, and for a moment I think that she is going to run me over, but instead she drives to the opposite side of where I was and parks the car about five parking spaces away. It brings a smile to my face as I stop walking and watch her do the maneuver to free up a path for the truck driver. I must be still smiling as I look up at the driver. I can read his lips as he says, "Thank you." I mouth back, "You're welcome."

Maybe sometimes people need to be shamed into doing the right thing. Now I'm glad I didn't drag her out of her car, and my faith in my fellow human beings has been restored.

I continue walking back toward the front of the store, thinking, "How do you like that! Sugar works better than vinegar." Back on the sidewalk, I look at my watch and it's about 20 minutes after nine and the store is still closed. I decide to go back to work because my half hour is fast evaporating. So much for the sign on the window for 9-to-6 open hours.

I hear my phone ding just as I'm getting back to work. I stop on the sidewalk not far from my shop's front door, and when I look at my phone, I see there is a message from my niece Nicla from Italy. We call her Nicla, short for Nicoletta.

When I open the message I see a picture. Not just a picture, but the picture of Italian comedian, actor, producer, writer, and superstar Roberto Benigni. My favorite Benigni movie is *Life is Beautiful*.

Life is Beautiful is one of his most acclaimed works. It got about 26 Academy Award nominations. It won seven awards and three Oscars, including one for best actor.

In the movie, set in 1940s Rome, Benigni plays the part of a smart, resourceful, Jewish waiter named Luigi. As the Nazis invade Italy, the madness engulfs both him and his family. They all get arrested and taken to a concentration camp. Luigi's resourcefulness gets put to the test to save his wife and child in the concentration camp.

Some might know him from the Awards ceremony. After the 26th nomination or so, the great Sofia Loren opens the envelope and announces, "And the winner is . . . Roberto!" The crowd goes wild as Roberto Benigni stands up and jumps on the back of his chair and starts making his way toward the stage from the back of one chair to another.

But for those not familiar with Benigni, at first look you might think that he is not a good-looking guy. He has a forehead that you can land a 747 on, framed by some unruly, crazy wild curly hair. He's not that tall for a man and maybe on the skinny side, but watch out! When Roberto smiles he becomes the most handsome man in the room.

The picture I'm looking at shows Roberto Benigni with his arms spread wide open toward the Heavens, and he has his best smile on. The picture is framed by a quote that says:

"*Questa mattina apri l'armadio e indossa un sorriso. Sta bene con tutto! BUONGIORNOOOOOOOOOOO!!*"

The closest translation to those words is:

"This morning, open your closet and put on a smile. It fits with everything!
GOODMORNINGGGGGGG!!"

Maybe smiles do work for everything, or it's just another coincidence.

I feel more and more relaxed as I adjust my body on the treatment table. Most times as the mask goes on my face and gets bolted to the table, the rest of my body seems to have reached an acceptance of the fact that this is life now and I should get used to it. I feel that my shoulders, instead of straining against the body part of the mask that holds me to the table, are more relaxed and my shoulder blades touch the table. As I hear the snaps closing in place, I have already taken a deep breath and closed my eyes.

I fall asleep even before my team leaves the room and I don't hear the "ding" to let me know the doors have closed and treatment is about to start. I haven't heard the sound of the thousands of bees yet, but it's comforting to know that it will be there as I close my eyes and drift off.

I'm standing in the lobby of a hotel and by the look of it, I know that it's from times gone. Every piece of furniture and all the drapes and floors are rich in color and feel. The ceilings are high and covered in mosaics. I realize that someone is near me, but I don't need to turn to know that it's my wife. She's spinning an open parasol over her head. I want to ask her, "Why do you have an open parasol? We are indoors."

Suddenly I see why she has the open parasol. That Victorian look has disappeared, and it has changed to a look found in one of those outdoor island hotels with a beach lobby and no ceiling. I can feel the breeze coming in and the warmth of the sun feels good on my skin. In the distance, I can see a sailboat with a white sail fully extended with the wind. On the sail I can see a big number 11 printed on it in a bright red color. As I turn toward the reception desk, I see a bellhop bell sitting on the very front of that desk. I can't see myself anymore, but I see my hand reaching for that bell and hit the top of it.

"DING!!!"

"Okay Bruno, you're done for today," I hear Frank's voice say over the speaker, and realize that the bell I heard is the bell that announces the beginning and end of treatments.

Back in the changing room, I see that all six of the cubicles are taken and that there are two other gentlemen waiting in line to get access to the rooms.

"This must be the busiest time of the day," one says to the other. For whatever reason, I answer, "Maybe it's two for one . . . or early bird . . ."

They both look at me in an annoyed way, for I interrupted them and I realize they didn't want any conversation with me. Maybe it's the funny gown I'm wearing, but on second thought, soon they will wearing the same gown. I walk to the water fountain and fill a cup with water, then just go into one of the bathrooms and ask myself, "What the fuck was that?"

The Whole Crew: 21 down, 11 to go.

Almost every time I open one of my rings it seems to reflect some of the happenings of my day. Earlier in the changing room, I thought I was cracking a joke with the two gentlemen waiting there, but they didn't seem to see it as that, and I felt almost a little hurt that they wouldn't engage in a conversation with me,. But reading the words in my next ring from my son-in-law makes it a little better. "*NEVER* be ashamed of a scar. It simply means you were stronger than whatever tried to hurt you. T2"

As I send my text, I remember the #11 on the sailboat. Maybe I was counting in my sleep.

I am at the hospital by 10:30 am for my appointment at 12 noon. Better early than late. I find myself looking around the room and looking at the people around me. Most seem to be around their eighties and maybe even older.

"Why I am here? I'm too young to be here. Why me?"

Today is a Monday, my day off. I should be sitting in a lounge chair by the shore with a beer and my fishing rod. I could be at the casino playing poker. I would be just as happy to be home cutting my lawn. Fuck, I'll even cut the neighbor's lawn and take out their trash.

I find a corner, sit down, and immerse myself in a book that I carried in with me. I'm wedged in the corner of my seat with an empty seat next to me, comfortably waiting for my treatment. I stop for a moment to take a sip of water from my cup, and as I look up, I'm pleasantly surprised as I see a gentleman who looks about my age, or maybe a little older, walking toward me.

He's wearing a fedora hat and he is accompanied by a young woman who I make to be his daughter. He stops in front of me and asks, "Hi! Is this chair taken?" while pointing toward the empty chair on my right. I can't believe that someone is actually talking to me, and with the brightest smile I can put on my face, I say, "No, nobody is sitting there."

"Oh, great!" he answered while extending his hand. "I'm Charlie!"

"Hi, I'm Bruno." We shook hands.

He then turns toward the young lady who was standing just beyond him and says, "This is my wife, Jen."

Holy crap! I think to myself.

I shake her hand and I can see a look on her face that is sad as she says to her husband, "I'll be there if you need me, Dad," pointing to an empty seat about three seats over.

Dad? Looking at the age difference I would say, "Sugar daddy anyone?"

I guess some couples refer to each other with terms like "Mom" or "Dad." If it works for them . . .

"If you like," I say to Jen, "I can move over so you can have your two seats together." But I spoke to her back as she had already turned to go to her seat.

"She's a great lady," Chuck says looking after his wife as she sits down and gets busy with her phone.

"Yeah!" I say. And pretty young also, I think, with a hint of envy.

"Guess how old I am?" Charlie asks. I am a little taken aback with the question coming from someone I just met barely ten minutes ago, but I answer, "Well, I'm 60. I think we are around the same age, about late 50s, early 60s."

"Do I look that old?" Charlie says with an almost insulted tone.

"I . . . I don't know, Charlie. I'm not too good at guessing people's age."

"I'm 56 years old!" he counters.

"Okay, I wasn't that far off," I say with a smile on my face.

"Are you having treatments, or are you with someone?" Charlie asks.

"I'm having treatments. And you?" I ask, while I think, "Doesn't my wearing this gown give away the fact that I'm having treatments?"

"I'm almost at the end of my treatments, but it's not doing much good," he says.

"Sorry to hear that. What's going on . . ." But I can't finish my question because one of the techs comes to look for Charlie, and suddenly he is gone. I go back to my book, but I barely read a couple of lines when I see Charlie's wife coming toward me. She takes the seat her husband had. I'm surprised by the move, but maybe she has the same problem I have: the fact of people not wanting to have much to do with others. She takes the seat and says, "Sorry about that."

"Sorry about what?"

"My dad."

Even before she continues, I am a little annoyed, and I think "Get over the 'my dad' thing. He's your husband." But I just smile as she goes on.

"When he introduced us I noticed the look on your face as he referred to me as his wife. I'm not his wife. I'm his daughter. My dad is a very sick man and some of the side effects from the cancer and maybe even the treatments are early onset of dementia. His mind and speech are not connecting too well and sometimes he may want to say something, but the words that come out are completely the opposite. By the time he comes out from his treatments, he may introduce himself to you again."

Shit. Open mouth, insert foot.

"So sorry!" I managed to say. "What's wrong with him?"

"It started one day with him sitting at his desk at work while ago, doing some work on his computer.

"He called to one of his coworkers to ask him if his computer was okay, because it was doing strange things. His coworker came to his desk and when he looked at my dad's computer screen, he saw a jumbled page of nothing. He asked my dad to write, 'Today is a nice day.' As my dad proceeded to type what he thought was 'Today is a nice day,' he said to his coworker, 'See? The computer is all messed up.' But the coworker knew differently, because he had watched my dad's fingers. When my dad was typing, he just kept on hitting the same couple of keys over and over again."

"Did he have a stroke?" I ask.

"That's exactly what his coworker thought. They called an ambulance and had him taken to Maine General."

"You guys come down from Maine for treatments?"

"Every day for the last six weeks."

"So was it a stroke?"

"No! It was not. They did a scan and they found a tumor on the right side of his head. They told us that because of the location of the tumor, it was inoperable. They told us the tumor was fast-growing and as the size of it increased it would put more pressure on the brain. One of the most common side effects, they said, would be amnesia and another would be that he wouldn't be able to put words together with thoughts. Also, that he had about six weeks to live."

"You said you have been coming down for treatments for six weeks. What changed?" I manage to ask.

"My dad is a very strong man and he wanted to prove all of them wrong, so he decided to come here to Boston's Mass General. After reviewing the scans, they believed they could do surgery, to be followed by treatments, and that he should be okay after that."

"So when is the surgery?" I ask.

"Oh, the surgery was done about seven weeks ago. Or, I should say, they tried to do the surgery. What they thought was a tumor on the right side of his head turned to be a tumor that traveled from about the front of his ear lobe, up the right side of his face, all the way up to his forehead, across it, and down to the front of his left ear lobe. One big fucking tumor that wrapped itself around his face. The doctors decided that they couldn't remove the tumor, but they still gave him hope that with chemo and radiation treatments they would able to slow its growth. The growth did stop, but it's still very big and the pressure on his brain is causing the side effects."

She stops talking for a moment and I don't have much to say as I look down at my phone, hoping for it to say something for me. But then, thankfully, she starts to talk again and as she points down the corridor where the treatment rooms are, she says. "You know those machines in the treatment rooms that the hospital uses to dispense the treatments?"

I look down the corridor leading to those infernal machines hoping for an answer, but Jen answers her own question. "My dad's job was to calibrate CT scan machines. He traveled all over the country and loved his job. He sometimes referred to those machines as his kids."

I can see Jen choke up a bit as she speaks, but she continues on without wiping the tears trickling down the side of her face. "Maybe now those machines are helping save his life. He has two more weeks of treatments. From there, we are going to South Carolina. We have been told that they're doing some experimental treatments, and for now it's the last resort . . ."

She stops talking when she sees her dad coming back toward us, accompanied by one of the technicians.

"Hi! Who's your friend?" Charlie says to his daughter. At the same time, he extends his hand toward me and says, "Hi! I'm Charlie ."

Sweet Jesus. Forgive me for thinking I was in such a bad place. After listening to Jen's story about her dad, I should stop complaining.

The Whole Crew: 22 down, 10 to go.

Like on most days, the next ring brings a smile to my face. There are a bunch of scribbles on the paper, and from one corner there is an arrow pointing at the scribble and then there is writing that says my granddaughter Autumn loves her *nonno*.

I call Dick and John on the way home. They both seem very happy to hear from me. I ask Dick about his schedule of appointments for treatments and he tells me they are still the same, with morning appointments. I say goodbye, and I resolve that next week on Monday I will go in earlier than my appointment and surprise them. Maybe we will have a cup of coffee together.

TUESDAY, JULY 11TH. DAY 24, 23RD TREATMENT

MY wife came in with me for my appointment and I'm enjoying her company. With the two of us in the car, we're able to take the zipper lane into the city. So the ride is smoother and shorter, but I'm still driving myself because I just need to know that I can.

Today as the thousands of bees spin around my head I find my gaze fixated on the ceiling above me. The room that I'm in is about 25 feet by 20 feet, in the shape of a small L. The foot of the L is the entrance to the room. On the ceiling is an area covered in some kind of pattern that looks like one of those pictures that a psychiatrist would show a patient while they ask them to express what they see or what they think they see. The ceiling pattern covers an area of a good ten feet by ten.

As I look up the ceiling, I'm getting into a staring contest with the ceiling, and soon my pupils seem to fix in place. I'm in a trance as the patterns around the ceiling come alive and take shape. One of the shapes is starting to look like Mickey Mouse, and the more I stare at it, I know that it isn't just Mickey Mouse. Could this be some kind of a vision?

Could it be that because my parents, instead of taking me to Disney World, made me clean my room and cut the lawn and feed the animals down at the barn, and do food shopping for the family, and dig potatoes at harvest, and graze the sheep so they would have fresh grass to eat so they could produce more milk, and then milk the sheep, and water the vegetable gardens, and do my school work after I finished all my errands and chores that I was expected to accomplish? . . . Is it possible that that's why I'm seeing Mickey up on the ceiling?

Too many responsibilities? How cruel my parents were to expect me to be part of that family and to impose so much on me. Is all of that in the recesses of my memory coming out now as I see Mickey Mouse galloping on the back of a pig? Or is that a rhino?

And imagine this, as not only do I see Mickey sitting on the back of what I take to be either a pig or a rhinoceros at a full gallop, but Mickey's wearing a chef's hat on his head, and to top that, he's got company on the back of the animal.

As my pupils dilate a little more, what do I see behind Mickey on the back of the pig or rhino? Minnie Mouse. It looks like poor Minnie isn't holding on too tightly as the rhino or the pig achieved a full gallop, because now she is clinging on with her feet. Do mice have feet? Or do they have claws? No! Birds have claws. Well, dinosaurs looked like they had claws. Do mice have paws? Felines have claws! Who the fuck cares? I hate the fucking dentist. Her whatever are up in the air and she's falling off the back of the pig or rhino.

Maybe Mickey is in a hurry to finish his ride so he can put his chef's hat to use and have a pork – or rhino – roast.

I can feel a smile coming onto my face. Wonder what a psychiatrist would think of my version of what I see up there. My gaze shifts, and amazingly I haven't blinked as I continue to look around the ceiling and . . . and what's that?

An angel.

A perfect Christmas angel with a cone body and spread wings. Not far from the angel, my focus shifts to something that puzzles me a bit, and I think I even blinked, but I'm not so sure that I did because I'm so focused on the next apparition that looks like a dove, an angel and a bat, all in one. What does that mean?

A dove = the Holy Spirit? An angel = St. Michael, the Archangel? A bat = the Devil?

Whoa! My parents really fucked me up by not taking me to Disney. Instead they gave me all of these responsibilities with accountability, and now look at the consequences of all of that as I look at my next vision. Yeah, that looks like a prehistoric bird of prey. I try to move my head some so that I can get a different visual of the ceiling, but there isn't much movement there as my head is bolted to the table through the mask.

DINGGG! See you tomorrow.

After treatment, we meet with my nutritionist. She is impressed that my weight has stabilized and about how good I look. She's asking questions about the way my wife has been handling my food and all of the diverse ways she has been finding to make it look interesting and appetizing to me.

I'm now about 170 pounds – a long way from my pre-surgery weight of over 190 pounds. All of the credit should go to my wife for all of the cutting and chopping and juicing and smoothies and frappes that she's been doing on a basis of five to six times a day for me to be able to keep up my protein intake. I'm able to eat those things that my wife puts together for me, but beyond that almost anything else is impossible because I can't seem to be able to chew on anything that gives any resistance. My nutritionist makes a point of giving my wife full credit for all of her work with my food, and I think she needs a pat on the back from someone because it definitely hasn't been coming from me.

The left side of my tongue is numb and tingling. I find myself catching it under my teeth and it hurts. I've got some nose bleeding, and while we were waiting for my appointment I texted my friend Peter to ask his opinion. He, like every other doctor and nurse, tells me that it's par for the course.

The Whole Crew: 23 down, 9 to go.

I read my next message from my ring, with my wife leaning in so that we can read it together. "Through good times and bad, never stop fighting. Cancer can never change who you are and what you mean to all of us. Tim 1."

"That's nice," my wife says as we both wipe tears from our eyes.

Wednesday, July 12th. Day 25, 24th treatment

I cancel my morning appointments at the shop because I'm getting a constant nosebleed. I texted Peter again this morning at 6;30 am, and God bless him, he answered me right away and told me to meet him at his office by 8:30.

Peter cauterized a couple spots in my nose and told me to use my new friend, the nose ointment, and to make it a close friend and use it at least three times a day. It hurts. Everything seems to hurt. My nose, my mouth, my teeth, my throat. When I touch my gums with my tongue they feel like sandpaper. I hate that fucking dentist.

As I'm sitting waiting for my treatments, someone got to ring their bell. My corner seat was taken so I am sitting in an area where I can see the bell. The gentleman who got to ring the bell is sitting in a wheelchair as his team and some family members are around him. I stop reading so that I can watch him and clap for him. He has a hard time reaching up to pull the cord and consequently the ringing is barely audible. I feel bad for him, but everyone around claps, and I join in. I have a thought in my mind: When my time comes, I will make sure that fucking bell will be heard all over the hospital for me, and for those who couldn't do it. God help me get through this. Another week.

My gums have a whitish look and a raspy feel. Jen, the nurse practitioner in Dr. B.'s office, wants me to try to explain how it feels, and the only way that I can describe it to her is to ask if she's ever been licked by a cat's tongue and felt that raspy feel. She shakes her head and asks me to remove my obturator and open my mouth

"Look at that," she says. "Thrush. I think you have a case of thrush."

"What?" I say in my mind, but the sound that comes out is more like, "...AATHH."

"It's an infection, or more like a fungus that often comes with radiation therapy. Very common. I will prescribe you an antibiotic and that should take care of it."

"Look everybody, another friend. Meet Mr. Thrush." I don't need another fucking friend.

The Whole Crew: 24 down, 8 to go.

Again it seems that every time I read one of my rings, it touches something in me that brings great memories and gives me great strength.

"Come a little bit closer, you're my kind of man, so big and so strong . . . Love, Chrissy." Followed by a smiley face.

In 1964 Jay and the Americans released their most popular song, *Come a Little Bit Closer.* I always loved the oldies songs and when driving I always kept my car, or the stereo at home, tuned to a station that played that kind of music. About the time my youngest daughter Christina was around five years old, she heard that song for the first time. I don't think that she understood the lyrics but she loved the upbeat sound of the song and she wanted it played over and over again. And every time she heard it she would say to me, "They are playing our song."

THURSDAY, JULY 13TH. DAY 26, 25TH TREATMENT.

I get a little surprise this morning when I come in for my appointment. John's schedule has also been changed to the afternoon, so it looks like for the next week, our appointments are going to be back to back with each other since he has the same team as me, in room #4.

It feels good to have someone to talk to again, as we get back into our routine of asking about family and about ourselves.

"Hi, is this chair taken?" a gentleman with a fedora hat asks.

As we turn around, I recognize the gentleman. It's Charlie, who I met few days earlier. His daughter is standing beyond him with a look that says, "Please, please don't say that we just met the other day."

My father-in-law dealt with dementia the last ten years of his life and I very much remember how every day most things that had been part of life for a lifetime became new.

"No, have a seat," John and I say at the same time.

"Hi, my name is Charlie, and this is my wife, Jen," he says as he points toward his daughter. As he looks at the young woman Charlie has introduced as his wife, John does a double take, just as I had done earlier. To his credit, he doesn't say, "Kind of young for you, isn't she?" Jen takes a seat next to Charlie and gets busy with her phone.

"What room are you being treated in?" Charlie asks.

John answers for the both of us. "We're both are in number 4."

"That's very good," Charlie says. "I'm in number 6. It's not too good. I have about three months to live, but I'm not giving up."

Now John has just met Charlie, and with this sudden burst of revelation, I see John ad-just his eyeglasses from the tip of his nose to the top of his nose, as if it would help him hear better what he just heard from Charlie. Maybe for some confirmation that he heard right, he turns toward me as Charlie finishes his sentence. He has a look of combined questioning and shock on his face, expecting to find the same look on mine. But this is nothing new to me, as Jen told me her dad's story yesterday.

I give him a little shake of the head and he seems to understand that there is more to the story. "I'm going down to South Carolina," Charlie continues on. "They're doing some experimental treatments."

John and I look at each other and I think we both have a question to ask, but I know most of the story and I can explain it to John later. So, I jump in with my question. "What do you mean when you say that number 6 is not too good?"

Chuck leans forward toward us in a conspiratorial mode and quietly says, "I used to calibrate machines like those back there. The both of you have the best of all six of them." He's shaking his head with a little back and forth rocking of his body, like he's agreeing with himself. "Number 4 is the best of the six of them. My number six is not too good." And he leans back with a knowing smile.

I look toward his daughter, as she says, "It's the truth. That was his job, and if he says that number 4 is the best, it probably is, because he did research on everything."

Charlie is called in. John, Jen and I remain seated, waiting for our turn. The three of us follow Charlie's progress as he disappears down the hallway. "There are always miracles," John says. And as he finishes his sentence, Frank calls John's name for him to go in.

About 15 minutes later as both John and Charlie are coming out toward the waiting area, Frank calls my name. I shake hands as I pass by John and Charlie in the hallway and tell them, "See you tomorrow."

As I keep on walking toward my treatment room, I think about what Charlie said about having three months to live, but wanting to keep on fighting.

The Whole Crew: 25 down, 7 to go.

My next ring is, "Love Autumn, Elisa and Tim," followed by some scribble that my granddaughter made.

FRIDAY, JULY 14TH. DAY 27, 26TH TREATMENT

THIS is the second day of ten taking antibiotics. I don't feel much difference; my mouth feels just as dry and painful. Maybe it needs a couple more days. Again, not much traffic driving in this morning. I guess normal people have taken the day off to enjoy a long weekend on Cape Cod, or maybe New Hampshire. As I'm checking in I see John sitting there waiting. So, before changing, I go to sit with him and chat for a while.

It's only 10:30 and my appointment isn't until noon, so I'll have plenty of time to change into my gown. At 11 o'clock, John gets called to go in, and as I'm sitting there deciding if I want to go and change, a lady sits where John was sitting. She doesn't have a gown on so she's probably waiting for someone. But I don't have a gown on either and I'm a patient.

Maybe like me, for a while she just wants to feel a little normalcy in her life.

"Good morning," she says.

"Hi. Good morning," I answer.

"Well, this place always seems to have plenty of business," she says.

"Yeah . . . maybe it's early birds, or two for one," I say, using my old standby line.

And she laughs. This is good. Someone who wants to talk,

"Oh, that's funny. I hope you are not making fun of us older folks!"

"No! No, I wouldn't do that. But you are right. This place doesn't lack business."

My God, this is the most action I'm getting in the all of the six weeks I've been here. Someone is actually talking to me. And she speaks to me again. "You must have just returned from a vacation, you have such a nice tan," she says, "and my God your skin looks so smooth. Do you use a special cream? Or what do you do for it?"

I'm a little annoyed by the comment and for a moment I don't know how to answer. I don't want to be rude, but I put on one of those fake half smiles as I say, "Yeah. I can give you the name of it but I don't recommend it. It's called six weeks of radium treatments after two cancer surgeries."

"Oh, my God, are you a patient? So sorry. I thought you were waiting for someone. I'm sorry, I . . . but you do look good!"

"Thanks," I say with a more sincere smile on my face as I take a sip of my water. I'm not quick enough with my Kleenex to block my nose, because when I take my drink, out comes the little river gushing out of my nose. Or maybe I didn't make or didn't want to make an effort to stop it. It has a little shock effect, as I see the lady do a little "oh" with her mouth, and she doesn't know what to do and say. Maybe she's embarrassed for me, but she stands up and says, "I think I just saw my sister going toward the changing room. Goodbye." And she walks away.

Well, there goes another one.

It's embarrassing to be in a conversation and have your nose shoot out liquid like a water cannon and not be able to stop it or control it. But maybe from now on if someone annoys me I can just take a sip and shoot at the same time.

I have to admit that if someone doesn't know what I've been going through with surgeries and treatments, and if I don't open my mouth and speak, I don't look so shabby. I've regained some of my weight, thanks to my wife and all that she does to make food appealing and taste good. The radiation burn that I have on my face looks like I spent a weekend on Cape Cod and I forgot to put on sunscreen. Normal life, just like all those people taking time at the shore.

"Bruno, we're ready for you," Frank says.

The Whole Crew: 26 down, 6 to go.

My next ring is from my son. "We all love you dad, stay strong. It will be over before you know it. Love, Anthony."

MONDAY, JULY 17TH. DAY 28, 27TH TREATMENT

OVER the weekend, I decide to do some yard work, and while using a weed cutter I must have gotten into a poison ivy patch. Well, it left me a nice present as my legs and arms are full of blisters.

The antibiotics seem to be working and my gum line doesn't seem to have that whitish look, and the sandpaper feel also seems to have decreased. But at the same time the pain in my throat has *increased*. My tongue feels like it's on fire and the numbness has increased. My nose is like a hose that has sprouted a leak. If I'm drinking, eating or just plain doing nothing, I need to have a Kleenex or a paper towel in my hand continually.

I have had a couple moments of distress at work while shampooing clients. A few times, I have blessed them with some drops while they're leaning back at the shampoo bowl looking forward to a couple minutes of being treated to a nice shampoo and head massage. The distress and discomfort comes as I lean over my client's head, and it never seems to fail as I feel the drops sneak out of my nose and in slow motion drop toward the top of the lucky client's head. I have learned to have some control over it by slightly turning my head toward my right, to divert the drop toward the back of the head and to mix in with the shampoo suds or in the shampoo bowl.

This morning, I came in early to the treatment room to surprise Dick. His appointment was at 9 am. At 8:30, I walked around the check-in station and saw Dick sitting in our old corner. We saw each other at the same time, and I was happy to see a great smile appear on his face at the same time as mine. We gave each other a great hug with shoulder slapping, and then held each other at arm length to appraise one another. "You look great," I said to him.

"You look great!" he said to me. We sat down and spent the next half hour catching up. At 9, he was called to go in. We hugged again and promised to keep in touch.

I had time to wait for my treatment and when I found a corner I did a little reading and looked at some mail on my phone. At some point, I fell asleep. I had a good long nap and when Frank came looking for me, he had to shake me awake. I stood up and felt a little wobbly as I followed him down the hallway.

After treatment, as I walked to my car, my legs felt like they were made of lead. Maybe it was the July heat getting to me, but I walked from the entrance to the Mass General Hospital parking garage feeling that every step was going to be my last one. I made it to my car, turned the car on, and cranked the AC at full blast. I leaned the back of my seat down as I closed my eyes. A minute? Five? Ten? I don't know how long I remained like that. Time doesn't seem to mean much anymore.

The Whole Crew: 27 down, 5 to go.

I looked at my kite and I saw that there were five rings left. The kite used to drape over the armrest into my seat. Now I needed to rest it on the seat because it kept flopping from the armrest to the floor. The next ring was from my son-in-law, T2.

"YOU *CAN* and you Will. T2, Sammy, Chris."

The Whole Crew: I Can and I Will .

I'll try.

TODAY I make my wife cry. Not purposely, but with my words and my actions. My wife this morning offers to drive in for me, but as usual I say, "You can drive with me, but I need to know that I can do it, so I'll drive."

"Okay," she says.

I go into the changing room and my wife goes to the waiting area. When I come out a few minutes later, I see her at one of the double seats waiting for me. I join her and turn my phone on. Over the last couple of months, with all of our doctor's appointments and waiting room after waiting room, to fill some of the time we have taken to playing a word puzzle game on our phones, called Wordwhiz.

The game involves finding words, and as each level progresses the words became harder to find. This morning's puzzle clue is "Things you find in the sky." After finding the few obvious ones like star, sun, moon and planets, there are two words left to be found, and neither one of us can come up with the answer.

For inspiration, I'm looking around the room. I don't know why I'm doing that because I should be looking up to find something that you see in the sky. But that makes no sense either as we are three floors down, about 100 feet underground.

Instead of inspiration, what I find, or what I see, is a sea of pain. There are about 40 people around the room. I can see that most of them are patients, because of the one-size-fits-all gowns we are wearing.

I count six people in wheelchairs and all of them seem to be keeled over asleep. I think I see more women than men, and as I do a visual count there are 16 women with a scarves around their heads. They probably have received chemotherapy and they are trying to cover the hair loss. Maybe they are just cold in here. There are ten more women with gowns on. Including me, there is a total of eight guys. The common thread around the room seems to be that both men and women are holding their gowns under their chins, either because they are cold or for modesty, and involuntarily I reach under my chin and tuck in the two flaps of my gown. I notice that even those who are asleep have their hand clutched near their chest.

There is a guy sitting a seat over from my wife and me wearing a gown, but no pants. He is also holding the flaps of the gown closed across his chest with one hand, and with his other hand he's been trying to adjust the gown around his crossed legs. In the last couple of minutes he has shifted at least three times to make himself comfortable, but without much success.

What comes naturally for a woman – to be able to sit and tuck a dress or a gown under her crossed legs or in between the legs, doesn't seem to be working for the man next to us and it seems that no matter how hard he tries, he's not having much success. I'm glad he is sitting next to us and not in front of us.

It's only Tuesday, and probably everyone is thinking it's a long way to Friday and the end of the treatment week, and maybe that's part of what makes everyone gloomy. I definitely feel that there is a lot of misery around this room, and I don't know why but I just blurted out, "It's going to claim all of us."

"What's that in the sky . . .? What did you say?" my wife says with a questioning look on her face.

"Look around this room," I said to my wife while pointing with my chin. "Cancer is going to claim all of us." My words come out matter of factly, without any emotion.

"Stop. Stop it. Don't say that," she says. I can see her face starting to tighten up, and I know she's trying to hold back tears. "Don't say that. I won't let it," she says again.

Now I can see tears coming down her face. I reach beside me and hand her some Kleenex. I try to patch up some of the damage as I say, "Well, not now. Five, ten, twenty years from now."

"Don't say that," she says to me again as she takes hold of my arm and buries her face in it like it was her last lifeline to save her from drowning. We silently sit waiting for my name to be called. I think of my wife next to me and how everyone is concerned about me and how I'm progressing, but rarely do people ask about those caregivers who silently stand by their loved ones and take just as many blows from Mr. C.

One of the few private thoughts I have shared with some of my close friends and family is that without my wife I wouldn't have been able to get through to where I'm now. By the end of second day, into the third day home following my first surgery, I found myself in a situation where I wasn't able to speak, drink, eat or even have a bowel movement. If it wasn't for my wife, I would have said, "Thank you for the 60 years, but it's time to check out." I would have found a nice tall bridge and I would have gotten my wings because God in His mercy would have forgiven my act. I had lived, and now I was living my hell. Without my wife and the rest of my family, it would have been time to go home.

There should be a special award for those people who, when you are at your worst and you are living in your hell, are always there for you to put your head on their lap. Their soothing hand is on your back as you hear them whispering, "I'm here . . . You'll be okay."

When you're throwing up at 2 am, or you have that embarrassing accident, they're there ready to help and to allow you to get lost in their warm embrace.

And yes, they are suffering with us. To those who love us, our pain is their pain.

The Whole Crew: 28 down, 4 to go.

One more ring off my kite. "HIGH FIVES FROM AUTUMN!" A hand print and heart and scribble from my granddaughter.

WEDNESDAY, JULY 19TH. 30TH DAY, 29TH TREATMENT

THE pain in my face is increasing. Last night I went to bed by 8:30, and I woke up a few hours later at 11 pm with a splitting headache. The radiation is affecting my sinuses, causing swelling. The area above and around my left eye and under it looks like a water balloon. The pain is so strong when I wake that I feel that I'm going to throw up. I go into the kitchen to take a couple of Excedrin (extra strength), and I grab an ice bag to take back to bed and hold over my face.

I fade in and out, but sleep still eludes me. My wife's soft snores next to me are very reassuring, and sometimes even comforting. But at this moment I want to scream as the snoring is pounding in my head. I bounce lightly on the bed to maybe make her shift some without awakening her. For a couple of seconds it seems to work, but then it's back on. I toss and turn and I succeed in waking my wife up. She gets out of bed for a bathroom trip, and as she goes across the foot of the bed, we catch each other's eyes in the dim light of the bathroom night light down the hallway. "Can't sleep?" she asks. A few minutes later when she comes back into the room she says, "Tonight you're going to take a couple of Tylenol PM if I have to shove them down your throat!" A few minutes later she's asleep again, lightly snoring.

The minutes crawl by like hours. Every time I look at the clock I swear the darn thing is stuck. Finally at 4:15, I quietly slip out of the room into the shower. By 4:30, I'm sitting on my living room couch looking at the still dark street. As I sit there, I realize that my mouth once again feels like sandpaper.

After treatment, I go to see nurse practitioner Jen at Dr. B.'s office. After exchanging the usual pleasantries and catching up on the past week, we get down to business as she asks me how the antibiotics are working and how my gums feel.

"Jen, have you ever been fishing?" I ask her. Jen stands back with a smile on her face, and I can see that she's taken aback by my question.

"No. I'm not much of a fisherman and I've never caught a fish in my life," she answers.

"Okay, have you have been to the Aquarium in Boston or anywhere else?"

"Yeah, I have done that," she says proudly.

"Did you ever get to those water tanks where kids get to feel and touch some of the fish, and specifically some of those small stingrays?"

"Yes! I took one of my nieces and it was fun. The skin on those small Stingray's felt al-most like sandpaper . . . Oh, I get it. You're telling me that your mouth feels like sandpaper."

"Yup!" I said.

"Okay, let's take a look."

It's amazing how often I get the "We're going to do something" or "Let's take a look." Everyone gathers around. It's always inclusive and we can't leave anyone out.

"It looks like you have a good case of candida…candida fungi."

"Where is she?" I want to ask. "And Jen, I'm a married man. Do you think you should be introducing me to other women?"

The name sounds so Italian, "CANDIDA." It flows right off your tongue. With a name like Candida you can be anything you like to be. The name has a sensual sound to it. It could also be the sound of a motherly embrace. It could be the sound of a smile in someone's voice. Yes! Some people's voices sound like there is a smile in it.

The name derives from Latin *candidus* meaning "white." The meaning is beautiful and the sound of it is candid, and it's a lovely name – but not for me.

"Your immune system right now isn't strong enough to fight the infection. What's this, your fifth day of antibiotics?" Jen asks me.

I can't answer as my obturator is out and the only thing that I can do is to try to sound like I'm saying "seven days," but what comes out is nothing like that. Jen surprises me as she seems to understand. She says, "Okay, finish the ten days of antibiotics and I'm going to start you on some medicated lozenges. You'll need to take them five times a day, or I should say they have to melt in your mouth."

Well, I guess Candida isn't working out too well for me. I didn't get a lover's kiss or a mother's embrace. Instead what I got is *fungi*. And for those who don't understand the Italian language or Latin, *fungi* is a mushroom. I got fucking mushrooms growing in my mouth. Then it makes sense as *fungi* like damp dark places, and what better place than the dark cave that resides where my palate used to be.

FUCK YOU, CANDIDA!!!!! AND TAKE THE FUCKING DENTIST WITH YOU.

MAYBE YOU CAN GIVE HIM A SWEET KISS.

The Whole Crew: 29 down, 3 to go.

I love my next ring: "Cancer is only going to be a chapter in your life, not the whole story. Chrissy." The quote is followed by two hearts.

THURSDAY, JULY 20TH. 31ST DAY, 30TH TREATMENT

I'M close to the finish line and still I haven't made any new acquaintances among the people who are here at the same time that I am. Like most of the past six weeks, beyond a good morning or a hello, no one seems to want to talk. I don't know why it bothers me. I feel very unsettled, almost restless, instead of being excited that it's almost over. Maybe it's the thought that it's almost over that's causing me distress. Is this the Stockholm Syndrome again; that no matter how bad things are, you start to assimilate to them and with them, and you don't want it to end?

Nah! No way. I want out of this dream. But I miss, and I will miss, Dick and John for the feeling of belonging that it gave me as I was able to sit and talk to them.

This morning while I was waiting, a gentleman took a fall and he landed right on my feet. I was watching him coming across the room when one of the technicians from his team called his name. He was accompanied by someone with a name tag who I took to be an aide who didn't seem to be too interested in watching over him, because he was looking at his phone. The gentle-man seemed very weak as he walked, and he was shuffling more than walking. Just like in a movie when they slow the action down, his foot caught on the carpet and he went down on one knee. Then he just fell to one side, not at my feet, but on my feet. I kneeled down next to him and helped him to a sitting position, "Are you okay?" I asked him.

Just when something comes out of your mouth you realize how stupid it sounds. The man has taken a fall and an almost full face plant on the carpet, and now some stranger is asking him, "Are you okay?"

"Sure! I do this for laughs," he answers.

No, he didn't.

He can't speak. He uses his finger to give me the universal "give me a minute" gesture to let me know that he's okay. At first, when I see him using his hands and no sound from his mouth, I think he is mute, but when he turns his head I see that he had a tracheotomy.

By now both the aide and the technician are kneeling next to me and they have him under his arms, one on each side, and get him to a standing position. I think, just like most cases of someone taking a fall, he is more embarrassed than hurt. Someone rolls a wheelchair behind him and they sit him in it. The aide says they should call a doctor because he thinks the gentleman had a seizure. The man keeps on signaling with his hand that he's okay, and I decide to get involved as I say, "No, I don't think he had a seizure. I saw him fall and I saw his foot catch on the carpet."

The gentleman gets very excited as he hears my words and keeps nodding his head up and down. I think he says, "Yeah, yeah, I just tripped." But the words are as jumbled as mine are when I don't have my obturator in place

He gives me a nod as he's wheeled away toward the treatment room. I hear the aide say as he passes by, to no one in particular or maybe to me, "I still think we should call a doctor." To which I want to respond, "If you weren't looking at the fucking phone and paid attention to him, maybe you would have got him before he hit the floor."

I look at my watch and it's only 11:30. I still have another half hour to wait. I look around the room, and as at many other times before, I see a lot of pain. There is a man across from me sitting back with his eyes closed. He's a big man, in the neighborhood of about six-four or six-five tall, and way over a couple hundred pounds. He looks close to my age, maybe a little older, around his mid sixties. His breathing sounds very labored, and it seems to me that he's trying to keep his eyes closed so that he can concentrate on his breathing. Looking at him, I'm thinking of a fish out of water.

I hear the bell ring and I join in the clapping, as a smile forms on my face. I'm thinking: It's almost my turn. Then I realize that it only rang one time instead of the usual three, and most people have stopped clapping and are looking around feeling that they messed up by clapping before the bell was rung three times. As I shift my body slightly to my left, I can now look down the hallway and what I see is a lady curved over in a wheel chair by the bell trying to reach up and ring the bell. One of the aides is now helping her stand up and she manages to ring the bell. The tone is so soft that most people don't even realize that someone is ringing the bell to indicate they finished their treatments, a signal to give them that good-luck clapping.

I see a gentleman in a gurney that's lined up on the side of the hallway. I find myself staring at that gurney. I don't know why he is there alone, but it makes me sad to see that man immobile on that gurney with his eyes closed, and nobody there to hold his hand.

Why do I feel that most people around here are sitting with their eyes cast down, trying to hide the shame that they are the ones who got the bad flip of the coin.

Are my eyes cast down?

I'm getting depressed as I see and feel the pain and despair all around me.

The Whole Crew: 30 down, two to go.

My next ring is covered by a hand-drawing of ten hearts. Four in each side of the ring, with two smaller hearts in between the four, that I take to be my grandchildren Autumn and Sammy's. Under the two small hearts is a note from my wife: "You have been very strong and thank you for making family time special. XOXOXO"

FRIDAY, JULY 21ST. 32ND DAY, 31ST TREATMENT

TODAY I'm feeling the opposite of how I did the last few days. I'm excited as I drive into Boston, or maybe even a little euphoric. I just can't figure out if it's the fact that after today I will just have one treatment left, or if it's my old friend OxyContin that's making me euphoric. The pain seems to be increasing as I get closer to my finish line. I'm supplementing OxyContin with Tramadol 50mg to help me through the day. And last night, I took a couple of swigs of liquid OxyContin, just for old time's sake and to dull the pain.

Sleep has become something of the past. By 8 pm, I fall into a trance-like sleep. By 11 pm at most, I'm awake like it was midday.

What was my routine of about five minutes at night to brush my teeth and go to bed, now takes me 10 to15 minutes. The removal of the obturator is painful enough, but what follows is even worse. The obturator needs to be brushed gently and then left to soak in Listerine to kill the bacteria that may build up on it. After removing the obturator I floss, but flossing now is an adventure as I need to stay away from my gums. Easier said than done. It doesn't fail that the floss will hit the gumline at least two to three times, causing a pain as sharp as a razor blade would. And then of course the bleeding comes. I brush very, very gently, using Biotene toothpaste that is supposed to be a very mild paste to soothe my very sensitive bleeding gums.

My next step is to use Neil Med Sinus Rinse. The process of rinsing consists of mixing a packet of saline solution with about eight ounces of warm water, not hot and not cold, because either would cause pain. If on the hot side, and I don't mean scalding, the tissue is so sensitive that it would feel like it's burning. If cold, and just cold out of the faucet, it causes brain freeze symptoms followed by pain around the area where the surgery was performed. I mix the solution in a plastic squeeze bottle with a nozzle about two inches long, shake well, and insert the nozzle into one of my nostrils while blocking the other. As I squeeze the bottle the liquid gets projected into my nose, up my nostril, and out through the cave where my palate used to be, into my mouth.

Each time I pump the liquid up my nose, I land a mouthful of I don't know what, or what to call it. It's a combo of snot, food, mucus, blood, and some particles that I don't recognize. As I repeat the process, I do the next step in reverse. I squirt the solution into my mouth and blow it out two times through my nostrils by blocking one side or the other. When I see the junk I spit out, in a way I'm almost glad that my taste buds are non-existent. As bad as it can be to spit something out of my mouth, it's worse to see what it blows out of my nose as it splatters around the sink bowl.

My next step is to use the fluoride treatment. The tube of fluoride has a little nozzle that I use to squeeze the cream around my gum line where the teeth and gum meet. After applying the treatment, there is a minimum wait time of two minutes. It's not easy, because the paste makes my mouth water, and my mouth fills with saliva. I try not to swallow in between, and spit it all out for the two minutes. Of course for me, spitting without the obturator in is nothing more than dribbling down my chin.

Next I apply the ointment for the nose sores using a Q-tip. I go all around my nostrils. Then the Aquaphor cream, from under my eyes around to my ears, and down to the line of my chin. As I look closely, I notice that my Charlie Chaplin/Adolph Hitler mustache is getting more and more distinct, with a perfect line running about a half inch above my lip to the corner of my earlobe. To keep the area clean and avoid infection, I repeat this process every time I have any kind of food or even liquid.

Food used to be fun, but now combined with the fact that food has no taste, and the nonsense of what I need to do to clean the area, I'm almost at the point that I eat only what's necessary to keep me going. My nutritionist told me that I should eat five to seven meals a day, each one of them no bigger than the palm of my hands, or a deck of cards. Well, it sounds great, but I don't want to do the work five to seven times a day.

On a funny note, and this is something that every man over 50 will understand, those pesky nose hairs that tickle your nostrils, or wrap themselves at the edge of your nose looking like spider legs, are gone. Not a single one of them to be found around the edge of my nose, and also the inside of my nostrils-- there's no hair left. Along with the facial hair gone from the radiation treatments, the inside of my nose was affected. That's good and bad. The bad part is that those nose hairs work to collect little particles that float around and prevent them from getting into our sinuses. The good part is I don't have to worry anymore about wild nose hairs curling around my nostrils or tickling me.

I finish it all up with moisturizing cream to hydrate the skin around my face and combat the dryness that seems to happen when my face gets nuked: Aquaphor and regular hand cream for my face.

I guess I'm saving money on razor blades. I wear a goatee, and the area under and above and around my cheek bones is now completely hairless. The only area where I seem to still have hair is lower on my neck, but because my skin is so sensitive, I haven't been shaving there, either. My checks look like the face of a puffer fish with the coloring of a red snapper. I use reading glasses, but lately I have taken to keeping them on at all times, because wearing them low on my nose, almost at the tip, helps hide some of the puffiness and redness.

I have a little surprise waiting for me when Frank walks me into the treatment room and accesses his computer on the side desk by the door. After hitting a few keys on the keyboard, he brings up my schedule of treatments for the last seven weeks and says, "Originally, Monday was supposed to be your last day—but we changed your last day of treatments to Tuesday."

He's looking at me and I'm looking at him, waiting for him to continue with an explanation of why the extra day.

"With today it makes it 32 days that you've been in, but today is your 31st treatment," he says. "Your first day was a dry run with no treatment. Someplace there was a mix up and it was entered as you're going to be having 32 treatments. But the prescription by Dr. B. is for 33, so we need you back on Monday and Tuesday."

"Okay," I manage to say.

Today I meet A.J.. a new technician as part of my team. He's a really nice kid. He reminds me of my son.

The Whole Crew: 31 down, 1 to go. Not. . . . Surprise, I got a bonus gift. I get to go one extra day on Tuesday.

As I sit in my car, I realize that I'm tired. I'm tired of the traffic that I have to face to get in and out of the city for my appointments, I'm tired of the hospitals and doctors, and now I have an extra day to come in for treatments.

Okay, it's only another day. What difference will it make?

My phone is lighting up like a Christmas tree with WHAT? WHY? HOW COME?

I decide I'm not going to answer any of it, because it will be much easier to talk to my family than to try to put everything in a text. I lean my head back with my eyes closed as I take a long deep breath. Maybe it isn't such a bad thing. 33. It's a good number, the age of *Cristo Re'*: Christ the King. I just hope I don't end up like him. With my hand I feel along the side of the armrest looking for my next ring, but I can't locate it. I open my eyes and turn my head sideways, and my kite isn't there. I panic for a moment, but then I realize that the one lonely ring that I have left to open is sitting in the middle of the seat.

I don't know if I'm ready to open this last ring. For almost seven weeks, every day after treatment, I have been opening one of these rings and looking forward to opening them so much. They have become part of my day and life. So what's happening, now that the ending is within my reach?

I'm having what? Survivor's guilt?

They say that every ending is a new beginning, so I open my last ring. I recognize my wife's handwriting as the one on my last ring.

"RING THE BELL!!!!"

Well, not yet.

On a positive note, I look into my rearview mirror with my lips pulled back so that I can see my gum line, and I notice that my gums are starting to have a pinkish look to them. Maybe ten days of antibiotics and medicated lozenges are starting to work.

Fuck you, Mr. or Mrs. Thrush!!! Or whatever you identify as.

While driving home, when I reach the intersection of Route 24, off Route 95, about four miles to my workplace, something new happens. I feel an itch in the arch of my right foot so intense that I have to take off my shoe, and even with my shoe off I can't relieve the itch. I pull my socks off while still driving at about 70 miles an hour. I'm driving with my left foot, because my right foot is on the seat by my groin so that I can better reach it to scratch. At this moment the only thing I can compare this itch to is a time that I got a bad case of poison ivy.

As I get to work. I'm able to take a closer look to my foot and I realize this is nothing like the time I got poison ivy. The skin on my foot is very smooth and I don't feel any bumps, but there is a shine to my foot, with a light redness. I put an ice pack on it, and that seems to calm down a little of the itch. But by evening not only do I still have the itch, but now the bottom of my foot has no arch. My foot is so swollen that the arch has evened out with my toes and heel. As I try to stand and put weight on my foot, it feels like as I have a roll of pennies in my shoe. It burns, it hurts, and the bottom of my foot has turned hard as a rock. Plantar fasciitis? Another new friend?

I work on Saturday for a few hours in total agony as the pain in my foot grows more intense. We need money now more than ever, and so I keep on working.

Sunday morning, magically when I wake up, my foot is back to normal. I decide to do a little gardening, so I just go out by my back patio and do some watering and weed pulling in some of the planters.

T-shirt and shorts and flip-flop—this is great. I have my big sombrero hat on to shield me from the sun and I even have gardening gloves on to help me pull those pesky clumps of crabgrass. I feel a little tingling around the ring finger on my right hand, but I don't pay too much attention to it as I'm busy doing my gardening. I give it a scratch through my gloves and continue on.

In about one hour I'm done, and I roll the hose back up, rinse my feet and take my gloves off to rinse them and put them away. As I take my gloves off I see that my ring finger looks like a mini sausage.

From the second knuckle to the tip, my finger is swollen in the shape of a lollipop. I'm looking at my finger about six inches away from my nose almost unbelieving what my eyes see. I'm expecting an explanation from my finger as I keep looking at it there in front of my nose, but nothing comes through. The feeling is growing that my finger is giving me the finger. It seems to telling me, "You got some 'splaining to do, Lucyyyy!" But still all is quiet.

No answer.

I see my wife looking at me through the second floor kitchen window, and probably she's wondering why I'm giving myself the finger. I wave at her like I'm trying to flag down a cab. "My finger is swollen," I yell as I hold up my middle finger. I can see that she's baffled by my rudeness and when she opens the window she says, "Why are you giving me the finger?"

"I wasn't giving you the finger, I was just showing you my finger," I say as I wave my hand over my head.

"What? I'll come out," she yells as she points to our back door.

I meet her halfway up on our back porch and even before I step on the deck she asks . "What's the matter? Is it your foot again?"

"My foot is fine, but my finger is swollen," I say while bringing up my middle finger.

"Oh, my God! What's the matter with it?"

"Don't know, just took off my gloves and there it was." She's holding my hand up while she reaches into her pocket for her eyeglasses. She studies the top of my finger closely, and she says, "I think you need to go to the hospital. Yesterday your foot, now your finger."

"I'm not going to the hospital!" I say while trying to take my hand away, but she doesn't let go of my hand. She says, "Is that a splinter on the tip of your finger?"

I look at the tip of my finger and I don't see anything. "Let me see your glasses," I say to her. With her glasses on I see a fleck of something on my finger. I try to brush it off because I think it's dirt sitting there. Some of it comes off, but despite repeat brushing with my glove some of it stubbornly clinks to my finger.

"You're right, maybe it's a splinter! Can you get me a needle so I can take it out?"

A few minutes later my wife comes back with a sewing needle, alcohol, a book of matches, Neosporin, a band-aid, and eyebrow tweezers. I used the alcohol to clean and sterilize the tip of my finger, followed by burning the tip of the needle with a couple of matches.

This takes me back to growing up on the farm. While working in fields, sometimes an hour or an hour and a half away from home, often some minor (and sometimes not so minor) cuts or scrapes would happen while working with sharp tools, or just by stepping on a stump. When some of those minor cuts happened, what we did was to spit on it to clean it, and then pee on it to sterilize it, and then we just kept on working.

In the case of a splinter or something stuck in your finger we had matches and a safety pin. Every man smoked, so there were always matches, and every woman around had a safety pin pinned to her apron, or pinned someplace. After burning the tip of the needle, with hands that were covered in dirt and anything else that you handled while working, you, or someone who was there if you couldn't do it yourself, proceeded to remove whatever was stuck in you. Well, what better way to clean a wound than to spit on it, wipe it dry on your pants or shirt full of dust and dirt, and then for good measure pee on it, and back to work.

I turn the tip of the needle a few times in the match flame, and satisfied that I have killed whatever bacteria was on the tip of that needle, I proceed to remove I don't know what from the tip of my finger.

"Son of a bitch! That's fucking hot!" I say, just as my wife says, "Wait! It's hot?!"

Too late. Now I have a burn along with whatever is stuck in my sausage finger.

"I can't watch this," my wife says as she walks back in the house.

I start to poke at the skin around the dot that I see on the tip of my finger, but I still can't decide if it's a splinter or a stubborn fleck of dirt stuck to my finger. I keep digging and I manage to make a nice little crater. Then I burn the tip of the tweezers and go at it again, removing a little more skin and bits of flesh. I hold my finger up like I'm giving myself the finger again and use one of the sterile wipes to remove the blood around the little crater. The good thing is that what-ever it was is gone, or maybe it's hiding under the blood that's flowing from my finger again. Neosporin and a Band-Aid should take care of it.

My wife is back out on the deck. "You should call the doctor or go to the hospital. Yesterday your foot, today your finger. Something is going on there."

I wipe the blood off the tip of my finger and say, "Look! Nothing in my finger." And at the same time I squeeze the tip of my finger, bracing for the pain that will come if something is still embedded in my finger. But there's no pain, just blood.

"I'm not talking about what is or was stuck in your finger. I'm talking about you going in to have them check out why your foot and now your finger is swollen," my wife says.

"Well, my foot is okay now. Let's see how my finger is tomorrow," I say as I need to use three band-aids to make it around my sausage finger.

MONDAY, JULY 24TH. 33RD DAY, 32ND TREATMENT

MY finger is back to normal, minus the chunks of flesh I removed chasing the splinter. No redness or lines running up and down my finger or hand, so those matches did a good job.

My wife is with me as we drive into the hospital. I like having her with me for company and again, the added bonus is we get to use the zipper lane that requires two or more people in a car to be able to use it. The pain in my mouth is constant and I'm breathing solely through my mouth, causing dryness and choking fits. I have taken to keeping some Altoids candy in my mouth. I found that Peppermint is my favorite kind, as that flavor seems to help with the flow of saliva around my mouth.

The feeling of excitement that I had about ten days ago, looking forward to today being my last day, has been very quiet, and now I'm silently glad that I have another day. Maybe it's the unknown of finishing treatments and having to have scans and find out, "Yeah" or "Nah."

I remember that today is my friend John's last day of treatment. It will be nice to be there to watch him and congratulate him when he gets to ring the bell. Unless he got an extra day also.

As I come out of the changing room, I see my wife sitting with John, his wife and their daughter. After saying hello, we form a nice circle. They are excited that it's coming to an end, and John says to me, "We did it . . . Our last day!"

"Yes, we did it!" I say to him and we exchange high fives, "...but I have another day."

I explain what happened and they all say to me, "Okay, just another day."

And then a pleasant surprise as we see Charlie coming into the room followed by his daughter and another lady. Charlie, John and I all hug at the same time and I'm happy to see that Charlie remembers us. The last time I saw him is close to two weeks ago, and my first thought as I see him is that he looks good. Maybe the treatments are working for him.

"Hi everybody...this is my mom," Charlie's daughter says, pointing to the lady behind her. After an introduction all around, I pull a couple more chairs close to where we were sitting. Our nice circle has grown a little bigger. Either we are becoming a little family, or misery loves company.

"Today, dad is graduating," Jen says with a big smile, putting her hand over her dad's arm.

"Me too!" says John, and for a moment I feel a bit left out, but then I realize I'm going to be part of both of them as they celebrate the end of their treatments. I will get to witness the same look of joy in their faces that I have seen many times over the last seven weeks on the faces of people I didn't know.

Later on, my wife and I do witness both John and Charlie ringing their bell, and we share in the tears of happiness as everyone hugs. I enjoy watching both of them ring their bell as we stand at the edge of their little circle. When John is ready to ring his bell, I stand up to follow the little group to the alcove that is home to the bell, but with her hand on my arm to hold me back, my wife says, "Give them a little space. Stay back and watch...this is their family moment."

"Okay," I say, a little disappointed and annoyed at my wife for keeping me back, but I have to admit that most times she reads things better than I do.

And then John, his wife and their daughter wave us into their hugs and welcome us to become part of their little family. At that moment, I know that this isn't misery wanting company. This is a genuine rejoicing that is touching all of our souls. A group of people who not so long ago were complete strangers – and now through bad luck or fate or whatever flip of the coin brought Mr. C. into our lives – are sharing hugs, tears and hope for the future. There's a lot of love flowing all around, with smiles and lots of red eyes being wiped dry. As I watch everyone around me, I wonder if all of this is wishful thinking that it's all over and everything will be okay.

I'm a little disappointed in John's ringing of his bell as he softly pulls on the cord. I can see that today, as much as it is a happy day for him, John isn't feeling his best.

I thought to myself: Don't you worry, John. Tomorrow I will ring that fucker for the both of us, and I promise that everyone in the room will be aware that the fucker is ringing.

Charlie surprises me as I go to shake his hand and I am being called to go in. Instead of shaking my hand he pulls me into a great bear hug, and he says to me the same words the blonde lady and the piano lady said: "You'll be okay."

Isn't it funny how complete strangers come to bond when faced with a common enemy? It doesn't matter if it's man or woman, Democrat or Republican, Catholic, Protestant, Jewish, or Muslim, Black or White, gay or straight—nobody cares and nobody asks.

John looks very proud as he receives his certificate of conclusion of treatments.

On the way home, my wife and I decide to have lunch at our local Papa Gino's and enjoy a couple slices of pizza. I get to eat the soft part, my wife eats the crust. I got my receipt when I placed our order, and as I'm looking for a number they will call when our order is ready, I see something that's a first for me, and I know my wife isn't going to be too happy about it. My receipt shows a 10% senior citizen discount. How you like that? I got my first senior citizen discount and I didn't even ask for it.

The Whole Crew: 32 down, one to go.

MY wife is with me when we leave work at 10 am. I want to be early for my 12 noon appointment. I woke up feeling good despite the pain in my mouth. The excitement of my last day is catching up and I'm glad that I feel this way and not the way I had been. With the use of the zipper lane we make it into Boston in less than 45 minutes. Not bad. But is this last trip just a tease? Every day one to one and a half hours, and today less than 45 minutes?

My wife suggests we go to the cafeteria for a snack. Earlier this morning we had a thunderstorm that knocked out the power in our street. We left for work, my wife without her breakfast, me without my smoothie.

We order a veggie omelet, coffee and a blueberry muffin. I sprinkled salt over everything, including the muffin, as nothing seems to have any taste.

At 11:20, I walk into the changing room. I look at the empty lockers and the ones available are #12, #18 and #7. I go with #7. Lucky #7.

I walk into the waiting area and sit next to my wife. As I sit, we lean into each other. Lean on me. There is strength in those words. I know that the weight of my sickness isn't just on my shoulders, as I can see the stress on my wife's face every day. It's about our finances, my health, and the uncertainty of my – our – future. I put my arm around her shoulder and pull her toward me so that her head is leaning into the crook of my neck. I close my eyes and take in her scent. I feel a tear coming down my cheek. Lord, I don't want to go. I'm not ready to die. This is supposed to be our time . . . for us, our children, our grandchildren.

"Hi, Bruno! Ready? One more to go." Amanda is the one who comes this morning to get me. My wife squeezes my hand as I walk away following Amanda.

At the computer station I get, "Name?"

"Still the same from the last seven weeks!" I'm the only one laughing.

"...and date of birth." It's the last day. What are they going to do? Keep me after class?

I comply. I make the turn toward the little plastic cup sitting on the counter next to the sink waiting for my obturator. As I remove the obturator I realize how easily I do it – not the physical act of removing the obturator but the removal of the obturator in front of strangers. Besides my wife and my doctors, I haven't removed my obturator in front of anyone . . . except the four people in this room who I have been spending time with every day for the past two months of my life. Not my kids, my best friends, or my brother. Nobody.

For a time as I look at my obturator, I feel it has a sad, lonely look that travels from my mind to my soul. The last few days I've had a sense that things were changing, but I couldn't tell what it was that made me feel that way. This morning on my last day of treatment as I'm looking down at my obturator resting in the tray on the countertop in front of me, I'm sure that I know what the change is. My sad, lonely feeling as I looked at my obturator has been replaced by a sense of understanding that this little blob in that tray allows me to eat, drink and talk. Each day, I feel more confident that I don't have to explain anymore that now I'm not able to communicate the same way I used to.

Those who know and love me are aware of my limitation. The rest will take care of itself with time. My team at the hospital is aware that once I remove the obturator, if there is any communication with words, it will come from them, followed by a nod of my head or a simple shoulder shrug. They know that if I try to talk, I will sound like a drunken soul with throw-up in his mouth. That thought makes me smile as I remember a news conference I watched on TV a few years back with former New England Patriots coach Bill Parcells facing a host of journalists. After some reporter asked a question the coach didn't think much of, his answer was, "I feel like I'm throwing up in my mouth." Well, that's the way I feel if I try to speak without the obturator in place.

When I'm ready to turn toward the table, I find myself reaching for my neck, and I smile because I had removed my necklace in such a routine way that I didn't even remember doing it. I touch it through the fabric of the front pocket of my jeans. My fingertips find the reassuring form of the Christ on Cross and chain. I lie back and I even welcome the mask as it comes toward me. As the snaps go into place, they don't sound as menacing or as loud. My chin and shoulder seem to know exactly what to do. I automatically bring up my knees as Frank puts the support cushion under them. My hands are flat on the table, but as usual my thumb and index fingers are under my hips to release the pressure that causes the pain in my back when I lie down flat on my back.

I see the laser light coming alive above me. Lisa is on one side and Marlene is on the other. Marlene pushes the gown down from my shoulders to mid chest. Even without eye contact, I can I feel both of them looking at me, and neither one says, "Chin up" or "Hips up a little" or "Scoot a little to the left" or "Shoulders flat to the table." Even my chin is lining up perfectly with the laser.

No fooling around today.

No sir! This is my last test, and I will pass it.

On one side of me, I hear Lisa say, "Okay!" Then Marlene puts the lollipop in my mouth and mimics Lisa's answer. "Okay!"

I get a shoulder squeeze from both of them as they turn and leave the room. I don't try to follow them with my eyes. I know they will be back, and soon I heard the DING! and the soft swish as the air-lock door closes. Normally, I close my eyes and rest, but today I want to see the three-headed monster, and I want to hear the thousands of bees as they say good-bye.

I see the checkerboard lowering itself in front of me and I count the 13 by 13 black and white squares. The checkerboard slowly rotates to my right and the UFO appears. I get a strange sensation that everything seems to be moving in slower motion. Even Mr. Conehead seems to be elongating in slower motion. I have been doing this for almost seven weeks, and this morning feels it like it's the first time. Or maybe I want to memorize every moment of it. Strangely, an episode comes to mind that involved my mom, on what was going to be her last visit from Italy to the States.

My mom was sitting by herself on our back deck looking across our back yard. I could see her through the kitchen window as I was there helping my wife prepare dinner. I asked her, while pointing outside toward my mom, "She okay?"

"Why? What's the matter?" my wife asked.

"I don't know. She hasn't moved in a while."

"Well, go out and see." Women always seem to know what to do.

I walked out and let the screen door hit a little hard so that the noise would warn my mom that I was coming out. She turned her head toward me and then turned again to look at the back yard.

"*Cosa ce'?* Are you okay?" I asked, as I sat next to her.

"*Si! Tutto bene . . . perche?* All is good, why?"

"I saw you sitting and not moving . . . You were so quiet."

"*Sto' facendo una foto mentale di tutto quel che vedo per poi ricordarmene a casa.* I'm taking a mental picture of everything I see so that when I go back home I can remember all of it."

As the UFO keeps on turning toward the right I see my elongated reflection disappear from my view, and . . . wait a moment! Is he waving at me?

"Goodbye, Mr. Conehead," I say. A thank-you note to Mr. Dan Aykroyd for creating this character that has entertained me for the last six weeks. And then the football stops above my face. I blink away from it as I want to look up and find all of my friends hiding in the ceiling. I hope that it's for the last time. I see Mickey with his chef hat still riding his pig or rhino, and Minnie is still falling off from the back of it. I see a dinosaur and my half-dove/half-prehistoric bird and . . . where is my angel? I panicked for a moment, but it's a very short moment, as I focus on my angel and close my eyes with that image. I hope I never have to be looking at this angel lying down on this table again. I contentedly blank out and drift in and out.

Before I see them, I hear soft footfalls coming toward me. The lights are on as Lisa and Marlene come back into the room. Marlene takes the lollipop out of my mouth, just as Frank comes into the room. He starts to unbolt the mask. He has a nice smile on his face as he says, "It's done. You finished your treatments."

I'm counting the nine snaps, and with each snap I hear I hope it's the sound of freedom and the beginning of a new phase of my life. As the last snap sounds, I give a sigh and stifle a cry. Frank notices, and still with a smile on his face, he puts his hand out to help me off the table like we were old friends that haven't seen each other for awhile. Contrary to what I have been doing the last seven weeks, pulling myself up to prove that I could do it, I take his hand and accept him pulling me up. As I sit at the edge of the table I feel Marlene's hand on my back as she says, "You're okay. It's all done."

It takes a couple of tries for me to put my obturator in place, because somehow my hands are shaking. When I'm done and I turn to leave the room, I see Marlene coming toward me, diploma in hand.

"Congratulations. You did it!" And she gives me a hug, followed by Frank and Lisa hugging me.

"Go and change. We will meet you in the waiting area. Bell ringing time!" Marlene says.

"Okay," I answer. A.J. gives me a couple of congratulatory slaps on my back.

I walk out without turning back, looking at my diploma. I feel proud, and a smile spreads on my face. I just hope I don't need continuing education.

When I come out into the waiting area, I see my wife looking toward the hallway, anticipating my emergence from the treatment area. As soon as our eyes meet, she jumps up to greet me. I get the biggest and strongest hug from her of our 40-some years together. It makes me think of those hugs that kids give you as they say, "I'm going to squeeze you like a lemon."

I proudly show her my diploma and ask her to hold on to it as I go in to change from my johnny to my clothes. I take my clothes out of the lucky #7 locker and go into the cubicle. I speed through my changing of clothes but take a few extra moments looking at the Christ on the Cross in the palm of my hand. I want to go and ring that bell. And then something strange happens on the way to the Forum.

I look for my wife when I come back out into the waiting area and I don't see her. Maybe she went to the ladies' room. I think, "What the fuck! She couldn't hold it for few minutes? I have a bell to ring."

I do one more sweep around the room to make sure I didn't miss her and ... there she is. I see her, with her back to me standing by the entrance to the hallway on the opposite side of the room near the area where the bell is waiting for me. Then I also notice something strange as I see my wife slipping a t-shirt over her head, over her blouse. That's weird! Was she cold and she went back to our car to get something to put on?

As I walk toward her, she's standing sideways to me and I can't fully see the shirt that she just put on. Maybe sensing that soon I will be out of the changing room, she turns and our yes find each other, and as she turns to face me, I can now see the front of the t-shirt that a few seconds ago she was slipping over her head. The t-shirt colors are red and blue, and in the middle of her chest there are two white boxes about six by six inches each, side by side.

Then I see that one box has my name above it: Bruno. And in the box under my name I see the number 3. The next box has Cancer written across the top of it, and under it the number 28.

Now, being a New England Patriots fan and a Bostonian, and having been a witness to the greatest comeback in football history, I know exactly what those numbers stand for. She must have had the shirt in her bag. As I get close to her, I see that these aren't homemade, stick-on numbers or letters. Definitely, this shirt was professionally made. I hear some commotion coming from around the corner, down the hallway. From where I am now I can't see what it is. She has a smirk on her face, and I should have known that something was up. As I put my arm out to hug her again, I can now see down the hallway in my peripheral vision, and I am stunned by what I see.

I break down in sobs in a way I haven't allowed myself to do in front of others in a long time.

All of my children are there. I see my daughters holding their respective children. My grandkids have balloons strings attached to their wrists. My sons-in-law are there, my son and his future wife are there, and all of them are wearing the same t-shirt that my wife has on.

They encircle me in seconds and all of them are hugging and touching me. I feel their love and I feel all of them melting into me. The floodgates open up. I can't stop it, and I don't want to stop it, because my family is crying with me, and in our tears there is happiness and relief.

Finally, I pull myself together, and my wife presents me with a t-shirt just like the one they have on. As I slip the shirt over my head, I see Frank, Amanda, A.J., and Lisa coming down the hallway. They complete the circle around me as I stand next to the bell. Every member of my family has their phone out to record this moment for posterity.

I have been imagining this moment from the first time I read this plaque on the wall next to the bell. This is my moment, and I'm not going to waste it. No weak ringing here. I want everyone within earshot to hear it loud and clear. No weakling here. I grab the cord attached to the clapper and pull.

OH, YEAH! That was loud and clear, and I have two more to go. Then my second pull comes with the determination of a novice monk in a monastery ringing the church bells and … nothing happens.

I broke the fucking bell.

The cord ripped right out and I'm left with this limp noodle of a cord hanging from my hand. I find myself stupidly looking at this piece of filament hanging from my hand while everyone is cracking up. Then I hear my little granddaughter say, "Don't worry, *Nonno* will fix it. *Nonno* is Mr. Fix It."

Everyone is looking at me. The clapping that usually comes from the waiting area is silent, but my circle of family and team is enjoying the moment. Marlene is laughing so much that she's holding her side. Frank has his head leaning against the wall, and he slides down the wall, and now he is sitting on the floor laughing. Lisa and A.J. are just shaking their heads.

I hear my granddaughter again say, "*Nonno* will fix it.'

Is this one last joke by Mr. C.?

At my expense? Fuck, no! And fuck him. I'll show you.

I look at the bell and see that the clapper had an eye hook that held the rope in place and with me pulling so hard I opened the eye hook that held the rope in place. I take the cord, thread it through the open hook and bend it back in place, and then for good measure I give a turn of the metal around the rope. I give it a couple of tugs while holding the clapper in place so as not to ring the bell. The cord feels solidly attached. Satisfied that it will hold, I announce, "ALL FIXED!!!."

I pulled on the rope a little more gently, but the sweet sound that follows is loud and clear, and it isn't a "ding, ding, ding" but a "DOOONG! DOOONG! DOOONG!"

My family and my team and all of those in the waiting area cheer and clap for me.

Again, everyone moves in to hug me and congratulate me. We take a bunch of pictures with my family and my team. I hug Frank, Amanda, A.J. and Lisa, thank them and walk out with my family in tow, showing everyone the back of our shirts.

BRUNO 34, CANCER 28

Fuck you, Mr. C. I broke it, I fixed it, and I got to ring it.

One for the good guys.

Tuesday, July 25th 2017

34-28 was the final score of Super Bowl LI, played between the Atlanta Falcons and the New England Patriots. Well into the third quarter of play, the Patriots trailed the Falcons by a score of 3 to 28. They came back and won the game. As we are walking out of the waiting area toward the elevator alcove I can't help taking one last look toward the waiting area. The thought that has come to my mind is the hope for everyone in that waiting area wearing a johnny, and for myself, that we can all have a comeback, as the Patriots did.

One week later

ON August the 5th, we make it down to Cape Cod. I take the week off following the end of my treatments to spend it with my family. This was my carrot on the stick: Get through those seven weeks and then have a week with all of those who love you the most around you to help restore you physically and mentally.

One of the few restrictions that I have after finishing treatments is to avoid spending too much time in the sun. Well, no big deal for me, because I'm just as happy to spend my time under the shade of a tree in the back yard or under a beach umbrella. The house we rented has a beautiful deck with a pergola over it for shade. A glass of wine, a book, and a lounge chair – that's a vacation.

Everyone goes about unpacking the five cars – yes, we drove down with five cars packed to the rim with everything from toilet paper to cookies, kitchen utensils, beach chairs, umbrellas and towels. Food and coolers filled with beer to cognac, and everything that you can fit in between. We are ready. We are not foolish enough to pay high Cape Cod prices.

I feel everyone being very attentive to y needs and wants. I'm enjoying the attention, but I'm so tired that I just let it slide over me, even as I acknowledge everything with a smile or a nod.

The week is marked by two happenings – one good, one bad. Number one is a message from my dad. My dead dad.

On Sunday morning, the day after we arrive down the Cape, I help set up chairs, umbrellas, and towels down at the beach. I take a little time there to play with my grandchildren, but as the heat of the day starts to intensify, and with me not being able to spend too much time in the sun, I decide to go back to the house and rest. I have a little snack with a cup of espresso coffee and choose to lie down on one of the couches in the living room instead of going up to the bedrooms. I turn on the TV and promptly fall asleep.

I dreamed. I dreamed one of those dreams where you can touch the people and smell the fresh air and feel the sun on your face.

I was in a railway station and as I walked by a coffee shop in one corner of the station, I could smell espresso coffee being made. Maybe it was because I just had a cup of espresso. I was there to pick up my dad. I don't know from where he was coming or why, but I just knew that I needed to be there to meet him. There were many people coming off the trains, and I kept on looking back and forth from one exit of the train to another but I couldn't locate him. Maybe he was still on the train, but as I looked up through the windows, I saw that the train cars were empty.

The crowds that came off the train had dispersed, and now I was by myself in the empty station. I was standing alone in the station's cavernous waiting room when the room started to spin around me. As the shape of the room changed, I noticed a long corridor I hadn't seen before, leading to another corridor crossing the end of it. I knew that I had to go down that corridor. I followed it to the end, and just as I was to turn into the next corridor, I saw my dad. He was leaning against a roof support column by the rails, with his arms crossed over his chest. I knew it was my dad, but he didn't look like the way he had the last time I saw him, as a 90-year-old man, just before he passed.

He had the look of a young man, but not a teenager. He looked more like a man in his thirties or forties. A glow of vitality surrounded him as if a spotlight was being held behind his back. For a moment it was so bright that I found myself squinting, but then it was as someone turned down a dimmer switch to allow me to see him.

His hair was full and shiny, with a touch of gray around his temples and sideburns. His face was tanned, just the way I remembered from when I was a child – tanned from the farm work he did his whole life. But his skin was smooth and freshly shaven.

He had on his Sunday best – a suit and tie. His vest was buttoned and I could see a gold chain looped into one of the buttons, leading to an invisible pocket watch in his vest pocket. Right above the last button of his vest I could see that he was wearing a tie pin. I had never seen him wear one, so I tried to look at it, but I couldn't distinguish the form of that tie pin. The cuffs of his shirt sleeves had cuff links. One of his feet was crossed over the other with the point of his shiny shoe touching the cobblestone pavement. One arm casually bent up at the elbow, and between his index and middle finger he was holding a lit cigarette.

In the distance I heard a train going through one of the invisible tunnels, and with the shift of air I got a whiff of the cigarette. As soon as it reached my nostrils I knew it was a *Nazionali* ,the popular, Italian-made cigarette brand. For a moment, I was eight years old and huddling with my mom in the back of a cart trailing behind my dad's brand new *Acria* tractor.

This was the first tractor that my dad owned. I was looking at his back, strong and straight. With one hand he was driving, while the other held his *Nazionali* cigarette. As the tractor moved and he blew out a puff of smoke, I could see it drifting toward my mom and me.

In my sleep, I find myself taking a deep breath, and I smell that pleasant aroma of a freshly lit cigarette. I know (in my sleep) that I'm actually smelling smoke. Did I shut the stove off after making coffee?

It doesn't matter because back in my dream the smell of smoke dissipated and my dad's eyes found me just as I was turning the corner. His face lit up in recognition.

"*Ciao papa', ti cercavo. Cosa fai li'?*" "Hi, Dad, I was looking for you. What are you doing there?"

His answer was simple and his face radiated happiness as he answered, "*Sto' aspettando.*" "I'm waiting."

I wanted to ask him, "Are you waiting for me to pick you up?"

He smiled, but he didn't answer, he just vanished.

I wake up and strangely, I can smell cigarette smoke. Maybe it's just someone passing by, smoke drifting through the open windows. Wait, the AC is on and all the windows are closed. Maybe I should check the stove. I did and the burners were nice and cold.

The following day, Tuesday the 8th of August, I was sitting on the deck with a cup of coffee when I saw a text from my niece, Nicoletta. She wrote, "Call me. I need to talk to you."

I called her. "*Ciao cosa ce'?* Hi, what's going on?" I asked, even before I greeted her.

"*Tutto okay per noi, pero'…*We are okay, but."

Before she finished answering me, I knew that this call was about my mom. The last few months, my mom's health had gone downhill to a point that for the last month she had been bedridden.

"*Nonna* has gone into a coma, and *mamma* needs your help to make a decision on what to do."

My sister Maria and I have been given power of attorney by our parents to oversee their affairs, financially and physically. My father and mother made it very clear that they wanted to die at home with no extreme measures to be taken to keep them alive. One of the last things that my dad said to me before he passed was, "Keep mom at home. You and your sister have control of everything and when the time comes, let her go."

I called my sister and these were her words to me:

"The doctor said that if we transfer mom to the hospital, they can put her on a respirator and she will probably last another week . . . ," but before she could finish the sentence I said, "No! Mom and dad were very specific." Before calling my sister I also spoke to my brother Vincenzo, and we agreed that it was time to let mom go .

"We need to let her go." I said to my sister

"Okay. I just needed to hear it from you. I just couldn't make the decision on my own."

We spoke at about 3:15 in the afternoon their time. Mom passed that evening at 6:20, surrounded by my sister and my nieces and nephews. When my niece texted to let me know that she was gone, it was 12:21 am, Eastern time.

That morning when my mom lapsed into a coma, the attending doctor had said there wasn't much brain activity and she wasn't going to come out of it. "We'll keep her comfortable with morphine so that she's not in pain, but her brain is gone," he said. That was the catalyst for my niece's text .

At 6 o'clock that evening, my mom had opened her eyes, and seeing her daughter and her grandchildren, she called to them with a weak voice and hand signal, "*Vieni*. Come," she said to them in a whisper. One at a time, she spoke to the five grandchildren who were there, and then last, she called to my sister .

"*Maria, figlia mia*. My daughter," she said to her, and those were her last words.

My sister recounted that mom's face lit up as she spoke those last words. The wrinkles in her 97-year-old face seemed to soften up and smooth out. Her eyes were clear as she looked at my sister, and my sister could feel the love in them. Then her eyes got big, almost like the eyes of a child seeing something for the first time. Her face lit up with a smile, and my sister felt that mom was looking beyond her. For a moment my sister thought that mom was going to stand up and get out of bed, as she tried to lift her head. With a smile still on her face, her head sank back onto the pillow and she closed her eyes. Her body relaxed and seemed to stretch out, and all of the hurts and pain were gone. Her last breath came and it was a soft whisper of a good bye. That was August the 8th, two days after I had dreamed of my dad. He got his wish.

Two days later I dream again and this time it is of my mom and dad. They were walking together in front of me, going away from me. I couldn't see their faces but I knew they were my mom and dad. For the last ten years, my mom walked with a bent back, and she hadn't been able to take a step without pain. The two people in front of me were young and strong and there was no pain in their steps. They had the body and look of young people, maybe even as they had been before they had children. There's no way I would know or remember them being that age or what they looked like then.

I was so close to them that I could smell them and feel their body warmth. I wanted to go to them. So, I picked up my walking pace, but it seemed that the faster I walked, the further away from them I got. I tried to walk even faster as I followed them, but I just couldn't catch up to them. They got further and further away from me.

I stopped so that I could look at them. I couldn't see their faces but I knew they were smiling. Their walk seemed to get even lighter, almost like they were floating away. Their backs remained tall and straight as they kept on walking. My mom had her hand through my dad's elbow and her head was leaning against his shoulder.

I called to them, '*Hey…aspettatmi!*' "Wait for me!" But what I got from them without any hesitation was my mom, with her back still turned, lifting her hand up with her index extended. Someone else might interpret that as her saying, "I'm number one." But I knew differently. It was her hand shaking back and forth saying, "No." I stretched out my hand to touch the two of them, but they just dissipated like fog in the sunshine.

This past May, three months before my mom passed, I had a trip booked to go and see her. Because of surgery and treatments, I had to cancel my trip. Over the last 42 years that I have lived in the USA, I've made the trip back to see my parents more than 30 times. The one year that I don't make it back, she dies. I didn't travel to Italy for the funeral because at that point I was neither physically nor mentally able to do it. I would have liked to see her one more time, but now I'm glad that my last memories and images of her will be of us having a glass of wine or a meal together, or taking her for a walk.

I have a memory of something I'm happy and proud to have done. To some, it may seem small and foolish. As my mom got older she started to have problems with her feet becoming arthritic and curled in. Her toes began overlapping one over the other, and her nails were growing into the skin and flesh. We had tried to have a podiatrist and a manicurist have a look, but no one seemed to be of much help.

Part of my training as I was going for my cosmetology license was how to do a manicure and a pedicure, but that was over 40 years ago and I never did either a manicure or a pedicure.

I watched our nail tech at work few times as she did a pedicure. I asked for a few pointers on what I could do to help my mom. On one of my trips, about ten years before my mom and dad passed away, I left home armed with a full pedicure kit including nippers, files, cuticle pushers, cutters and creams. Remembering the way my mom's feet looked, I took with me a couple of tubes of antibiotic ointments, just in case I did too much cutting instead of pushing those cuticles.

"*Che devi fare?* What are you going to do? "*Ma chi si pazz!* Are you crazy!" my dad said in an indignant voice.

I explained to him that I was going to give mom a pedicure, and now I needed to convince my mom. After a few minutes of talking to her she said yes, and she sat down at one of the kitchen chairs. My dad placed himself about two feet away and turned the TV on.

I took a *bacinella* bucket, filled it with some warm water, and told my mom to soak her feet. Liliana, our manicurist at the shop, told me to file her nails first and then soak, but as I looked at her feet, I felt it was going to be better to soak and then try to cut some of the nails embedded into her skin. I took a seat by her feet in *la siggette.* (In our dialect, the word *siggette* means a small chair.)

La siggette is a small, wooden children's chair with a straw seat. And coincidentally, this was my *siggette* from my childhood. I was sitting at my mom's feet with a towel across my lap and her foot on my knee. The moment I touch her foot she jumped back saying, "*Fa lu solletico.* You're tickling me," and laughing like she was a small child.

I touched her foot a couple of times, and after a few bouts of laughter she settled down and I was able to clean and cut her nails. During the hour or so that it took me to do her feet, I noticed from the corner of my eyes my dad looking at me. Every time I looked up he would turn the other way, making believe he was watching TV. But I knew better. He was checking on me. Just as I was about to finish, as I was putting some ointment on the couple of little cuts around my mom's cuticles, I saw my dad taking his shoes and socks off. He said, "*Puoi fare pure a me'?* You think you can do mine, also?" And as he said the words, he came to my mom's side, encouraging her to get up from the chair so that he could have a seat.

"*Si papa'.* Let me get some clean water."

Leave it up to my mom that even in her passing, she was doing for others. In a normal week, my kids, their spouses, my wife and I would all be at work at this time on a weekday. If I had received the call about my mom passing while I was at work, I would have gone home and taken the rest of the day off, and my children and family would have done the same, but it would have been hard to be able to have the whole week together.

Very few workplaces allow more than a day or two for the loss of a parent or grandparent. I'm glad that when I got the call from my niece informing me that mom had passed, my family was all around me. We did our best to comfort each other. We cried and hugged, and after a while all of my kids seemed to come up with a story about *Nonna Assunta*. A few hours later, after dinner, we sat out on the deck. My two grandchildren were playing around the floor and they entertained all of us. The distraction was good, but I could see the somber mood all around me. I made a decision to ask my family to do one thing for me.

"Sure, dad! What do you need?" they all asked.

"If you want to honor your *Nonna*, I ask you to spend this week like nothing happened. I want you to go to the beach, go shopping, go out for dinner, have fun! You have loved and honored her in life. Now celebrate her life."

I'm glad I made that little speech because, unknown to the family, my son had planned on this week to propose to his then-girlfriend Christie. When the news came that my mom had passed, he decided he was going to wait. After my little speech, he changed his mind, and on Thursday, the two of them went out for lunch and then took a walk on the beach. My son got down on one knee and proposed to her. She said, "Yes!" and they were married the following year, June 2nd, 2018.

I found a quote on Facebook, and I don't know who to attribute it to. But I love the words used to describe a Mom.

AVERE LA MAMMA E COME AVERE SEMPRE LA COPERTA PER IL FREDDO,

Having your mom is like always having that warm blanket when you're cold,

L'OMBRELLO PER LA PIOGGIA

having an umbrella in the rain,

IL PANE PER LA FAME,

bread when you're hungry,

L'AQUA PER LA SETE.

water when you're thirsty.

Three months removed from the end of my radiation, I have my first PET scans. After a week of waiting, we get the good news that everything looks good. "We'll see you in three months," Dr. B. says.

But . . . most of the late summer and early fall, I am experiencing the need to urinate too frequently, and at night I'm getting up two or three times. I see my urologist the week before Thanksgiving and after examining me, he recommends that before we do another biopsy I should go for an MRI of my prostrate. At the same time, he prescribes a medication called Tamsulosin to help with the frequent urination. A new friend.

The week leading up to Christmas I get the news there is a spot on my prostrate and it is likely to be cancerous. Merrrrrry Christmas!

The good news is that the spot is very small, too small to do a biopsy. We should wait a year and do a follow up MRI in a year to see if there are changes. Doing a biopsy at this point could yield either a false negative or a false positive. My blood test showed that my PSA is over eight.

I love the continuation of the "We." All inclusive. Don't want leave anyone out.

"Is the medication helping with the urination?" my urologist asks.

"Doing okay. I'm up one, two times a night instead of two, three times a night."

"I'm going to give you something else to try along with the Tamsulosin. This is a prescription for Finasteride. I want you to take it until we do another MRI next year."

Soon I will have to put an addition to my house, as my friends are expanding daily, and in no time I'll be like all of the other 90-year-olds with a pill box for every day of the week.

Wait! I'm only 60!

I still wake up every morning with a moment where consciousness and oblivion are mixing and fighting to control my mind, and for that moment I still feel and think that I'm whole. Then as my tongue makes its way around my mouth to bring some moisture to my gums . . . BANG! The taste of the metal hooks from the blob in the cave in my mouth where my palate used to be registers on the tip of my tongue. Back to reality.

The dripping from my nose is constant. Sleeping is an adventure as I use four pillows to prop my back up. During the day I seem to do a little bit better with breathing, but when I lie down at night, everything shuts down.

My family, my friends, my coworkers, have all done a great job helping me get through my valley of tears, and I'm thankful for all of it. But as the weeks and months pass by, people have their own sets of problems and when they ask me how I am, my answer is not as important, because most times they're telling me about their own problems before I have answered their question. When you're a downer, people sense that, and they tend to move away from you and your problems. So I have taken to giving my standard answer: "I'm doing great!"

"You look great!" is the standard answer I get back. Everyone is happy that everyone is great, and doing great, and they don't have to listen to other people's problems.

In the third week of January 2018, on Monday the 22nd, I go into the bathroom to brush my teeth. When I remove the obturator, I see some blood around the edge. I don't think much of it and I'm not too alarmed because in the past I've had some bleeding. Most of the time it happened because I pushed too hard when putting in my obturator, causing some bleeding, and most of the time it would only be a little staining around the now pink blob.

I brush my teeth, and when I drool the wash and spit out of my mouth -- because I couldn't spit even if I had a mouth full of shit – what I see is a red mix of saliva and toothpaste. I rinse again as much as I can and red is still the prevalent color. I fill my medical squirt bottle and go to work on my nose and mouth, and squishing and drooling.

What comes out of my mouth are globs and blobs of blood clots. After a couple more rinses and spraying, the redness and blood diminishes as I go along.

I'm moving my tongue and feeling along gingerly, exploring the area around the cave in my palate and . . . what was that? I go backwards with my tongue and feel around . . . there!

What the fuck is that? Is something missing? Or is something there that wasn't there yesterday? I feel around with my tongue again, knowing that the area around the part that was surgically affected doesn't feel normal. Now, my normal is not a normal that anyone else would experience, but at this point my tongue has learned to feel around the area and know what belongs and what doesn't. This morning, there is something there that doesn't belong. And what's with the blood and blood clots?

Maybe I didn't do a good job last night before I went to bed, and maybe some bits of food got embedded in my cavern and now need to be brushed out. I look into my medical basket next to the sink and see my eyeglasses and a flashlight. Okay, let's take a look.

I have my eyeglasses on the tip of my nose with the flashlight shining up so that I can look into the cavern.

"WHAT THE FUCK IS THAT?"

And by the time my mind registers what my eyes are seeing, I have to clean the drool that is coming down my chin. After wiping I look again and what I see is little bubbles, bubbling out of the roof of my cavern. I can feel myself starting to breathe harder and that warm feeling creeping into my stomach. I'm trying to figure out what is happening, as I see more and more bubbles coming from the roof of my garage without the Mack truck. It's my day off. I'm in the bathroom alone and I wonder if I should share this with my wife. I rinse my mouth again and look up again and this time I try not to take a breath.

Great! No bubbles, and with no bubbles comes a clearer view of the roof of my mouth and what I see is an opening about a half inch long and a quarter of an inch wide next to the opening created by my surgery.

Another hole? Another fucking hole? No, that can't be. Holes don't just appear from one day to the next. I hold my breath so long that when I let it go, my glasses fog right up.

I'm leaning over the counter holding on with both of my hands looking at my reflection in the mirror, hoping that someone will give me an explanation for what I just saw. Honest to God, I look around my bathroom hoping this is a joke and someone will say, "Ha, ha, got you. April Fool's in January!"

For the third time, I rinse and make sure that I blow out of my nose so that anything hidden or stuck there comes out. With each time I rinse out, the hole becomes clearer and clearer. You know the saying, "You need that like you need another hole in your head." Well, now I have two extra holes in my head. The cave now has a chimney. Soon I can rent space next to the Mack truck.

Two days later, I'm in Dr. L.'s office. My wife had called with desperation in her voice and they gave me an appointment on Wednesday morning.

The physician's assistant says, "Let's take a look."

"Okay," I say, as I remove my obturator.

"I never saw one like this. We have to consider whether this is a cancer recurrence. But Dr. L. will be in shortly and he'll take a look." And she softly closes the door as she leaves the room.

The words feel like a punch in the gut. Any hope that was in the room has been completely obliterated along with the air in my lungs.

"How dare you have any hope," Mr. C., the thief in the night, whispers in my ear.

My wife is sitting at her usual spot by the window overlooking the Charles River while I sit in my examining chair. I'm looking at the little paper tray in my hand that my obturator is in, trying to find an answer to a question that I can't formulate. Even if I could, I don't know what I would ask, but what I know for sure is that if I keep looking at the little tray, I don't have to look at my wife's face because I know what I will see there.

From the corner of my eye I can see that she has her head turned to look at the river, but I don't think that as beautiful as the river looks this morning that my wife sees any of it. I can see a little rivulet on the side of her face from a tear running through her makeup. Either she doesn't realize that it's there or she doesn't care, because she makes no effort to wipe it away.

Dr. L. comes in and he is his usual happy, bubbly self. We exchange the usual pleasantries, but soon Dr. L. realizes that the mood in the room isn't good.

"Let's take a look." Again I hear this very peculiar "we." Maybe I'm the only one who gets annoyed by this way of seeming to include someone in a decision when they really have no choice and no power over what or where or when anything happens.

"We will do a scan to make sure that's not a cancer recurrence . . ."

"Well, Dr. L., what do you think it is?" my wife asks, just like she could read my mind. That was the question I wanted to ask.

"We'll do a scan. With the scan I will able to see and know better what's going on." I could see my wife try to jump in with another question, but Dr. L. puts up a hand like a stop sign as he continues on. "We are going to set you up for PET scans, and I'll have Dr. B. also see you. Judging by my experience, and I want to say that this is only an observation of what I have seen over the years, I think that what you have there is radiation damage from your treatments. It's good and bad. Good that there's probably no cancer recurrence, bad that we don't know how wide that hole will open or what else it will do."

A little air comes back into the room.

The following Wednesday I'm in Dr. B.'s office. With her usual bubbly manner, Jen says, "I don't think it's a cancer recurrence, but we will have Dr B. take a look."

"Look at that! That's definitely a new hole!" Dr. B. says, as he's taking pictures of the new cave in my mouth. My cavern now has a mini me. How cute.

"I'm almost sure that this is radiation damage, but the scan will tell us more."

Okay, a little more air, and with that air a little hope comes back into the room.

On Monday, February the 26th, I had my PET scans. Wednesday I was back in Dr. B.'s office.

"The hole that opened up is a result of radiation damage," he said. "In your case as the teeth and the bone were removed, there wasn't much there to hold your sinus in place. We were pretty sure before your scans that this was the problem with that opening . . . but!"

Fuck! Here it goes. There is always a "but!" Every fucking time.

"One of your lymph nodes is very swollen and inflamed. I don't want to do a biopsy yet. We'd like to wait another three months and we will repeat the PET scans. By then we should know what our course of action should be. We hope that when we repeat the scans in three months that your nodes remain the same, or maybe they'll be even smaller."

Three months is not a long time, but it's very hard to distance yourself from the specter of cancer. It's the Sword of Damocles. Every day I labored under the specter of anxiety with my friend Mr. C. looking over my shoulder. At some moments I felt like I was hanging from a thread made from the same horsetail hair that held the sword that hung over the head of Damocles.

"We have an opening for your scans on May 21st," the receptionist at the front desk said. I nodded a yes, but immediately I said, "No!" Both the receptionist and my wife looked at me with a questioning look. "Why not?"

"The wedding!"

My son was getting married the 2nd of June and I didn't want to have to be getting scans and waiting for reports just before the wedding. I wanted to enjoy the happy occasion.

"Wouldn't it be nice to get the scans done before the wedding and get it out of the way so you don't worry?" the receptionist said.

I nodded but said, "What if the scans don't come out as we hope?"

"Okay. We'll wait," she answered.

On Monday, June 25th, I had my scans done. I got to the hospital at 7:30 in the morning and left at 5:30 in the afternoon. It was a marathon of a day.

WEDNESDAY, JUNE 27TH 2018.

WE are sitting in Dr. B.'s office, my wife in her corner, me in the examining chair, and neither one of us wants to talk about the elephant in the room. We sit quietly waiting for Dr. B. to come in and give us our verdict. We both turn around toward the door as we hear the door knob move and the door starts to open. Showtime.

Almost a full year to the day has passed since my last treatment. The pain that cancer has introduced into my mind and body is beyond what words can describe. The physical pain sometimes is easier to deal with because of old friends like Tramadol and OxyContin. The mental anguish my family and I are going through, waiting and waiting, doesn't seem to have a pill for it. I think of Charlie and wonder how his experimental treatments went and if he survived. I talk to Dick every few weeks or so, but we haven't seen each other since the end of treatments.

When we speak we both seem to have the same comment: "I feel good, but I'm always tired."

Most nights I'm in bed between 9 and 9:30. I had an episode that scared the shit out of me. I was in my car driving home at about 9 o'clock in the evening from my weekly *bocci* game. The traffic was light and I found myself traveling at about 70 miles an hour. I don't know why or how, but I just passed out. Not passed out as fainted, but just fell asleep.

The next thing I remembered was my car shaking, and the ruckus that the tires were making traveling over the side strips at the edge of the road and then on the gravel. I was lucky that I was in the right lane with no guard rail and no other cars near me. I was able to get the car back onto the highway and into my lane. And I don't drink. Much.

After my PET scans, I had asked Dr. B. why was I feeling more tired now than I did during or after my treatments.

"Sometimes, for some people, it takes up to two years to reverse the damage that radiation causes to their body, and to flush it out. For some people it happens much faster, and other people don't feel anything until six months to a year out from the end of treatments, which stretches the time and process for the body to flush it out." Dr. B. took a little pause while looking at me and then continued. "You were so busy proving to the world and yourself that you were stronger than radiation and anything else that we threw at you. You didn't allow your body to slow down or affect you. And maybe now this is the accumulated effect catching up to you."

I do know that some of what Dr. B. is saying is the truth, and I'm hoping that I'm one of those people that get affected later. When I was going through my treatments, I needed to prove to myself that I could take it. I had to prove that I was stronger than Mr. C. I had to prove that I could take a licking and keep on ticking like the Timex watches of old. I think that I did well through it, but now I feel it's catching up to me. Please no tap, tap.

Is this a losing battle? Am I giving up? Tired of the uncertainty in my life?

In my private moments as I run my tongue around the inside of my mouth, I still can't get used to the feel of my plastic palate. I try not to think ahead, but I can't help thinking that if I'm lucky enough to reach my seventies, eighties and maybe even nineties, what will happen when I'm an old man with shaky hands full of arthritis. How will I be able to take care of my obturator?

The obturator needs to be snapped in place in a very specific way: Hook on the right side while balancing it on the ball of my right thumb. The pressure to snap it in place needs to be applied softly but evenly and in a continuous motion so that it's a smooth progress of the hooks over the teeth.

As the right hook snaps in place, the left hook needs to follow at almost the same time, but not exactly the same time. To remove the obturator, the process needs to be done in reverse, starting on the left side.

The two hooks that hold the obturator in place are pointy and sharp. My gums are always very sensitive and inflamed from the obturator and the hooks rubbing against them. The area above the obturator is very sensitive to any pressure. When I rinse after a meal, just using the medical squeeze bottle brings pain. On a couple of occasions when I was either in a hurry or wasn't paying enough attention, I snapped the obturator in place from the wrong side. By going in on the left side first, the hook got embedded in my gums. Pain is pain, but I swear that I felt like someone had taken a butcher knife and was slicing open my gums. The hook punctured the gums and got stuck under the ridge of the cap that my oral surgeon put in after surgery so that it would accommodate the hooks from the obturator.

The first time that happened I was at work on my lunch break, and after finishing my lunch I had gone into the bathroom to rinse my mouth. I was running late for my next appointment and wanted to get back behind my chair so that I could make that money to pay for those medical bills.

I had the obturator half sticking out of my mouth with one of the hooks stuck in my gums. I thought of going to the back room so that I could sit down, but I didn't want to take the chance of coming out of the bathroom and running into either clients or coworkers. Being a Friday, the shop was packed, and the last thing I would want was to have everyone see me like this. I decided to just push the other side of the obturator in place. I did. I pushed the obturator in and I could feel the hook on the left ripping through my gums, and the part of the plug on the top of the obturator that fills the hole in the top of my mouth slammed in place the wrong way, hitting the edges of the hole. The only way I can explain the sensitivity of that area is to compare it to the time after my first surgery, when the P.A. stuck her finger in the side of my face. The pain was like lightning bolts shooting out of my eyes, and it made me kneel down on the floor and cry.

What will happen when I'm 90 if I can't do this for myself? Is an aide making $15 to $20 an hour at todays rate, or a hundred dollars an hour thirty years from now, going to take the time and care to do it the proper way?

What about as I get older and my teeth are removed one by one because of radiation damage, or simply because I'm getting old and there aren't any more teeth to hook the obturator to?

I sleep with four pillows and as long as I stay on my back or turn on my left side, I can hardly breathe, but I do breathe. The moment I turn on my right side it's like someone pinches my nose and puts a pillow over my face as my airways get completely blocked. The scans showed that the mucosa is thick and enlarged from radiation damage. The cancer hiding in the lining of the nerves needed to be chased with the radiation. They got the cancer, I hope, but the surrounding areas have also taken a beating.

The dripping from my nose is constant and I'm always trying to catch those pesky little droplets before they land on someone's forehead while I'm shampooing their hair, or on my shirt. I walk around with a constant companion in my hand: a Kleenex, paper towel, or toilet paper. Anything to catch those drips.

Over the last six months I had the obturator adjusted three times to try to block the dripping and avoid food getting into my nose. Every time we made an adjustment it lasted about two weeks and then the dripping got worse. I came to find out that the soft palate is a muscle. It's a muscle that doesn't like to be touched. Let me explain.

The hard and soft palate are attached to each other, and they function well together. When surgery was done to remove the cancer, the part of my hard palate that was removed was what could be defined as the shield for the soft palate. The soft palate, left exposed, functions well enough to allow me to swallow food or liquids, but that changes when something is put in place, like in my case wearing the obturator. The obturator does a decent job of allowing me to eat, drink and speak, but the soft palate doesn't like the nearness of the obturator and shrinks away from it. That creates open

spaces that allow fluid or small particles of food to get through and consequently come out of my nose.

Every time we adjusted the obturator to close the space between the
soft palate and obturator, the soft palate shrank away and created a bigger
and bigger space. So we stopped making adjustments and I needed to get
used to the fact that the space cannot be closed. At the edge of the meeting
point of the obturator and soft palate, the obturator creates a little ledge
raised about an eighth of an inch above the soft palate line. That area
becomes a collection point for everything: bits of food, mucus, phlegm – in
particular, any food that is stringy or gritty.

To give it a positive spin, what I can do on those nights when I wake
up and want a snack at one o'clock in the morning and don't want to get
out of bed, I can just pull up those bits of food. Combined with mucus they
should be nice and moist. I'll be like sheep, cows and camels, with my own
cud. And then, we don't want to talk about when I need to clear my throat
and bring up a stubborn piece of phlegm. But let's talk about it. When I do
try to clear my throat and that blob travels up from my throat and meets
the little shelf between the soft palate and obturator and . . . nothing. It just
gets stuck there, forcing me to send it back down where it came from.

WHEEEEEEE. YUCK!

Jumping ahead a bit ... After I saw my urologist and I got to read the
reports from the ultrasound of my prostrate, I saw words like "mega." I
don't think they were talking about my private parts.

I find it easy to deal with the day-to-day happenings of my life because
I keep myself busy with work or home. If I don't have a project lined up, I'll
create one for myself. But lately what I find it hard to do is to look to the
future. The now is easy. The future is scary, so my dilemma is this:

TRAVEL
_____

NUMBER one.

Should I be consumed by thinking of my cancer and what report I will get another three or six months from now?

Should I worry about November 2018 when I go for my ultrasound if the results show that I have prostrate cancer?

Then what? Surgery again? Treatments? Radiation or chemo? I don't know if mentally I can deal with that again.

Should I worry about not being able to take care of my obturator as I get older?

WALK

NUMBER two.

Should I focus on the fact that I made it through stage 4 cancer and treatments?

I belong to a support group called "ACC WARRIORS" and their motto is:

FEAR can be what we *FEEL*

But BRAVE
Is what we *DO*

The group has a worldwide membership of under a thousand people. Sometimes if I'm sad about my situation or feeling drained and having a bad day, or feeling "Why me?" I'll read some of the postings on the group website from members looking for advice, or with news of new treatments, and maybe sometimes just to vent to others who will understand you.

Most times it takes only reading through a couple of postings to be reminded that there is always worse. But the old saying is that someone else's pain doesn't take your own pain away. I do find that by reading through some of the postings I gain some resolve and strength. And talking about strength, some of these people have strength beyond strength. With recurrence after recurrence of cancer, and with the loss of an eye, nose, ear or vocal cords, with a tracheotomy or a total collapse of one side or the other of the face, they still fight on and on, and always with the hope for a cure and always offering advice and prayers for others.

As hard as my last year has been dealing with Mr. C. and all of his friends, I have been blessed with many good things. Along with my granddaughter Autumn and grandson Sammy, I now have a second grandson. His name is Grayson. After my son's proposal last year to his girlfriend and her saying "Yes," we just had their wedding. Who knows, maybe in another year or so I will get my fourth grandchild.

I'm back to a semi-work schedule. It's no way near what I did before my surgeries and treatments, but I'm doing enough to pay our bills. Both Mass General Hospital and Mass Eye & Ear allowed me to get into a payment plan to satisfy what we owe, and I'm getting caught up with my other bills. But Mr. C. and the cost of my health care insurance sucked away what we worked for and saved in the last 40 years. My car is 10 years old, and every month I send that check to the hospital I think it could be a payment for a nice new car. I can't take a bite from an apple, drink from a straw, or blow out a candle. The grandchildren can blow out those 60 or so candles for me. Occasionally I try to chew on a piece of gum just to help with the dryness in my mouth, but of course the gum catches the obturator, making it move up and down.

Exchanging a kiss has become something of the past. I can't blame my wife, as the obturator always has a slimy feel to it. But without that slimy piece of plastic I wouldn't be able to speak, talk, drink or even take a breath.

So what are my choices?

Should I focus on all that is good in my life? When I try to go to sleep and I can't breathe, should I be thankful I have a nose and I'm not like some of the people from my support group who have lost their nose to cancer? Poor me, I have no shoes. But look – he has no feet.

When I try to swallow my food and I happen to look up and talk at the same time and I choke on it, should I be thankful that I don't have a tracheotomy? Or that I'm not on a feeding tube?

Do I need to find balance in my nervous system between my parasympathetic and sympathetic divisions? Can I find and separate my sympathetic responses of fear and anger from my parasympathetic responses, to conserve the body energy that supports internal body functions such as digestion, blood pressure and heart rate?

When I think of that dentist, my sympathetic response kicks in. My heart rate accelerates, my breathing gets heavy, and I feel the heat from the pit of my stomach that makes me want to throw up. Maybe writing my thoughts down will help my parasympathetic take control. Or maybe I'm starting to forgive him, as he is only human.

Regarding our meeting with the attorney and trying to recoup some of the medical expenses: We were told it would take close to two years, but about ten months into it we heard from Sharon, the attorney, and what we heard was not what we wanted to hear.

"We are sorry, but we have decided not to pursue the case. But we're not telling you that you can't pursue it with another firm. There are those who will take the case and tell you have a great case, but unless they do it on a contingency basis . . . Our advice to you is to move on and live your life."

"But what about the fact that over two years went by?" That was my wife's and my response, our words echoing each other's.

"Our medical board concluded that since ACC is a very slow-moving cancer, there is no way to prove when the cancer started."

About two days after Sharon called to let us know they weren't going to take the case, we received a UPS delivery of a packet containing all the information that the law firm had collected about my medical history, along with information about ACC.

With the recommendation of a client-friend, we made an appointment to meet with another law firm. The attorney we met with was very impressed with the packet of information we provided them from Sharon's law firm. "This should speed things up," the new attorney commented, flipping through the pages.

Less than two weeks went by, and we got the same answer that Sharon had given us: "Move on with your life."

Easy for them to say.

My wife, the voice of reason, sat the two of us down and her words that helped me were, "We will be okay." So we are moving on with our lives, and I think I have moved on from hating that dentist, but I still just wish he had practiced the *primum non nocere*. I'll never know whether it would have made a difference, but the thought and the doubt will always remain in the back of my mind.

I saw a post on Facebook by a friend of mine. The post was the picture of a plaque in front of a hospital entrance in Italy. The post said:

Ce' chi sposta un sasso e ne parla

come se avesse spostato una montagna.

E poi c'e chi sposta una montagna in silenzio.

There are people who would move a pebble

and talk about it as if they have moved a mountain.

Then there are people who move a mountain in silence.

The majority of people plan their lives from the time they get out of bed and have a bowel movement to the day they are going to retire. But as we get older , and those that who we love and care about also get older, the loss of family and friends comes into our lives .With that comes the knowledge that we are getting into the autumn of our lives, accompanied by those little pains and aches our bodies seem to spring on us every day. The expressions, "One day at a time" and "day to day" become part of our vocabulary. Before Mr. C., I never used those expressions or others I heard from my grandmother – or from my parents when they said, "Some day you'll understand." I didn't pay much attention and I didn't fully understand the meaning of those words.

This last year of my life I have become to fully understand the meaning of "day to day." And I have found how hard it is to adapt to the true meaning of day to day or three months to three months. I'm hoping that when the next three months pass by I will hear, "See you in six months." Then, "See you in a year" or "See you in five years." So for now, I'm living with the real day to day.

It was ingrained in me since childhood that we plan ahead, no matter if it's the day you tilled the ground, or seeded or harvested. Planning gave everyday life continuance and normalcy. At times, I feel that my life is not even day to day, but almost moment to moment, and as the moment passes I don't seem to give much attention to what the future or the decision of that moment may be.

YOUR FEET WALK, YOUR MIND TRAVELS

AS the door opens, I see Jen the nurse practitioner coming in, followed by Dr. B. My wife, maybe sensing that soon the doctor will be coming in, has moved to stand next to me as we are waiting to get our results.

As she stands there next to me, I see our reflection in the computer screen and it makes me think of one of those old photos you see from 1870s that has a couple stoically posing – one standing, the other sitting. Usually the man is standing and the woman sitting. Well, the world has changed. We do this pose in reverse, with my wife standing and me sitting down.

She's leaning against the side of the chair with her arm and hand across my shoulder. I don't know if her arm and hand are there to give me comfort if our news isn't too good, or to hold herself up. I can feel her grip on my shoulder tighten and I can feel her body shifting closer to the chair and me, almost like she's trying to hide behind me as Dr. B. and Jen walk in.

Jen has a smile on her face and Dr. B. seems to have the same look on his face. Before any greetings are exchanged and any words are said, I see Dr. B. putting up his right hand with his fingers up and spread, followed by him putting up his left hand with just his index finger extended, like he was going to say, "I'm number one!" But instead as he waved his hands back and forth he said, "All is good, see you in six months!"

And then the tears come.

HAD a CT SCAN on 7/15/19, with a follow up appointment with Dr. B. on 7/18/19.

Met with Dr. L. on 7/22/19.

Results?

Two thumbs up from both doctors and a "See you in six months."

As of June 2019, my PSA numbers were down from over 8 to 1.5, and the tumor hasn't grown in size.

BUT!

On my visit with Dr. L. on 7/22, in our usual meeting with his P.A., there was a glitch that has put the little black cloud back in play. This is how it went:

There were hugs and greetings all around as the P.A. came into the room.

"Mr. Di Carlo, you look great! How are you feeling?"

"Doing good," I said as I gave a little shrug of the shoulder.

"I saw that you had your scans. Have you seen Dr. B. yet?"

"Yes, last Wednesday."

"And?"

"He has me scheduled in six months for another scan."

"Hmmm. Usually by now they go to the one year scan. Let me look up your scans," she said, without waiting for an answer as she accesses the computer on the table next to her.

I saw her scroll down the scans as my wife and I quietly sat in our designated areas. I didn't know the reason yet, but I felt a golf ball forming in the very, very deepest pit of my stomach.

"Oh, nodules. That's why he wants you back in six months."

The ball is getting a little bigger. Tennis, anyone?

"Did Dr. B. talk to you about those nodules?"

What nodules?

Is that a softball that I felt?

My wife seemed to pick up the football a little quicker than me because I was still stuck on the question about those nodules.

How the fuck was it possible that for every ounce of decent news, there was always that two-by-four that was about to hit you on the forehead.

"What do you mean?" my wife asked.

The P.A.'s back was still turned to us as she said, "There are some good size nodules on your lungs, and I think that's why Dr. B. wants you back in six months instead of a year."

What the hell was this? Did I just hear Arnold's voice again? Yeah, and I think he was playing with the basketball in the pit of my stomach. I hadn't said a word, but I knew the ball was definitely getting bigger. At that moment I was upset that neither P.A. Jen nor Dr. B. mentioned anything to us about those lung nodules. Maybe this was the old, "We'll keep an eye on it." Or maybe even better, it was like in the old day: If you don't talk about it, it isn't there.

My wife and I didn't seem to know what to say, or what questions to ask. The P.A. knew she had thrown something out that maybe was meant to remain in the corner of the "cloud." She couldn't miss that both of us were stunned. Four days ago, we got the thumbs up for another six months, and now we were getting hit over the forehead with a word. Nodules.

"I'm sorry if I upset you. I thought you would want to know," she said.

And remembering the old "Be polite, no need to be rude," we gave the polite answer. "Sure, we want to know. Definitely, I want to know."

I had been fine with the, "See you in six months."

"Dr. L. will be in shortly," she said as she was leaving the room and softly closed the door.

And there we were, just the two of us again, looking at the river. Looking at that beautiful river flowing by. I wonder how many times people have looked at that river after receiving some of the news that these visits bring, and I wonder why something so ugly should be told while looking at something so beautiful.

For a moment I didn't see any movement on the river. I thought: Has the river stopped flowing? Is it a trick of the sun's reflection?

Neither one of us said anything. I think my wife just got drained of her last ounce of strength, but she surprised me. "We'll deal with it. Let's wait and see what Dr. L. has to say," my wife, always the rock, said to me.

I shook my head yes. As if on cue, the door opened, and Dr. L. came into the room, followed by the P.A. and the computer man, woman or x-person note-taker.

Dr. L. was always an inspiration when he walked into the room with his smile and charm. He greeted my wife and me as if we were old friends, and he knew that the mood in the room was a little sour because the P.A. had passed on the news about the nodules and the way it affected us.

"Mr. Di Carlo, you look great. If you can give me a minute before we do anything I want to look at your scans."

Both my wife and I nodded our consent. A few minutes went by waiting for Dr. L. to finish reading the report. I checked on the river to see if it was still flowing. We need the river to keep flowing because it takes all of the pain out to sea, I thought to myself, just as Dr. L. swiveled his chair toward us.

"Lung nodules are a very common happening. Yours are pinpoint nodules that appear on your scans. Your cancer likes to jump to the lungs, so Dr. B. has decided to keep your scans at six months intervals, so as to make sure we can keep a close tab on it."

He was looking at us, but our faces didn't seem to react much to the explanation that the good doctor had given us, so he gave another try by pointing to the young man/woman/x note-taker by the door as he said. "He has lung nodules." I could see a little crease on his/her/x's forehead as the typing stopped.

"What the fuck? Why me?" the typist must have been thinking.

Even Dr. L. noticed. "Okay, everyone in this room has lung nodules," he said.

Now everyone was looking at each other, wondering: What the fuck? This was getting better by the minute.

"Pinpoint lung nodules are very common in both men and women. Just because there are lung nodules, it doesn't mean that they are bad or cancerous," he said, "but in your case ..."

"I'm baa ... " Shut the fuck up, Arnold.

"... the reason Dr. B. chose not to say anything," I saw Dr. L. turn toward his P.A. as he said the word anything, "and to reschedule your scans at six months, is so that he can keep a closer look on those nodules, knowing that you have a cancer history and your cancer likes to jump to the lungs. This is very normal, just routine ..." As Dr. L. stopped talking, I wondered if he was thinking, "Do I have to repeat this again?" But the moment passed.

Walk ... and the river flows again.

As my journey with cancer weaved in and out from people to places, some people and episodes helped me cope and also gave me the strength to continue on to see where my journey would lead, and whatever would be ahead.

Certain things will remain with me for the rest of my life, while others will be forgotten before the ink is dry. (Try to explain to most people the expression "before the ink is dry." For myself in kindergarten and first grade, 1961-62, we still had an inkwell at our desks.) And I will always be thankful for those things and people that are embedded in my mind and soul and helped me cope with cancer.

CAREGIVERS, AND GRATITUDE.

I want to close these pages by giving kudos to a bunch of people who made it possible for me to get through my journey. At the top of the list is my wife Pina.

Yes, that's her name.

Throughout this manuscript I have purposely referred to her only as "my wife." Omitting her name was my attempt to bring attention to those caregivers, and if even one individual reading the above words has the thought, "Doesn't this wife have a name?" I feel I have successfully achieved my goal to point out that our pain is the pain of those warriors who walk with us but don't always get the attention or the support they need.

And to put another exclamation point on the awareness toward caregivers, I want to bring my wife's perspective into the story. To do that, we need to backtrack to where, during my Calvary, I was diagnosed with cancer, and the surgeries that followed.

The fear and pain I was experiencing were so deep that I failed to see that those around me were experiencing emotional pain at a parallel level. Physical pain is hard, but emotional pain is a close second. Those who love us cry and despair just as we do, but it seems that both sides are so intent on protecting the other that both sides cry alone instead of together.

For my wife and I, it took close to four years to reveal our thoughts to each other, and the catalyst was that I finally tried to put it all in writing. As she read through the words and pages and saw all of the tears I had shed privately, one of her first comments to me was, "I needed to be strong! I couldn't fall apart, but in retrospect I shouldn't have tried so hard not to fall apart. Maybe we could have fallen apart together and cried together, instead of separately."

As she continued reading through my manuscript, we had a few back-and-forths that brought out some details about the time following my first surgery.

"...you didn't know?" she asked.

"No, I didn't! You knew?" I answered, then asked.

"Yes, but I thought that you knew."

A veil of darkness comes over me as we are sitting at our kitchen table having dinner on Wednesday the 17th of February 2021, just about four years removed from my diagnosis.

It feels like the times of old: "Don't talk about it, and it isn't there."

The following account is a very small sample of my wife's side of the story. As I was living through mine, she had her own Calvary, just as full of tears, fears and worries. And her story could be applied to any of the care-givers who live anonymously among us. This is a small part of her story, as she told it to me.

Pina's story

MY first awakening that this was oncology was the day I walked into Dr. L.'s office with my husband. That's not to say I didn't know what oncology was. With older parents and relatives, we had heard and seen plenty, but this was hitting home, way too close. The word oncology is scary, and it was giving me a lot to process.

When all this started, at each step we had taken, it seemed at first that thing be okay, and then, never fail, the hammer would hit. WHAM!

I felt we were walking into an abyss as I watched my husband being wheeled down a long white hallway by a group of nurses and doctors, soon disappearing behind a set of double doors.

I was still watching the closed doors as I heard my name called. "Mrs. Di Carlo?"

"Yes," I answered as I turned toward the voice.

"The family waiting area is on the 7th floor," the receptionist said to me.

"Okay," I replied without moving.

I think she felt for me. I heard a kinder, softer tone in her voice as she said, "There is a TV screen on the wall of the family waiting room. It gives updates on the time surgeries are done and when patients are moved into the recovery room." And for emphasis, she had her hand on my forearm. I wasn't sure whether she did it to give me a squeeze for strength or to point me toward the side alcove where the elevators where .

Of course, I knew all of the information about the the family waiting area and how the progress of the surgery would be posted, but at that moment I had no thread to follow and guide me in that broken bundle that our life was becoming.

There were about a half dozen people in the family room when I walked in. The room was so quiet that I felt I was walking into a sanctuary. I saw a loveseat in a corner and sat down. As I looked around the room, I noticed that everyone seemed to be in a place of their own, with none of the back and forth banter that a group would normally have, even when they are all strangers to each other.

I also noticed that most people were looking up, and for a short moment I thought that they were praying and looking up for inspiration, but I soon realized that everyone's attention seemed to be focused on the big-screen TV beside the entrance to the room.

The screen showed many names that I took to be patients, followed by a doctor's name and then the time of surgery. I heard a couple of comments from different parts of the room. One was from someone who had come into the room and was dressed in doctor's garb: "All went well and she's in the recovery room." That was followed by a sign of relief on the family members' faces.

But almost at the same time I heard a comment from someone sitting behind me. "Why is it taking so long? Is everything okay?" I could see the profile of the person who the question was being asked of. And on that profile I could see dread of the unknown, when those uncertain minutes turn into hours. Then I saw her turn toward the family who had just received the good news that all was well, and I noticed a little sense of jealousy toward those others who seemed to be rejoicing with the doctor's good news.

I prayed as I kept looking up, just as most everyone else around the room seemed to be doing. Finally, almost three hours later, I saw that my husband's surgery was done, and soon he was going to be moved into the recovery room.

Just then I heard a ding from my phone, and as I looked down I saw a text from my daughter, Elisa. "I'm here, coming up."

A few minutes later, she was there. "Hi ,mom!" she said as she hugged me. "Have you heard anything?"

" Yes! They just posted that surgery is done and soon he should be moved to recovery."

I sat with my daughter at my couch-for-two, and both of us tried to carry on some small talk. I tried not to think of what Dr. L. would say. Thumbs up? Thumbs down?

I needed to put a little more fervor into my prayers.

"Hello , Mrs. Di Carlo!" I heard, just like in a dream. And when I turned, there was Dr. L. with his usual reassuring presence and demeanor. My daughter and I stood up at the same time. "Let's go and talk in the cafeteria," he said as he pointed across the way from the family waiting room.

From the 7th floor where the cafeteria is located, there was a nice view of the Longfellow Bridge that spans over the Charles River, leading toward the Museum of Science. There were a few regatta boats gliding by so smoothly over the water that they seem to be gravitating over the water. Everything seemed to be shining on this mild, sunny, March morning. But my heart was bouncing in my chest. As we found a table, Dr. L. sat down, and we took the seats across from him. We were looking at him expectantly, and I knew we would be hanging on every word.

Dr. L. had both of his forearms on the table as he said, " I'm not sure yet, but pending the biopsy results , I think that Bruno may need another surgery."

This felt unreal and I didn't want to believe it. How's Bruno going to deal with this news? I thought to myself as Dr. L. continued on.

"I suspect that there is cancer in the soft palate," he said. And then he stopped again and reached into his pocket and took out a blank folded piece of paper and spread it in front of him. He started to draw what looked like a set of teeth and what I thought to be the back of the hard palate. He said, "This is the hard palate where the tumor I removed was, and this is where I removed one of the teeth." He pointed to one side of the oval. He looked up for a moment. "This is the soft palate," he said, "and I suspect that the cancer may have gone there."

Dr. L.'s words were like a bucket of cold water being thrown at me.

"But I wanted to have the biopsy results before I went any further with the removal of the soft palate."

There aren't words to describe the tightening that I was feeling in my chest. Maybe this is what people feel when they're having a heart attack. But the good doctor continued. "When the soft palate is removed, there is no going back, and his quality of life will change. It makes it very hard to fit a prosthetic, and sometimes it's not possible at all."

"What happens then?" I asked.

"If we can't fit a prosthetic, the next step will be to put in a feeding tube, and that could be permanent. The rest of his life."

Neither my daughter nor I at this point seemed capable of formulating a question. Dr. L then said, "I didn't want to take that chance, so I removed only what I needed to around the growth. The biopsy results will help me know better what I need to do in the next surgery. I will talk to Bruno."

"Can we wait to tell him?" I asked.

"I don't think I can do that," Dr. L. answered.

"Well, you said you won't know for sure until the biopsy results. Why put him through this?"

"Mrs. Di Carlo, he has the right to know."

Either through some divine intervention, or because Bruno seemed high on something, my husband surprised me by how well he took the news of more surgery and the possibility there was cancer in the soft palate. Or maybe it was the way Dr. L. presented it, in the most positive way. But now, four years later as I read through the words Bruno had written, I realize that he never fully understood the reality or the gravity of that moment, and the dilemma that I was dealing with because his focus was on "When you wake up, your cancer will be gone."

I wondered if he was being strong to protect me and our children and putting up a front, as I was doing for him. So why not give him a few more days of a reprieve before dealing with the news of more cancer, surgery and the specter of a feeding tube.

Everyday it was a full-time job to try to bring him to a better place. I knew I needed to be strong for him and at that point my only priority was getting him better.

I had confided in my daughter Christina the anguish I felt at having to wait the two weeks until our appointment to get the results of the biopsy. "Call and find out. Why do you have to wait?" she said.

"I don't know if I should," I answered.

"Won't it be better to know? I'm sure it will be good results."

I did call Dr. L., and he confirmed that there were cancer cells still present and that a second surgery would be needed.

I was devastated. My heart dropped for Bruno. My world was shattered. I knew I should tell him. But how?

I didn't know what to do or how to make a decision. Should I live with my knowledge and hold back the information until our appointment with Dr. L.? Or should I tell Bruno?

Fate, in the form of our friend Peter, helped me make a decision.

When Bruno was admitted to the hospital for bleeding and his palate needed to be cauterized, it was a chaotic morning, and after a couple of hours in the emergency room he was moved up to the eleventh floor. It seemed that as soon as he was brought to his room he fell into a deep sleep. Maybe it was the blood loss, or just the pain from the cauterization that just knocked him out. I sat there and watched him sleep, and I think I also started to doze off. But I heard his phone ring and grabbed it on the first ring to shut it off, as I didn't want to wake him up. Just as I was pushing the Off button, I saw the name on the caller ID.

"Hi, Pina!" Peter said when he heard my voice. "How's the patient?"

"We're at the hospital," I answered, after a short pause.

"Why? What happened?" Are you at the M.E.E.?" I heard the concern in Peter's voice as he asked the question.

"Yes!" I simply answered.

We spoke about the conversation I had with Dr. L., and then I said to him, "I don't know what to do, Peter."

"About what?" he asked.

"The results of the biopsy…more surgery…feeding tube…" I said, as I looked toward the bed where my husband was.

"You did the right thing, Pina. It isn't your job to tell him."

"But Bru ..."

He didn't let me finish. "As doctors, it's our job, Dr. L.'s job, to talk to Bruno."

"But I'm afraid that Bruno isn't going to want another surgery."

Peter interrupted me again, asking, "What makes you think that?"

"He's been through so much suffering and pain. I don't think that he'll agree to another surgery." And my tears were flowing.

"Pina, I have been around Bruno long enough to know the way he thinks of you, the children and your grandchildren. Bruno will do anything to be around and watch them grow."

In the end, he was right.

"I'll be over in about twenty minutes to see you," Peter concluded as he said goodbye.

THIS IS BRUNO AGAIN.

I give thanks to my children, their children, spouses, extended family, friends, co-workers, my ACC group, clients, and even complete strangers.

But most of all, I would like to acknowledge the people from the two hospitals, Mass General Hospital and Mass Eye and Ear. There was one thing I found was constant for me while going through my surgeries and treatment, and all of the following scans and appointments: From the parking attendant to the receptionists, the cafeteria workers, Sweet Bea, the nurses, my friend Dr. Peter Friedensohn, P.A. Bob, Dr. L. and his staff, Dr. B., his P.A Jen, the rest of the staff, Dr. J., Dr. C. and many, many more, all of them gave me the same incredible gift: COMPASSION.

My hope and wish with this account of my journey is to bring a smile or build a little hope, or even draw a happy tear from anyone who is suffering through cancer. There is help for those who search, and there is light at the end of the tunnel. Yes, sometimes the light is a train coming, but there are among us those angels who will help you get off the train tracks. We just need to choose to see them, and I hope you will be as lucky as I was.

God Bless.

The names of patients and technicians have been changed to protect their privacy, and some of the doctors names have been omitted or changed or abbreviated .

Epilogue

AS I wrote things down, I chose to omit certain episodes because sometimes personal moments are meant to remain in our hearts and souls and between the individuals involved. But as time went by, I started thinking about a happening that at first I had decided to omit, not because it was personal or private, but because I didn't realize until later what it meant to me.

The moment didn't come from a family member or a friend, a doctor, or a casual acquaintance. It came from a complete stranger. I should specify that this stranger is fictional, but his name is known worldwide.

Rocco Balboa, a.k.a Rocky.

I never been one who loves movie sequels. They never seem to live up to the original. And by the time "Rocky III" came along, I had moved on from going to movie theaters and watching sequels.

I enjoy a good story in a movie and I love to watch a ballgame no matter if the players are skating or using a hoop, a bat, a pigskin or a soccer ball, but I'm tired of being lectured every time I turn the TV on. I don't have many of those few-hour blocks of time to sit in a movie theater, and by the time those movies make it to TV, there are just too many commercials. I wonder what happened to "If you pay for cable, you'll have TV without commercials."

So for myself, when I do have those few hours, I prefer to go out for dinner with my wife, friends, or family.

But! One of those mornings during the time I was receiving treatments – or I should say one of those nights that I couldn't sleep – I quietly slipped out of bed to avoid waking my wife with my tossing and turning, and made my way to our TV room.

I piled three pillows behind my back and pulled a blanket over me. The clock on the TV box said 3:50 am. After going through the local station listings – and the not-so-local stations that covered every letter of the alphabet – the only programs I could find were those that offered vacuum cleaners, or the best sex toys, or a glue that could fix anything.

I decided to check the movie channels like HBO or STARS. Most of the movie titles didn't seem to hold my interest, or the subject wasn't appealing to me. I was on my second pass through the listings when I spotted something that made me push the information button on my control to get a synopsis of the movie. The clock on the cable box turned to 4 o'clock as I clicked on the movie, and as I did I heard a familiar song. The movie was *Rocky Balboa*.

In the first ten minutes of the movie, I am reminded that Rocky still has the biggest heart in the world, but his life is all fucked up. His wife Adrian is dead and his son is ashamed to be around him, or to be in his shadow. Rocky tells the same story about his time in the ring to those who come to his restaurant, appropriately named Adrian.

I doze off for a moment, or maybe longer, and as I'm awoken by Rocky's voice, I hear, "I . . . yeah. It was a woman cancer." From earlier in the movie, I knew she had died, but I now know that Adrian died from cancer. At the end it gets all of us. Even at 4:20 in the morning, with just the first glimpse of day starting to show beyond the tall pine trees that circle my backyard, the beast makes itself heard.

I thought that I was going to watch a movie about a boxing match.

I feel the tears flow freely…but what's new. Tears are my new friends, and just in case, I have my blanket tucked under my chin on this chilly, late June morning to catch those tears.

I couldn't stay asleep in bed, but on the couch I seem to have no problem going in and out of sleep. And as I come out of another one of those moments, I hear and witness the first of three moments in the movie that just bring more tears for me .

"Are you angry?" Paulie, Rocky's brother-in-law, asks. At this moment I don't know what he's asking what Rocky might be angry about .

"Angry?" Rocky asks back.

"Are you angry because Adrian left you?" Paulie presses on.

And what came next was for me the *pièce de résistance*. This was Marlon Brando in *On the Waterfront* or *A Streetcar Named Desire*, or anyone else who has ever received an Academy Award.

"She didn't leave, Paulie." And after a brief moment, in a broken voice worthy of a thou-sand Oscars, Rocky says, "She died!"

That's it for me. The floodgates open. There it is. The beast that takes anything it wants. I feel a nice, wet pool just about where my chin meets my chest as I am lying down on my couch.

"Okay, okay," Paulie says as Rocky continues. There are few words Rocky says that I can't distinguish. I don't know if it's him or me, because the sobs seem to have blocked my ears and eyes. But as I look at the screen again, I see Rocky with tears on his face and I hear his voice saying, ". . . feels like this beast is inside me!"

Oh, my God! Home run. And, he continues, "Just never knew it was supposed to be this hard . . . It wasn't supposed to be like this, Paulie." And as Rocky wipes tears with the back of his hand, I let mine run.

Maybe it's the cancer or my hormones or the effects of radiation, but I am shedding way too many tears before 5 am.

As the movie develops, Rocky will get a chance to fight for the championship belt. Just before he's ready to leave his dressing room, my second moment of the movie comes as one of Rocky's friends, a former fighter but now a pastor, comes into the room to recite a prayer with him. "Zechariah 44 says it's not by strength, not by might, but by His spirit that we have already claimed a victory in our Lord Jesus Christ ...Good luck, Rocky."

I let the blanket catch the tears that I shed in my new found belief in God.

How convenient to find God in our time of need.

The fight starts with a fury of punches and blood and spit flying everywhere, and on the tenth round Rocky goes down . . . but wait! He isn't down. He is on one knee with one glove on the canvas of the ring and the other on his thigh.

He's stunned and hearing voices – including his own voice during a conversation that he had with his son. But I missed that part of the movie as I had fallen in and out of sleep: "It ain't about how hard you can Hit, its about how hard you can get hit and keep moving forward."

Now he's having flashbacks as he sees Adrian on their wedding day.

I swear that time slows down. Maybe it's the movie or maybe my imagination, but I see my wife walking down the aisle toward me on our wedding day as I stand at the altar of St. Anthony's church with my brother Vincenzo next to me as my best man.

Rocky sees his son being born. I see my children being born at the old St. Margaret's Hospital.

And tears continue to roll.

"GET UP ... LET'S GO, GET UP!" His son is yelling at Rocky from the corner of the ring. The crowd is at a crescendo with the Rocky chant. "ROCKY .ROCKY ROCKY." And finally, just before the count to ten, Rocky does stand up and finishes the fight. And no, he doesn't win, but he is standing at the end of the fight.

I wipe my tears and I find a new resolve in me.

Yes, I would continue to walk, not just for me, but for those who were walking with me.

Thanks, Rocky.

I needed to write down the words in my mind to help me cope with cancer, but even as I tried to formulate those words, I didn't know the words to express what I was and am feeling. When I managed to dig some up and thought I found the right words, it took me about three to four tries with spell-check to get the proper spelling or meaning. Heck, I finished high school at 14 years old and at this point of my life, my vocabulary and punctuation were at a 4th grade level. Maybe 5th.

As I managed to put my thoughts into words, I read them over and over, hoping that each time I read them it would become something my mind assimilated to, and at the same time I was trying to become oblivious to the emotions the words brought out. But instead, each time I read them over, the wounds became a little deeper, and the tears came.

Bob, the physician assistant, told me that tears are okay. But he also thought I was depressed.

I just wanted to take some sleeping pills so that I could fall asleep at 10 pm and wake up the next day around 11 am and realize it was nothing but a dream.

Cancer.

Cane che na' conosce padrone.

Dog with no master.